Philip Larkin and His Audiences

Philip Larkin and His Audiences

Gillian Steinberg

palgrave
macmillan

First published 2010 by
PALGRAVE MACMILLAN

Palgrave Macmillan in the UK is an imprint of Macmillan Publishers Limited, registered in England, company number 785998, of Houndmills, Basingstoke, Hampshire RG21 6XS.

Palgrave Macmillan in the US is a division of St Martin's Press LLC, 175 Fifth Avenue, New York, NY 10010.

Palgrave Macmillan is the global academic imprint of the above companies and has companies and representatives throughout the world.

Palgrave® and Macmillan® are registered trademarks in the United States, the United Kingdom, Europe and other countries.

ISBN-13: 978–0–230–23778–0   hardback

This book is printed on paper suitable for recycling and made from fully managed and sustained forest sources. Logging, pulping and manufacturing processes are expected to conform to the environmental regulations of the country of origin.

A catalogue record for this book is available from the British Library.

A catalog record for this book is available from the Library of Congress.

10   9   8   7   6   5   4   3   2   1
19   18   17   16   15   14   13   12   11   10

Printed and bound in Great Britain by
CPI Antony Rowe, Chippenham and Eastbourne

For Mark

Contents

Acknowledgements

Reprinted by permission of Farrar, Straus and Giroux, LLC:

Excerpts from *All What Jazz: A Record Diary* by Philip Larkin. Copyright © 1985 by the Estate of Philip Larkin.

Excerpts from *Collected Poems* by Philip Larkin. Copyright © 1988, 2003 by the Estate of Philip Larkin.

Excerpts from *Required Writing* by Philip Larkin. Copyright © 1983 by Philip Larkin.

Excerpts from *Selected Letters* of Philip Larkin, 1940–85 by Philip Larkin, introduction by Anthony Thwaite. Copyright © 1992 The Estate of Philip Larkin. Introduction copyright © 1992 by Anthony Thwaite.

The quotations from 'Places, Loved Ones,' 'Lines on a Young Lady's Photograph Album,' 'Reasons for Attendance,' 'Maiden Name,' 'Church Going,' 'Poetry of Departures,' and 'I Remember, I Remember' by Philip Larkin are reprinted from *The Less Deceived* by permission of The Marvell Press, England and Australia.

I owe enormous thanks to the many people who read versions of this manuscript and helped me to improve it in countless ways. To past and present members of our Yeshiva College writing group, Lauren Fitzgerald, Chaviva Levin, Jess Olson, Evan Resnick, Allison Smith, and Rob Stretter, I offer thanks for great patience in reading and commenting on drafts as well as for their ongoing moral support. Thanks to Ariel Schwartz of the Yeshiva College Writing Center for his help with my concluding chapter. I am grateful to Karen Mills Courts and Steven Helmling for their wise counsel and willingness to serve as mentors and cheerleaders. This book would be quite different without the advice and insight of Adam Zachary Newton, the most dedicated and supportive department chairperson a young scholar could hope for, as well as a wonderful colleague and friend. And I owe profound thanks to two people without whose help this book would not have been possible, Minda Rae Amiran and my father, Theodore Steinberg, both of whom read every chapter and offered pitch-perfect advice at every stage of this process.

Finally, I am tremendously grateful to my amazing family: to my father, who taught me to love literature and to pursue that love; to my mother, Phyllis Steinberg, who has never waivered in her belief that I could work full time, write a book, and raise two children simultaneously (and who has always been available to fill in the gaps when I couldn't pull it all together); to my in-laws, Andrea and Steven Davis, who are as proud of me as my own parents and who truly are second parents to me; to my siblings, Dan Steinberg, Annys Shin, Miriam Steinberg-Egeth, Marc Egeth, Howard Davis, and Adinah East, who constantly demonstrate the true meaning of family through their love and friendship; to my two sons, Akiva and Gavriel, who have offered their own kind of moral support and have provided me with endless entertaining distractions from my work; and, of course, to my amazing husband Mark Davis, who doesn't care that much about Larkin but listens to me talk about him all the time anyway, and who has convinced me that I am capable of anything. Thank you.

List of Abbreviations

AWJ *All What Jazz*
CP   *Collected Poems*
FR   *Further Requirements*
RW   *Required Writing*
SL   *Selected Letters*

Preface

I came to write about Philip Larkin because, above all, I love his poetry. When, as a teenager, I first read 'Home is So Sad' and reached the final devastating words – 'That vase.' – I knew I had stumbled upon a poet different from the many others I had read and admired. It took many years before I could see what made Larkin's work so very different from others. One answer to that question – and my answer in this volume – is that Larkin, perhaps surprisingly, is constantly thinking about his audience. In other words, my reaction to his poetry is not merely a reaction to the scenes he describes, the themes he return to, the diction or rhythm or rhyme he uses – although, of course, it is a reaction to all those elements as well – but also to his anticipation of my reaction. To some degree this give and take is true of any writer or conversationalist, as has been demonstrated by linguistic theorists and Reader-Response critics alike.[1] But, as I argue throughout this volume, Larkin's involvement of the audience takes on dimensions beyond the straightforward interplay of poet, speaker and reader generally assumed of him and instead unsettles assumptions about readers' roles and the traditions of form, voice, and poetic narrative.

That consideration of audience, hardly one of the hallmarks of Larkin's popular perception, manifests itself in numerous ways, ranging from the obvious desire to cause aesthetic pleasure in his readers to a stated interest in recreating his own emotions in readers. But it extends much farther as well, through the creation of spaces in the poems into which readers can insert themselves; the regular use of first-person plural pronouns that include the reader even when he wishes not to be included; the positioning of the poems' speakers as audience members themselves to create an alignment with the poems' readers; the explicit calling into question of the observer's role in any scene; and the use of media outside the poems to play games with audience expectations.[2]

In spite of all the statements of Larkin's simplicity – offered both as condemnation and as praise – he remains a man of contradictions. He is at once revered and reviled, profoundly self-deprecating and shockingly arrogant, an aesthetic traditionalist and a religious renegade, a professed misanthrope who expresses profound concern for audience, a quiet recluse with many friends, a university librarian who eschews scholarly reading, a quiet and nervous stammerer who carries on numerous romantic affairs, a literary critic who ridicules literary criticism, and an Oxford-educated poet who claims to despise the study of poetry.

These contradictions contribute to Larkin's continuing appeal and his continuing mystery, but they are not restricted to his life; the poems – while brief and, at least superficially, simple – also contain numerous contradictions. In fact, among the primary difficulties in fully understanding Larkin are the brilliantly contradictory intonations of the poems, which can be read at once as overly accessible and painfully obfuscating. The desire to read the voice of the poems as the precise voice of Larkin is evident in much scholarship, and that tendency certainly has a reasonable basis. He creates poetic speakers so close to his own cultivated persona that one cannot help but assume that the speaker of 'The Whitsun Weddings' or 'I Remember, I Remember' *must* be Larkin himself. As Anthony Easthope confidently proclaims, 'Though the poetry and a writer's critical voice do not necessarily coincide, in Larkin's case they do.'[3] At the same time, though, Larkin offers significant clues throughout his works that such a biographical reading of the poems is false and should not be relied upon. And beyond the difficulties of reading the poems' perspectives lies the complication of the interviews and prose writings. Logically, readers look to these pieces to find answers about both the man and his poetry, but, in many cases, the voices of the interviews are as intricate and puzzling as Larkin's other voices.

My goal in *Philip Larkin and His Audiences* is to examine the different ways that Larkin approaches his relationship to audience in order to explain some of his contradictions and to highlight the sophistication and deliberateness of his poems; my study builds on earlier works that argue effectively for Larkin's masks and personae to show a unique positioning of audience in his poems. While some readers, like Stephen Cooper and Richard Palmer, have argued that Larkin's masks protect him from judgment or hide uncomfortable aspects of his personality and beliefs, I explore the poems in conjunction with his other writings to show that the personae serve not (only) to veil the author but also to expose the reader. This uncovering of the reader's place in readership – of his assumptions and his usually comfortably displaced role in the reading of a poem – brands Larkin's poetry and separates it from the formal and linguistic traditions to which it appears to belong. Thus I argue that what separates Larkin's poetry from others' and what makes it both so powerful and so distinctive is its constant attention to the role of the reader.

Mikhail Bakhtin contends that all speech, including secondary speech acts like poems, necessitates the existence of others 'for whom the utterance is constructed... From the very beginning, the speaker expects a response from them, an active responsive understanding. The entire utterance is constructed, as it were, in anticipation of encountering this response.'[4] Throughout this volume, I argue that Larkin constructs his poems – just as he claims to – expecting a response from the reader, but that the poems anticipate multiple levels of reader involvement, not simply the recreation of experience he claims to desire but also an interrogation of the poems' speakers and characters and, ultimately, of the readers themselves.

Much scholarly work on Larkin has attempted to reconcile some of his many seeming contradictions, by, among other things, engaging in Freudian psychoanalysis, as Richard Bradford does, finding some of Larkin's contradictory beliefs and behaviors rooted in similar contradictions inherited from and imposed by his father, Sydney;[5] or by privileging one behavior over another, as Andrew Motion does by suggesting that Larkin's letters and diaries show the more genuine but less publicly acceptable man.[6] Stephen Cooper approaches the contradictions by arguing that perhaps they are not contradictions at all and offering, instead, an alternate reading of Larkin's (mostly prose) writings as subversive; this analysis suggests that Larkin's writings should not be taken literally and instead are meant to send up many of the very qualities – provincialism, misogyny, racism, conservatism – with which he himself is often associated.[7] For any of these approaches, acknowledgment of the role audience plays – both explicitly and implicitly – in Larkin's writings can inform the literary analysis by adding an important dimension to the discussion. Rather than offering a linear model of Larkin's life and poems, a triangulation that includes the reader along with the life and the art, not only in the poems but as a constant presence in the prose and interviews as well, clarifies the nature of Larkin's apparent contradictions and opens the discussion of his poetry to more of its complexities.

Larkin himself has little to say on the subject of his seeming contradictions, treating them very offhandedly, if he addresses them at all. About the tone and content of the letters, of course, we have nothing from Larkin, who certainly could not have anticipated the uproar they would cause or even, likely, the fact that they would be read by the public at all.[8] Concerning some of his other personality quirks, we have only the highly cultivated persona of the interviews, which uncover much about his creation of a publicly presentable poet character but much less about his real depths and intricacies. Reading the interviews, one has an ongoing sense of *déjà-vu*. The same answers are offered again and again, with slight or no variation, leading some critics to suspect that the Larkin persona of the interviews is a disingenuous creation. Many close readers have noted various contradictions in the interviews that support this view, most notably that Larkin claims to be less learned than his answers generally indicate, for instance claiming to know very little about American poetry and then, just a few lines later, invoking both John Ashbery and John O'Hara as well as Archibald MacLeish. In addition, his answers seem to have become so rote as to be almost divorced from his 'real' voice. In response to questions about his failed career as a novelist, for instance, Larkin told Neil Powell, 'I think someone once said – I did, actually – that poems were about yourself, novels about other people' as though the statement were removed from himself and yet entirely familiar to him. Because of this sense of distance from his own interviews, some of which were conducted in writing rather than in person, we may overlook some of the contradictions contained therein because his answers are so predictable and scripted. And those readers who find some disingenuousness in the interviews also rely heavily on answers in the very same interviews to provide insight into Larkin's true beliefs. The question becomes how accurately we can read the tone of those answers to determine which ones are jokes (like his answer to *The Paris Review* that the idea of toads as a symbol of work was 'sheer genius,' something he would almost certainly not say seriously), which ones are straight-faced attempts at creating a common and curmudgeonly but likeable public persona (like his asking 'Who's Jorge Luis Borges?' after being compared to him),[9] and which may have been honest and authentic. These obvious levels of self-presentation heighten our awareness of Larkin's game-playing and encourage us to consider his answers carefully at the same time that we take into account Larkin's own awareness of voices and readers' responses to them.

John Shakespeare's recent revelations in *The Times Literary Supplement* underscore Larkin's profound interest in self-presentation and self-creation and the ways in which he controlled the interviews that are so often taken as complete truths about the poet. Shakespeare provides dozens of examples of Larkin's controlling nature, his desire to appear to *The Times'* readers as 'less of a simple-minded spineless book-drunk, if you can manage it; I want to sound more guarded, more complex, more like a person who could possibly write a good poem.' To that end, he largely rewrites Shakespeare's profile, changing descriptions of his physical appearance, his manner of dress, his friendships, his attitude toward work, his writing habits, and his private life, among other characteristics. Shakespeare asks, in response to this early experience, conducted well before Larkin had written his greatest work or reached much fame, 'Why was Larkin, unlike his fellow poets, so obsessive about his profile?' Shakespeare's answer, and one that will be explored throughout this volume, is that 'he seized this as the perfect opportunity to say exactly what he wanted about himself and his writing as he stood on the cusp of fame, and to direct all future inquirers after him to this article so that he could avoid submitting to further interviews.' As we will see, Larkin did just that, and used future interviews as opportunities to slightly tweak, and mostly repeat, details that he had decided early on to use as the foundation of his public self-presentation.[10]

The approach to his multilayered relationship with audience has long been part of the critical discussion of Larkin's work, albeit often implicitly. While the work that has gained the most attention in recent years has been biographical, quite a number of writers have explored, in part, the ways that Larkin keeps audience in mind. Andrew Swarbrick, for instance, analyzes Larkin's performativity, his manipulation of dramatic action, and his appropriation of 'other people's words.' As Swarbrick finally posits, 'Larkin's poems speak to us and for us in their unique and representative individuality,' thus emphasizing Larkin's 'dialogic negotiation with otherness,' a category in which Swarbrick includes the reader as one of several manifestations of otherness. My study, however, privileges the reader above Swarbrick's other possible categories of other (personae, caricatures) and argues that the multiplicity of 'the reader,' in his stark reality as well as in his possible membership in categories of difference (class, race, gender, age, and nationality) positions him as the primary site of Larkin's contradictions and his uniqueness.

Tijana Stojkovic examines Larkin's relationship with his reader primarily in terms of his 'empathy,' which she reads both in his plain style and in the prose writings that most clearly articulate his attitudes toward audience: as she explains of 'Mr. Bleaney' and 'Toads,' 'a more vulnerable tone, coming from fear, sadness or disappointment with the self often encourages our imaginative participation in the speaker's mental predicament.'[11] While I certainly agree with Stojkovic on this point and offer my own analyses of Larkin's evoking of emphathy in Chapter 5, I also argue throughout this volume that empathy is only one of many ways that Larkin connects to his readers. And while, as Stojkovic points out, Larkin presents a twofold argument for writing for a reader in 'The Pleasure Principle,' – 'It is not only irresponsible on the writer's part to neglect clear communication to the reader, but this neglect is also contrary to the very nature of poetry, as Larkin defines it' – his enactment of such reader-centered writing in his poetry is more complicated than his simple statements of 'neglect' and 'attention' to readers indicate.

Others have noted, more than identity crises or empathy on the part of the speaker, the places left in the text in which readers can insert themselves. Damaso Lopez Garcia, for instance, remarks that the poems present ambiguities that invite 'the reader to compare his own recon-struction [of meaning] with that which necessarily underlies the poem' and move 'the reader to consider the kind of world where such things take place unnoticed.'[12] Others read those spaces as 'bullying' the reader into moving in a direction to which he is resistant. Indeed, the 'blanks' in Larkin's poetry (to borrow a term from Wolfgang Iser's theorizing about fiction) invite readers to make connections that are not fully articulated in the poems and to find a place for themselves not only as readers but, dually, as participants in the poems and as their readers. Whether read as a positively inclusive technique or a negatively abusive one, the silences in Larkin's texts speak as profoundly as the words. As Nicholas Marsh notes, 'the "silence" is a place where we expect to find a causal rela-tionship between two ideas explained, and the poem does not explain... There is no explanation, only a silence.'[13] And I add to this analysis that those silences offer a unique *entrée* point for the reader into the text.

In addition to the multiple voices of the poems complicating interpre-tation, a significant difficulty in analyzing Larkin's work, as we will see in the following chapters, is that the slipperiness and complication of his poetry is not limited to that genre, and critics' logical turning to the interviews and prose writings to find clarity raises its own difficulties, especially since, as John Osborne has amply demonstrated, 'sometimes he lobbed misquotes and false attributions at his interviewers as though testing their fitness for the job.'[14] Given the false leads and obvious manipulations of the interviews (despite their often frank and disarm-ing tone), they cannot generally be used as proof of Larkin's beliefs or the impetus behind the writing of his poems. Nonetheless, Gary Day argues, using 'The Pleasure Principle' as his starting point, that Larkin is only able to find community through his reliance on 'traditional English metres' since he 'takes an authoritarian attitude towards the reader, cir-cumscribing his or her experience of the work by insisting on its one meaning which, moreover, never changes. Indeed the reader is envis-aged as someone incapable of seeing things as the poet sees them...'.[15] This interpretation might be true if we could trust the voice of the prose above the voice of the poems – to use it as a straightforwardly honest interpretive tool – but very little about the prose suggests such hon-esty. On the contrary, Day's assertion that 'Larkin's engagement with an implied reader not only undermines his view of the poem as a one-way message but it also suggests that his poetry is not as self-contained as he seems to think' might be reconfigured to demonstrate instead an undermining of the prose. In other words, if the two genres do not accord, we need not necessarily give primacy to the truth of the prose writings. My approach throughout this volume is always to privilege what is enacted in the poems, even above what Larkin charmingly presents as his 'real' objectives and beliefs. Thus I find not that the poems are undermined by the prose but that the prose is repeatedly and profoundly undermined by the poems.

Although the central contradiction (or consistency, as the case may be) between the voice of the letters and essays and the voice of the poems has caused the greatest damage to Larkin's reputation, his other contradictions are similarly puzzling and potentially problematic in considering him as a poet. One of his great strengths is the familiarity of his poetic voice and his ordinariness as a speaker, in terms of both his subject matter and his view of the world, qualities which suggests that the poems do not require a great deal of interpretation, that, as Larkin himself said in his interview with *The Observer*, 'there's not much to *say* about my work. When you've read a poem, that's it, it's all quite clear what it means.' This statement, like many of Larkin's others, attempts to discourage readers from looking too deeply into the poetry. A number of critics, particularly those sympathetic to Larkin, have commented explicitly on the difficulty of proceeding with Larkin scholarship in the face of his disdain for such a pursuit. As Andrew Motion, the greatest of Larkin's biographers, writes, 'It is hard to write a critical book on Philip Larkin without feeling guilty. ... His comments on his poetry are clearly designed to embarrass or even exclude [critics], either by denigrating their methods or by revealing little about his intentions.'[16] This discouraging of scholarship about his poems, coupled with the ideas that the poetry requires no such analysis, that the literary critic is 'in the unprecedented position of peddling both his work and the standard by which it is judged,' and that a reader who feels he needs assistance with explication must not be reading the poems correctly leads to some of the resistance readers may feel at advancing the study of Larkin's poetry and at carefully examining the contradictions between the man and his work.[17] And yet the poems cry out for analysis, both because they are not simple despite the appearance of simplicity and because Larkin's protestations in favor of simplicity seem a bit too emphatic, particularly once one begins to notice the depth of allusion, symbolism, shifting perspectives, and conflicting interpretations of these 'quite clear' works.

Part of what we learn from Larkin's contradictions is how polarizing a figure he has become, but we also find among Larkin's readers a frequent hesitation to privilege the life or the letters over the poems. Even as Larkin has been brutalized by critics, many readers (with the notable exceptions of Tom Paulin and Lisa Jardine and a few other of the most vocal anti-Larkinists) return to his poems and find in them a value and a voice that transcends and ultimately supersedes the baseness of the letters. As John Banville writes, 'All this, of course, is incidental to what matters, which is the poetry. ... And, *pace* Eliot, Larkin was – is – a great poet.'[18] But others who do admire Larkin's poems find it hard to reconcile what they know of him from the poems with what they have learned of him from his other writings. The question of which voice to privilege – the sensitive speaker of segments of the poems or the bigot and misanthrope of the letters and diaries – looms large over how readers judge Larkin and into which camp they fall.

Nonetheless, we find reviewers like Banville noting that, despite the letters' 'violence and virulence,' 'one finds it difficult to see why at the time of publication so much was made of the misogynistic and misanthropic aspects of them. Larkin had never sought to hide his views...'.[19] This idea is further articulated by Joseph Bristow, who writes that, far from disliking Larkin's obscenity, readers loved it and found it endearing until, through the publication of the letters, they found that 'the use of "fuck," "crap" and "piss" now enjoys a far more disturbing authenticity. It seems as if Larkin actually *meant* what he was saying.' In other words, just as readers have suspected that the interviews did not show the true Larkin, they have suspected – consciously or not – the same of the poems, thus allowing for the ongoing charm of the neurotic, vulgar, low-brow speaker of 'This Be the Verse' or 'Wild Oats' who was, for the readers, almost another Jake Balokowsky of 'Posterity,' a writerly creation; but by privileging the letters and believing, as nearly all readers have, that these private correspondences speak the voice of the 'true' Larkin, they find that he is himself the Balokowsky, not a poetic voice at all, but a real bigot and actual lowbrow. In the manner of good New Critics, readers of the 1970s and 1980s seem to have believed that behind the persona of the poems' speaker was an ordinary guy about whom no assumptions could be made from the voice of the poetry, or only such assumptions as were supported by the curmudgeonly but nonetheless charming speaker of the interviews and radio shows. The shock of the letters hit almost as though readers had found, after reading 'My Last Duchess,' that Robert Browning had actually done away with his first wife before meeting Elizabeth and had had a lovely portrait made.

Such a misperception, while never applied by a creditable reader to Browning's work, is consistently used in analysis of Larkin's poems. As James Phelan presents it, Browning's role in his poem is made gradually more evident 'when we realize the audience and the occasion for the Duke's speech.' The poem's construction, unfolding a story as it does, offers the Duke as a character who might be initially reliable but whose situation, as the poem develops 'would seem an obvious contrivance by Browning.' In other words, 'as Browning follows the mimetic imperative, he also increases the effectiveness of the poem as a constructed object.' Larkin's poetry, while remarkably similar to Browning's in its creation of character, development of narrative lines, and attempt at creating 'the *illusion* that we are not reading a poem but overhearing part of a conversation' (or, more frequently in Larkin's case, witnessing an internal, rather than a dramatic, monologue), is seldom read as Browning's is, with a precise separation between speaker and author.[20] Part of the reason for this conflation is the obvious choice Larkin makes to present speakers who seem like himself and therefore more open to potential confusion with himself. A more significant reason, however, and one that I argue for throughout this volume, is that Larkin's subtle insertions of the reader into the text decrease the effectiveness of the poem as a constructed object, to borrow Phelan's language, and increase its effectiveness, misleadingly, as an offering of self that is more true than illusory.[21]

The structure of *Philip Larkin and His Audiences* develops an argument for Larkin's multifaceted inclusion of audience in the poems that begins broadly, presenting in the first chapter several ways that Larkin leaves room for readers, encourages their participation, forces them to take sides, and unsettles their expectations for lyric poetry. The second chapter expands this argument by examining his use of multiple tonalities in complex and unexpected contexts to acknowledge layers of readership and further to destabilize readers' positions. The last three chapters focus on three subject areas of particular concern to Larkin that persist throughout his poetic career: temporality, jazz, and religion. In each case, I argue, Larkin engages readers and positions them as active participants in the poems, inviting them to take responsibility for their interpretive acts and to view the reading – as much as the writing – of poems as a consciously synthetic act of artistic creation.

1
Larkin and Audience

Often, analysis of Larkin's writing emphasizes his artistic development over time. Based on Larkin's own comments, critics frequently remark on his imitations of Yeats and Auden, hierarchizing his poetry volumes into those that have little poetic merit on their own but might prefigure the later poems (*XX Poems* and *The North Ship*) and those that best illustrate Larkin's mature talents (*The Less Deceived* and *The Whitsun Weddings*, generally, and, somewhat less often, *High Windows*). The differences among these volumes, for many critics, are not merely of poetic diction and style but of substance and subject matter, with the later poems more often referring to loneliness and the onrushing of death and the earlier poems showing more concern with romantic and sexual relationships. While of course we can find significant generalized differences among the volumes, we also see that some of Larkin's primary poetic concerns remain constant throughout his life. He himself states that he is not interested in poetic development, and although he says it jokingly, the similarities among the volumes are at least as pronounced as the developments and differences. Although the subject matter does shift noticeably in the later volumes, I would argue that the shift is less significant than the numerous ways in which the later poems demonstrate almost identical concerns to the poems of the early volumes.

Indeed, the sense of community created in both the earlier and later published poems remains nearly constant, and although the later poems deal less with sex and the earlier ones (somewhat) less with death, they ultimately show a remarkable constancy in their concern for the audience's place in the poem itself. Larkin is explicit about the important relationship between artist and audience in many of his writings, but he expresses this interest most clearly in 'The Pleasure Principle' and the Introduction to *All What Jazz*. Although his prose writings are

1

notoriously untrustworthy, his many statements of attention to audience are not only consistent throughout his life but also across genres, including, importantly, in the poems themselves. He writes, of the writing of a poem, that 'the third stage is the recurrent situation of people in different times and places setting off the device and re-creating in themselves what the poet felt when he wrote it... If there is no third stage, no successful reading, the poem can hardly be said to exist in a practical sense at all.'[1] He reminds readers, in 1957's 'The Pleasure Principle,' that 'poetry is emotional in nature and theatrical in operation, a skilled recreation of emotion in other people.' He goes on, over a decade later, to say that there are 'two tensions from which art springs: the tension between the artist and his material, and between the artist and his audience,' and he suggests that ignoring the second of these tensions leads to a decline in 'people using their eyes and ears and understandings to report pleasure and discomfort.'[2] The audience in Larkin's view, at least as expressed explicitly in these two pieces, is necessary to production. Acknowledging readers is not merely a byproduct of writing, nor are readers simply consumers of an artistic good; they are part of the creative process.

Larkin does not articulate what he sees the audience's role to be, precisely, but the frequently stated sense that the reader is 'essential' and 'fundamental' to the writing process begs the question of how Larkin regards his reader, particularly since, as a poet, he is judged so often as insular and self-absorbed. He certainly seems to consider real readers, particularly those who read for pleasure rather than scholarship. But as I will demonstrate in this chapter, he includes as well – intentionally or not – a variety of the 'narrative audience' of which Peter Rabinowitz writes, 'a role which the text forces the reader to take on.'[3] For the genre of poetry, however, Rabinowitz's terms must be slightly redefined, as the poem does not precisely mimic a nonfictional form (although it may pretend to express historical truth in verse) and therefore circumvents a reader's implicit knowledge of his adoption of a narrative audience stance; actual readers of poems do not ask themselves 'What sort of reader would I have to pretend to be... if I wanted to take this work of fiction as real?' because the mere form of the work, its self-evident artistry and, certainly in Larkin's case, its brevity, offers resistance to an audience's full novelistic absorption into the work.[4] More significantly, it denies its own fictionality by not being an obvious work of fiction, about which readers have long been taught to differentiate between narrator and author.[5] Because his poems seem to inhabit a middle ground between fiction and nonfiction, Larkin is able to manipulate his readers at the same time that he engages them; the simple attention to readers' concerns in his prose is both expanded and complicated in the poems, which do not simply please (as one might assume they would based on Larkin's prose statements) but also discomfit and challenge.[6]

In Larkin's prose, we find an overt preoccupation with audience that is reflected in his poetry, his criticism, his feelings about music, and his private correspondences, albeit in far more sophisticated ways than his accessible prose indicates. Aside from two youthful and uncharacteristic comments, that 'a poet never thinks of his reader. Why should he? The reader doesn't come into the poem at all,' and that 'poetry is nobody's business except the poets' & everybody else can fuck off,'[7] Larkin shows a great interest in what his reader thinks and how he interacts with the poem.[8] Larkin talks and writes repeatedly about the necessary tension he feels between artist and audience, for example in 'Subsidizing Poetry,' in which he discusses 'the fundamental nexus between poet and audience, which is something he has to struggle for in the same way that he struggles with his medium of words,' and in his introduction to *All What Jazz*. There he writes extensively about modernism's loss of the tension 'between the artist and his audience' which has 'slackened or even perished,' and, 'in consequence the artist has become over-concerned with his material, and, in isolation, has busied himself with the two principal themes of modernism, mystification and outrage.'[9] Larkin's anger at this loss of the 'artist-audience nexus' seems to be not only on his own behalf but also in defense of the 'romantic loiterer who recalls the days when poetry was condemned as sinful'.

As we will see in Chapter 4, that romantic loiterer may be Larkin himself, not as poet but as reader. The loss of the slightly subversive nature of poetry, which Larkin senses has come about with the wider acceptance and study of poetry, disappoints him because he hopes to appeal to the person who looks to poetry as a place, much like jazz, for the intellectual outsider. Frequently Larkin presents himself (untruthfully) as such an outsider, and jazz – because it did not strike Larkin as a formal academic field of study – fulfills the caricature, if not the reality, of a genre for the pleasure-seeker. Similar sentiments of pure audience empowerment can be found throughout his prose writings, as in the review 'Armstrong's Last Goodnight': 'He listened to what the audience applauded, and tried to give it to them.' Throughout these prose writings, we can find readers very like Larkin – those romantic loiterers, perhaps – and also those who share certain basic poetic assumptions with him but are otherwise undefined.

Larkin has an enormous respect for and trust in his audience and claims in places to know what it wants from him: a recreation of the poet's own experience that elicits genuine and deeply felt emotion. In 'The Pleasure Principle,' for instance, Larkin laments that 'We seem to be producing a new kind of bad poetry, not the old kind that tries to move the reader and fails, but one that does not even try,' a claim that he repeats in a number of other contexts as well.[10] The goal of pleasing the reader is presented as foremost in Larkin's mind, and abandonment of that goal seems practically equivalent to abandoning poetry itself. If a poem is commissioned, for instance, then 'the poet is paid to write, and the audience is paid to listen. Something vital goes out of their relation, and I am afraid that something vital goes out of poetry too.'[11] Furthermore, readers must begin 'asking themselves more frequently whether they do in fact enjoy what they read, and, if not, what the point is of carrying on,' which essentially encourages readers to divorce themselves from those poets who do not aim to please.[12] He neglects to mention what, precisely, causes that pleasure, but his openness to the general readers' desires here trumps, at least in theory, all other concerns. For all his professed dislike of social situations and self-cultivated perception of his solitary and lonely life, Larkin presents himself in 'The Pleasure Principle' and in 'Subsidizing Poetry,' as having greater regard for the intelligence and ability of his readers – not to mention greater concern for their personal enjoyment – than most other artists, and certainly than the castigated Modernists. This relationship is nonetheless deeply fraught, in that Larkin publicly idealizes certain readers (the pleasure-seekers) and publicly dismisses others (students and scholars, particularly).

But, as we know from the plethora of contradictions contained therein, Larkin's prose writings and interviews cannot be taken at face value. In recent years, critics have presented irrefutable evidence that Larkin, for all his professed shunning of allusion and the 'myth-kitty' of Modernism, was quite allusion-heavy himself, in both his poems and his interviews. John Osborne, among others, has argued that Larkin, despite publicly dismissing Modernism, was profoundly influenced by the movement and used a number of Modernist techniques in his poetry. Osborne goes so far as to say that Larkin 'misled interviewers,' that he 'loved many aspects of Modernist music but lied about it,' and that the influence of Eliot is 'so pervasive that it is possible to detect echoes of his work in nearly forty Larkin poems.'[13] Critics have shown, variously, that Larkin claimed not to be well-read but had obviously read quite a bit; that he ostentatiously dismissed foreign literatures but was very familiar with and admired quite a number of foreign writers; and that he cultivated a persona as a quiet and reclusive bachelor but actually had a fairly active social and romantic life. These contradictions are evident in some places: in the single *Required Writing* volume, which Larkin collected himself, he says to the *Observer* on page 53, 'I virtually read only novels, or something pretty undemanding in the non-fiction line, which might be a biography. I read almost no poetry. I've always thought the reading habits of Dylan Thomas matched mine – he never read anything hard' and then on pages 85 and 86, 'I've always been a compulsive reader. ... Within reach of my working chair have reference books on the right, and twelve poets on the left.' However, in the area of Larkin's attachment to his audience, no such contradictions exist. This is a concern he wrote and spoke about for decades of his career and, far from disproving Larkin's interest in his audience, the poems show his attention to and engagement of audience in ways well beyond even what the prose indicates. In fact, the poems demonstrate a more sophisticated and broader attachment to audience than one might guess based on the prose statements, and they deliberately appeal to a wider variety of audience: the pleasure-seekers, certainly, but also the scholars, students and critics who are dismissed in his prose.

While Larkin may describe a particular sort of reader, as he does in the Introduction to *All What Jazz*, who resembles his own public persona and shares his poetic interests, his poems demonstrate a broader approach to satisfying readers and expands the definition of 'the reader' far beyond the 'sullen, fleshly inarticulate men' described in *All What Jazz*. Throughout his volumes of poetry, Larkin emphasizes his alignment with an audience and his nearly constant awareness of that audience's presence. The poetry highlights, in other words, the truth of Larkin's stated interest in the audience and the enactment of that fundamental writer–reader tension to which he so frequently refers. Most importantly, this concern is evident throughout the body of his poetry and not merely in the poetry of a particular period of his life. In other words, despite all of Larkin's slipperiness in pinning down his real beliefs and ideals, one that seems to remain constant from the beginning to the end and across all genres and types of work is a particular attention to the relationship of writer to reader. The important difference among genres, though, is how that concern is enacted. In the prose, Larkin writes of a very specific audience (the pleasure-seekers) and of a more general audience (those in the artist-audience nexus), but the poems also reach out to scholarly readers that, in the prose, he claims to at least ignore and at most disdain. In any case, the concerns of pleasure, which sound relatively simple in the prose, are vastly complicated by the poems' reaching out to different kinds of readers in ways that unsettle as much as they please.

In a number of the poems, we find the speaker sounding very much like the Larkin readers have imagined, and naturally the relationship between speaker and poet is significant; but again and again we find that the more important – and the more compelling – relationship is between the speaker and his readers. The readers figure implicitly in so many of Larkin's poems that it is surprising how seldom critics comment on their presence. Instead, the focus is almost always on the 'Larkin' character himself and on that character's real-life relationship to Larkin; his fears, his insecurities, and his pedestrian opinions capture the critics' attention far more than his frequent reaching out to his audience. Bradford's emphasis on this connection is most stark, generally focusing almost entirely on the experiences in Larkin's life that have led to the poems' being written; for instance, Bradford's analysis of 'The Old Fools' claims that it was written in direct response to Amis' writing *Ending Up* and, further, to a birthday card from Winifred Arnott, the return of Colin Gunner, and the institutionalization of Patsy Strang. Most other critics are less interested in finding perfect parallels between the poems and Larkin's life, but the emphasis remains on the relationship between Larkin and his speakers. Larkin halfheartedly reinforces this interpretive approach by explaining to John Haffenden that 'I think we *want* the life and the work to make sense together: I suppose ultimately they must, since they both relate to the same person.'[14] Larkin likely recognizes the complications in this statement, though, and his own resistance to it, which is exemplified by his creation of a 'Larkin' character.

Larkin goes to great lengths to present himself as an ordinary kind of guy who just happens to be visited by a poetic muse now and then: he tells *Paris Review* that, just like everyone else, he's not particularly talented.[15] Through this cultivated modesty and disarming self-effacement, he presents himself as understanding the desires and motivations of the regular reader because he, too, is so plain and simple. He further emphasizes this point through many of his answers to interview questions, particularly those about his own scholarship. In keeping with his professed belief that student and critic audiences for poetry ruin its beauty and disrupt that fundamental tension between artist and audience, Larkin presents himself, somewhat misleadingly, as neither a student nor a critic. His interviews often highlight his 'ordinary reader' status, and he intentionally cultivates the sense that he is an average working man with plain tastes and middlebrow interests. He claims to have 'always been right-wing' and to associate particular virtues with conservatism, including 'thrift, hard work, reverence, desire to preserve,' and shortly thereafter reinforces that ordinariness by remarking on his own lifestyle: 'I don't really notice where I live: as long as a few simple wants are satisfied – peace, quiet, warmth – I don't mind where I am.'[16] He further encourages the view of himself as not particularly intellectual (and not particularly respectful of intellectuals) by saying that 'maybe the average reader can understand what I say, but the above-average often can't.'[17] To show his passivity and distance himself from those artists with a 'higher purpose,' he explains that Betjeman, whom he claims to love and admire, 'is always against uglification, greed, vulgarity, and the rest of it. I just accept them for the most part.'[18] In all of these cases, the 'Larkin the librarian-poet' character presents a necessarily oversimplified and publicly palatable version of himself for easy digestion. He offers himself as a particular 'type,' and while many of these characteristics – or less severe iterations of them – may be true of him, his answers generally indicate a willingness to oversimplify his own character in a way that commonly leads to similarly oversimplified readings of his poems, beginning with the presumption that so simple a man must be a simple poet as well.

Larkin tells John Haffenden about his time at Oxford that he loved it but always felt 'a pressure at the back of my neck at being surrounded by about six thousand people who are cleverer than I am.'[19] And, about his poetic prominence, he says, 'Please don't think that I'm great. If I'm noticeable, it's because we're in a trough at the moment.'[20] He is similarly self-effacing with the *Paris Review*: 'I don't read much. Books I'm sent to review. Otherwise novels I've read before. ... Nothing difficult.'[21] These comments, and many others like them, underscore Larkin's public presentation of himself as a person who simply reads what he likes and one who is, as much as possible, unlike Pound or Eliot in their synthesizing of the 'poet' and 'critic' roles. He refers emphatically to his dislike of literary criticism and his intention to have nothing to do with such a pursuit. As he tells *Paris Review*, 'I should think chewing over other people's work, writing I mean, must be terribly stultifying. Quite sicken you with the whole business of literature' and, later in the same interview, "I've never been much interested in other people's poetry.' And yet, as we well know, Larkin had an elite literary education and wrote reviews and critical essays prolifically, both to promote writers he admired (John Betjeman, Barbara Pym) and lambaste those he did not (the later W.H. Auden, Roy Morrell, Rupert Brooke). His self-presentation in the interviews is pleasant and modest and means to highlight his similarities to 'everyone else.' He is not particularly gifted, not special or different in any way; and many readers have taken these comments at face value and found in the poems precisely the kind of simplicity of language and thought that would complement a man such as the one Larkin presents to Haffenden. And yet even the casual reader of Larkin would easily discover how misleading these self-presentations are.

In addition to being perceived as ordinary and anti-intellectual, Larkin is often considered a kind of hermit, both because he asserts that he has 'withdrawn from what you call "the contemporary literary community" and because he describes his daily routine as 'as simple as I can make it... I almost never go out.'[22] What we find, however, by reading the poems with the relationship between speaker and reader in mind is not that Larkin reaffirms his 'recluse' persona by creating speakers who model anti-social behavior, but that the poems actually create a very social atmosphere in which the relationship between the speaker and the reader is constantly reaffirmed while the reader's role in the poems is challenged. Readers want to believe in 'Larkin the loner,' (and Larkin wants readers to want to believe) and he encourages that belief through various aspects of his self-depiction, including his own descriptions of a colorless, lonely childhood; an intimidated, nervous college experience; a resigned acceptance of isolated, small-town librarianship; and an adult bachelorhood in cold, quiet rental flats. But while the poetry, on the surface at least, could, with some embellishment and some deletions on the reader's part, further encourage such beliefs, it could also demonstrate the kind of communities Larkin created around himself and the kind he continues to create through groups of readers who feel a connection not just to the speaker but to other readers as well.

Larkin claims, in several of his prose pieces, to desire a preservation of experience in his poetry. He most famously tells D.J. Enright in 1955, 'I write poems to preserve things I have seen/thought/felt... both for myself and for others, though I feel that my prime responsibility is to the experience itself, which I am trying to keep from oblivion for its own sake. Why I should do this I have no idea, but I think the impulse to preserve lies at the bottom of all art,'[23] and he repeats this idea in interviews and other writings on at least three more occasions. The many poems in which Larkin presents his speaker as separate from the so-called experience of the poem lead to the frequent analysis of his poetic character as isolated, lonely, and unhappy. And the poems do, in many ways, ask for this sort of explication. 'The Large Cool Store,' 'Ambulances,' 'An Arundel Tomb,' 'Home is So Sad,' 'Faith Healing,' and 'Reasons for Attendance' all feature a central first-person figure who does not seem to participate directly in the experience that the poem describes; he watches shoppers or watches ambulances or watches worshippers or watches dancers. Unlike 'Aubade,' 'Sad Steps,' 'Letter to a Friend About Girls,' and 'A Study of Reading Habits,' which feature the speaker in the action of the poem, these others show a speaker far removed from the experience that Larkin claims he wishes to preserve. But as we know, the preserved experience for Larkin is indeed the experience of observation; so, for example, in 'Reasons for Attendance,' the preserved experience is not that of dancing but of watching dancing, which is itself an important experience for Larkin and, he suggests, for his readers as well. The speaker of this poem feels called by the music of a trumpet to a bright window, where he stands and watches young couples, simultaneously solemn and happy, dance in pairs, holding each other tightly. While Larkin might be critiqued for placing a speaker outside the action of the poem, the speaker's distance from the 'action' is only true if one defines the action, rather narrowly, as dancing; what Larkin's poetry emphasizes, though – particularly through the prominent image of the 'lighted glass' against which the speaker places himself – is that observation is itself a powerful action and one that his speakers (and, by association and temperament, his readers) engage in very well.

In this poem we find necessary layers of audience that highlight the importance of the reader for Larkin's poetry. Written in 1953 and published in *The Less Deceived*, 'Reasons for Attendance' shares the audience concerns that we see throughout his poetry and prose, both earlier and much later. Because it is so often read as a poem of almost devastating loneliness, it is an especially effective one to consider when arguing that Larkin in fact works against that sense of isolation. This poem, like many of Larkin's others that seem initially to highlight solitude and the solitary experience, actually plays with the idea of a lonely poetic speaker by implicating the reader in that same loneliness. The regular misreading of these poems may stem from the discomfort of being affiliated with this seemingly anti-social speaker, which leads most readers to judge the speaker rather than recognizing their essential similarities with him. 'Reasons for Attendance,' along with many of the other first-person poems, creates not only a solitude but also a solidarity between speaker and reader – and, almost necessarily, with the poet as well – but only if readers are willing to put themselves in the slightly discomfiting position of viewing themselves with the same brutal honesty with which Larkin forces his speakers to approach the poetic mirror.

Most analyses of this poem emphasize Larkin's, or sometimes the speaker's, separation from the action of the poem and the consequent sense of depression and even misery that accompanies this solitary, separate figure. Andrew Swarbrick argues that the speaker is 'an outsider looking in,' 'drawn towards an individual fulfillment in art rather than the dancers' search for happiness with a mate'. Swarbrick goes on to explain that the speaker, in his 'bachelor's vocation to Art,' 'knows all too well that the individuality he thinks is preserved in Art might in fact be nothing more than an imprisoning loneliness.'[24] His emphasis, like that of most critics, is on the speaker's isolation and, implicitly, on the speaker's similarity to Larkin himself. Simon Petch, examining the sentence structures and rhymes of the poem, similarly argues that the poem underscores the speaker's separateness and says that the speaker's 'sudden acknowledgement of the falseness of his rationalization makes explicit what has been apparent all along to the reader. The poet has conclusively exposed his speaker through structure and versification.'[25] Janice Rossen says, about Larkin's poems in general, that 'for the most part, though, the poet remains an outsider and an observer of others and their rituals, rather than becoming part of the crowd with them. On a larger scale as well as a small one, he prefers solitude,' and she calls this attitude part of 'a larger misanthropy.'[26] All three of these, whether reading the poem as autobiographical or not, make much of the speaker's separateness and isolation and of his false rationalization. And yet the persona of the poem need not be read this way, and instead , in this Prufrockian scene, might be saying 'Let us go then, *you and I.*' The speaker's individual insecurities are additionally directed outward, implicating the reader rather than allowing him to maintain an attitude of smug superiority to an isolated, neurotic speaker.

Throughout 'Reasons for Attendance,' the speaker uses the first person voice, calling attention to his own place in the scene he observes. Seemingly offhanded phrases like 'as far as I'm concerned' and more grandiose statements like 'I too am an individual' serve to remind readers of the loneliness of this experience and the self-conscious choice on the speaker's part to be alone. The problems with finding direct parallels between Larkin's life and this speaker in this moment should be obvious: Larkin's regular participation in romantic coupleship, among other things. But a problem also exists with finding the speaker buttressed in his isolation, for where is the reader during this poem? Inside with the dancers, 'all under twenty-five'? Certainly not, and Larkin is well aware that he has positioned his readers with his speaker, outside and watching.

The poem seems so solitary, in its repetition of 'me' and 'I' and in its arguments in favor of finding happiness alone, listening alone, and watching alone, that readers may overlook the very poignant lack of loneliness in the poem. Certainly the speaker is not part of a couple in 'Reasons for Attendance,' but he seems to have found something better: a community. We might believe initially that he is speaking to himself in this poem and that the monologue is really only intended as a justification to the speaker himself for not participating in the dance. But we find two important moments when he moves outside of the first person voice in ways that change the tone of the poem. First, in the parenthetical aside, which is easily overlooked, the speaker addresses his readers directly:

> What calls me is that lifted, rough-tongued bell
> (Art, if you like) whose individual sound
> Insists that I too am individual.

While the subject of those three lines is individualism and the way that the music speaks directly to the poem's speaker, proclaiming for him his individuality, the parenthetical 'Art, if you like' says something entirely different. The 'if you like' has the same kind of throwaway tone as 'as far as I'm concerned,' but the change from first to second person is hardly incidental. All along the speaker has been addressing us, watching with him through the glass, but in this aside, which is generally analyzed more for the word 'art' than for the second person address, he gives us a moment to respond and to participate in the conversation. Leaving open the possibility of an ordinary and meaningless colloquialism, that 'you' also serves as both an invitation and a reminder: we are invited to watch with him – and, by watching, to experience – and we are reminded that we, too, are individuals, in 'attendance' 'here' and not 'there.' The 'if you like' practically admonishes us not to judge the speaker for remaining separate, for what are we if not just like him?

The conscious attention to the 'here' and 'there' of the poem and to the poem's sense of place – a characteristic central to Larkin's poetry generally, as in 'The Importance of Elsewhere' and 'Here' – is presented with the reader in mind since we, having no choice in the matter, are positioned 'here' rather than 'there'. This principle is, to some extent, necessarily true of lyric poetry, which places a reader 'here' alongside the poem's speaker. So Larkin's speaker might be no different from Wordsworth's in 'I Wandered Lonely as a Cloud'.' And yet the reader's role is significantly different in these two poems because Wordsworth describes for us his experience without any suggestion or hint that we have experienced it too, or ever will. We are allowed to see, over his shoulder, or through his eyes, what he saw, and we are told what the experience meant to him and how it continues to affect him, but our own attendance in the episode is perfectly unquestioned.

Larkin, on the other hand, presents himself not merely as separate from the dancers but as aligned with the reader. He offers reasons for our attendance – both our physical presence and our careful attention – as well as his own. The subtle inclusion of a 'you' in the poem begins to open it to something well beyond a Wordsworthian depiction of experience, but the final line of the poem departs from the Romantic first person voice in a simultaneously less subtle and more unsettling way. Rather than changing to the second person here, as he does in line 13, Larkin writes the final line in third person voice, thus creating a new kind of relationship with his reader. This very personal poem takes on such a clearly communal sensibility in its last line: 'If no one has misjudged himself, or lied.' Larkin makes perfectly clear here that the speaker doubts his own arguments, just presented with such superficial confidence, and he also points out, through the use of the third person voice, that the dancers (if they were more thoughtful and a bit more self-conscious, perhaps) would also doubt their choices. But the generalized 'one' here includes a further subject, and that is the reader himself. Have we misjudged ourselves? This poem is as much an accusation as it is a self-assessment, and that final line insists on a reconsideration of the reader's – as well as the speaker's – confidence in his own decisions. Throughout the poem, the speaker is particularly reflective and explicit about his outsider status and the fact of his conscious choice thereof, unlike the reader. His frankness is then compounded by the explicit self-doubt about that choice. This self-doubt places the reader in one of two positions: either finding himself connected, through his own insecurity, to this lonely speaker, or passing judgment on the speaker while willfully overlooking the fact that he is positioned alongside him. The last line prevents the honest reader from separating himself fully from the speaker, and if he considers himself and his own position as honestly as the speaker does, he will recognize their kinship. Being a critic does not prevent the reader from being implicated here, and only the reader who is able to ignore or disown his relationship with that speaker can force on the speaker the title of 'misanthrope.'

Whether the readers believe in the poem's argument concerning love – that the popular belief that being part of a couple is a perfect recipe for happiness is a fallacy – is hardly the point of including the readers with the speaker rather than having the speaker truly stand alone. Instead, that thoughtful placement reminds readers that they, too, often remain outside the most obvious action and that doing so is a choice, and not necessarily a bad one. The dancers are 'other' to everyone conscious of the poem: to speaker and reader alike. And while Rossen and Petch and many others make much of the speaker's lack of compassion and his purposeful separation from the love and action of life, they subtly place themselves in a superior position, implicitly suggesting that by having such insight into Larkin's speaker, or Larkin himself, they are aligned with the dancers – with those who experience their full lives – not as judgmental observers but as active participants. The poem is clever in its manipulation of the reader, though, and, if we look at it not as an indictment of Larkin or as a demonstration of what we would like to believe Larkin to be, we find in it the kind of relationship between speaker and reader that Larkin long argued was one of his primary interests in writing verse. The 'fundamental nexus' here is not that of a misanthropic writer removing himself from the life of the world, but of a shrewd observer connecting himself to other observers who, instead of dancing and making love, are sitting somewhere by themselves reading poems.

In addition, we must consider that the poet is himself separate from the speaker here, as Eliot is from Prufrock. Swarbrick suggests that Larkin's use of a jazz motif in this poem says 'something about his own love of jazz either as an involvement in a shared popular culture or as the pursuit of a solitary aesthetic. Even here, it seems, Larkin is divided between communality and privacy.'[27] And yet this idea of a clear divide between 'communality and privacy' (attributed in this case not to the poem's speaker but to Larkin himself – and to jazz, which is not mentioned in the poem as being the music to which the dancers listen) dismisses the important communality created by the mere fact that the poem is being read. It pretends that the speaker (or, perhaps, Larkin) is truly alone in 'Reasons for Attendance' rather than recognizing the obvious community created outside of the dance hall. Just because no one stands next to the speaker in the poem does not mean that no one is there. *We* are there. The readers are not dancing, flushed, cheek to cheek. They are watching, right along with him. In fact, the speakers of Larkin's poems often perform this translator or guide function, which leads to the superficial sense of isolation from the world, but, more deeply and more positively, also leads to a greater affinity between reader and writer. Because the reader finds himself so seamlessly integrated into the action of the poem through both the speaker's positioning and the poem's use of pronouns, he is able to disregard his own place alongside the speaker, but closer attention to the place of the reader – and Larkin's direct address of him – forces us to recognize a community in the poem that is often more easily, or more comfortably, ignored.

In addition, the preservation of the experience in 'Reasons for Attendance' is far more complicated than Larkin's simple statement to Enright would allow: the poem is not merely a maintenance of the speaker's own experience as a viewer. The sight is real enough for the speaker, even from outside the glass, to know 'the wonderful feel of the girls,' which he hopes, presumably, the reader can feel as well, even at the same time knowing that we are all individuals and cannot share his precise happiness: he can only hear for himself, as others can only hear for themselves; and this individual reaction to music is paralleled in people's individual reactions to emotions. And what is this sentiment but the writing of a poem, the idea that he may express the experience as well as possible and yet never fully recreate it for the reader? But that is the goal nonetheless, to create that 'enormous yes' and remain true to the experience, even while recognizing that the reader is necessarily outside of the 'true' experience. So as much as the reader stands alongside the speaker, Larkin recognizes that the speaker has a perspective the reader cannot have – that of a lived experience rather than an experience through words – and the question becomes how effectively the speaker can convey his experience to those of us standing just behind him, straining for a view, and perhaps for an emotion as well.

Ultimately, this poem suggests that reading *is* doing and, simultaneously, that readers may be deluding themselves in this belief. The poem offers no easy answers but does present possibilities. There is a comfort in being outside, and at the same time a necessary justification for remaining a reader rather than a participant. But, in addition, being a reader *is* being a participant, just not in the way generally valued by a society that emphasizes touch and sex and contact instead of one that recognizes observation as its own kind of experience. 'Reasons for Attendance,' while often read as a misanthropic work and as a poem that emphasizes loneliness and externality, can also be read as a poem of connection and community. That interpretation, though, requires a willingness, at least temporarily, to distance Larkin's biography from his poetry: to reconsider the popular perception of Larkin as a loner and to face the universality of the observer. More importantly, it asks for an awareness of the very individual loneliness of the poetry reader, of which Larkin is acutely aware and which he points out through both the direct and indirect address of the reader in this poem. Larkin possesses this kind of self-awareness in abundance, but most readers seem to feel uncomfortable perceiving themselves as mere observers, as though the fact of separateness is an insult rather than a simple truth.

Robert Crosman asks if readers make meaning, and he answers with a confident 'yes' that he posits against E.D. Hirsch's argument that the author makes meaning. In fact, Larkin's poetry may address this question in a roundabout way with the applicable metric that the author makes readers who make meaning. The conscious layering of readers, speaker, and author in Larkin's poems demonstrate his awareness that readers have a necessary role and are inseparable from the either the author's or the text's creation of meaning (a possibility that appeals to neither Crosman nor Hirsch). And so while the Larkin persona of the interviews scoffs at those who 'trust the tale and not the teller,' the poems move beyond a question of tale and teller and instead focus on the implied 'you' of the verb 'trust.' In fact, the important part of Larkin's quoting of Lawrence is neither the tale nor the teller but the implicit statement that someone is doing the 'trusting.'

Larkin's allowance of a space for the reader in the poem may hint, too much for Crosman's taste, at the possibility that author's meaning is that readers should create meaning – a clever bit of simultaneous holding on and letting go – but it also splits the reader into the one who is implicitly included in the poem through the observing speaker and the actual person who reads the poem and may, or may not, react as Larkin anticipates. Crosman remarks that authors make meaning 'in exactly the same way we all make meaning: as interpreters, as readers.'[28] Larkin's frequent remove from the subjects he examines – his positioning of the speaker as 'an interpreter, a reader' – seems to acknowledge the inherent truth of the reader's power more overtly than does other lyric poetry. That additional level of remove places a gap in the text into which readers are invited.[29] Furthermore, the speaker's near compulsion to offer multiple interpretations of the scenes he observes – to double back on and rethink and undercut previous ideas and opinions – opens for the reader more profound places for themselves in the text, a kind of polyphony that will be discussed at greater length in the next chapter. Historically, critics have often filled these textual gaps with details from Larkin's life, but the poems do not necessarily ask for that treatment and instead invite readers themselves to step into those gaps. The significant differences between Larkin's lyric and, for instance, Wordsworth's (the poet Crosman uses to prove readers' making of meaning), is precisely in the consciousness of this reliance on the reader, particularly since the speaker himself is so often positioned as a 'reader' of what he observes. In poems ranging from 'Triple Time' to 'Essential Beauty' to 'Show Saturday,' spanning the length of his poetic career, Larkin merges the visual and cerebral perspectives on a scene to recreate the readerly experience, first for his speaker and, secondarily, for the reader who watches, hears, and internalizes the 'reading' speaker.

Andrew Swarbrick remarks that the 'personae or 'masks' by which Larkin ventriloquises attitudes evolve from his command of idiom' and that his poems can be read as '"performative" in being constructed with an explicit consciousness of the impression they are creating.'[30] Stephen Cooper extends this analysis to suggest that this quality of multiple voices, which he examines through Larkin's adoption of a female voice in some early stories and poems, 'is a phenomenon more usually associated with the novelist than with the poet.'[31] This tracing of Larkin's various voices to his lost career as a novelist is valuable, but it may prevent readers from noticing the distinctly poetic qualities of this 'multivocal polyphony,' as Stephen Regan calls it, or the style's associations not merely with Larkin's novelist ambitions but also with his desire to appeal to an audience, even one 'who has never met you and perhaps isn't even living in the same cultural society as yourself.'[32] Larkin's use of voices is not merely novelistic, just as it is not merely autobiographical, and another relatively early poem allows us to see how Larkin moves away from his novelistic roots to create layers of audience and layers of viewership.

'Lines on a Young Lady's Photograph Album,' also from *The Less Deceived*, speaks to a fascination with photographed women, and although the poem's photographs are not technically pornographic, nonetheless a voyeuristic sense of titillation is present in this poem. As Cooper points out, the poem includes 'stereotypical images of male sexual desire' while 'the girl is presented as both innocent and sexually suggestive.'[33] The sense of audience is very powerful here because of the speaker's self-awareness as an audience member and his implication of the reader in his voyeurism. In many ways, this poem resembles Larkin's letters to Robert Conquest that discuss their shared interest in pornography, which also have a heightened and extremely self-conscious approach to the reader who is, in the case of the letters, a particular individual. For instance, Larkin writes to Conquest on March 5, 1966, a passage that demonstrates his own awareness of his pornography viewing and how it appears to others: 'I've rather gone off the mags: I sent a 6 months sub to *Paris Hollywood*, but after sending one issue they've gone dead – next sign will be the heavy tread of the British law enforcement officer, come along o me, my bucko, we know your sort. Librarian charged.' Here Larkin self-deprecatingly acknowledges, in three voices, his own unwholesome habit, the accusations with which he might be faced, and the newspaper headline in which the announcement of his arrest would appear. And although most readers have been more taken with the letters' statements about the pornography themselves than about the self-aware statements that almost inevitably accompany discussions of pornographic images, what Larkin proves even in these private correspondences is how fully aware he is of his personal proclivities' potential impact on others. In other words, he thinks about audience, even in his private letters, on multiple levels, speaking directly to Conquest but never forgetting how various audiences might view the same set of circumstances.

In 'Lines on a Young Lady's Photograph Album,' the speaker's relationship to his subject and the speaker's relationship to the poet are often misread as providing the central tension and emotional connection of the poem. In fact, though, a close reading of the poem, particularly noting the development of the speaker's ideas as the poem progresses and the audiences he addresses, shows that the most fraught, tense, and meaningful relationship in the poem is not between Larkin and his speaker or between the speaker and the woman of the photographs but between the speaker and the reader.

The poem opens in the confessional first person, suggesting the same kind of lasciviousness which Larkin accuses himself of in his letters. The 'I' of this poem is himself an audience member, not acting but watching, using his viewership to contemplate action but not actually to take any. The poem begins with a first-person depiction of a speaker looking at a book of old photographs that feature a woman he knew at the time the pictures were taken. The speaker, who is the photographs' viewer, notes how the subject's life is visually depicted and compares the pictures to rich dessert. 'I choke on such nutritious images' and 'My swivel eye hungers from pose to pose' tell us of the kind of speaker we are dealing with here – a consumer of images who uses them, inappropriately, to satiate his own perverse desires – and highlight the vague repulsiveness of his lust over old photographs.

After three stanzas, though, that initial tension of the poem begins to collapse on itself as the voice, while still in first person, becomes distant from itself, able to step back and analyze its own voyeurism and question how photography, in particular, encourages this kind of one-sided emotional response. 'But o, photography! As no art is,/ Faithful and disappointing!' The reader is thus brought along on a brief journey, first as a revolted viewer of the speaker, thinking disgustedly to himself, 'This pervert is looking at pictures of this girl so lasciviously' and soon as a thinker about photography in general and the ways in which it forces us to view. Of course, since the poem's reader does not see the photographs himself, he is not likely to jump right in to sharing the speaker's lustful reaction in the first three stanzas. Instead, as the speaker views the young woman's pictures, the reader views the speaker viewing the pictures. The pictures are not important to us as readers; the speaker, viewing the pictures, is. When the poem moves, in the fourth stanza, to a more distanced, analytical discussion of the nature of photography, though, the readers move closer to the speaker because they, too, are analysts. The speaker suddenly becomes more palatable at the same time that the reader is able to use the speaker's generalizations about photography to think of his own examples rather than his imagined examples based on the speaker's earlier lewdness.

Larkin fully captures and implicates the reader in the seventh stanza, in which the very prominent and necessary 'I' of the poem's opening becomes, without warning, a 'we' and an 'us.' Here 'we cry' together, and we share in 'our grief' at the loss of the past. This conflation of speaker and reader lasts for only one stanza, but it is the crux of the poem. After having involved the reader with his musings on the nature of photography, the speaker recognizes that the reader is with him now, not as an outsider watching him watch the photographs' subject but as another viewer of the photographs. The speaker knows now that we, too, are crying at the loss of the photographs' truths, at the *'what was'* of them. And he knows we are no longer separate from him but joined with him, all of us excluded together. The subject of the photographs – the imaginary, disappeared, unreal beauty – is in many ways the real lonely figure of this poem, while the speaker actually finds himself in very good company. In this poem, as in 'Reasons for Attendance,' we find that the primary connection – the one on which the poem hinges and the one that contains the most meaningful and *real* emotion – is not the one between the speaker and the subject but between the speaker and the reader, and claims of the speaker's solitude are undermined by his creation of allegiances with the reader. The reader, in this case, may begin as the typical narrative reader of fiction Rabinowitz describes, but the expectations established by the poem's opening – a first-person speaker with second-person address, a distanced judgmentalism on the part of the reader – are dismantled as the poem incrementally involves and implicates the readers themselves and then moves gradually back to the narrative conventions of the opening stanzas (albeit with an altered tone). Audience is everything in 'Lines on a Young Lady's Photograph Album,' not just the obvious audience of the speaker viewing the photographs but the subtler and deeper relationship between the viewer of the photographs and the reader who views this viewer and find himself swept up with him, part of him.

Cooper argues that this poem's 'consistent objective is to show that the speaker's dated sexual politics are just another facet of a world-view that is resentful of social evolution' and that 'the "theft" of a photograph of the girl "bathing" suggests the speaker's attempt to regain what he perceives as the "heaven" of former times when women were defined by the controlling male gaze.'[34] While this view does exonerate Larkin, like earlier interpretations of the poem, it ignores the audience's place in the poem as well as the significance of that placement. If we read the poem while keeping in mind Larkin's interest in and concern for audience, we may extend Cooper's analysis. These 'dated politics' are not merely those of the speaker, as separate from Larkin, but also of the poem's reader who acts with double voyeurism, watching both the photographs and the watcher of the photographs. The poem does not merely implicate some vague past, in which the male gaze controlled viewership, but the current mode of looking as well: the one performed by the reader by proxy, in which the male gaze continues to control viewership. Keeping in mind Larkin's youthful writings as Brunette Coleman, we might also note that the speaker of 'Lines on a Young Lady's Photograph Album' is not clearly defined as male but simply most often assumed to be male. What the pronouns of the poem and the discussion of photography's fundamental nature highlight are not just the subversive politics of Larkin but his accusations against the reader regardless of gender: the speaker of the poem is far from alone in his (or her) voyeuristic tendencies, and we lie to ourselves if we pretend we are not present.

Larkin's implication of his reader in these and other poems differs markedly from the reader's relationship with first-person speakers in earlier poets' works. Consider, for instance, Keats, another poet who wrote in the first person about his fear of impending death (and in whose case death was a lot more impending than it was for Larkin). Although one can read Larkin's poetry as personal in the way that Keats' poetry is personal, Larkin's voice is a more universal one too, as it envisions a reader very much like the speaker, bridging the gap between the loneliness of the speaker and his surroundings by creating connections between speaker and reader. If we imagine for a moment that Keats and Larkin are the speakers of their own poems, we can see the difference in connection to audience quite starkly. Keats, in 'When I Have Fears That I May Cease To Be,' a poem read almost universally as autobiographical, covers the thematic ground that Larkin constantly revisits, imagining his own death in the starkest terms and expressing his dread of that event. That poem does not, however, draw the reader in as Larkin's fear-of-death poems do. That is, readers certainly understand and empathize with Keats' terrors, but the fears of the poem feel nonetheless very much like Keats' personal fears rather than the more general fears of the average reader.

When I behold, upon the night's starr'd face,
Huge cloudy symbols of a high romance,
And think that I may never live to trace
Their shadows, with the magic hand of chance;

Part of the emotional beauty of that poem is its eliciting of our empathy, but clearly Keats' teeming brain was vastly superior to ours, and so what we lament in that poem is not the inevitability of death (or of *our* deaths) but of *Keats'* death.

In addition, the sub-genre of sonnet in which Keats writes – the 'you'll miss me when I'm gone' sonnet – includes an internal audience and leaves the poem's narrative audience to understand that it is witnessing one side of a conversation with another, implied, individual. In Larkin's 'Aubade,' on the other hand, the audience becomes part of the poem in a strikingly personal way; the fears we read in that poem are undoubtedly Larkin's fears but the movement after the first two stanzas from 'I' to 'we' reminds us that we are as implicated in the whole affair of death as the speaker is. The lack of an implied internal audience leaves readers themselves to fill that gap, to become the absent lover who laments the speaker's loss, at the same time that we are aligned with the speaker himself, lamenting the loss of ourselves. In 'Aubade,' it is not 'my mind' that 'blanks at the glare,' but 'the mind.' Similarly, what readers might expect to be personalized, possessed nouns are preceded by neutral articles: 'the love,' 'a life,' 'the extinction.' This almost awkward neutrality draws attention to the lack of possession, the purposeful distancing of the speaker (and the reader) from these ordinarily personalized things. Larkin's poem goes out of its way to avoid singular first-person pronouns despite its very personal nature and the fact that it begins in a stark and lonely first person voice. We can easily see Keats' death as imminent and not quite related to our own – 'such a shame that he had to die so young and with so much brilliance yet unaccomplished' – while 'Aubade' reminds us of 'what we know,/ Have always known, know that we can't escape.' The speaker here is presented not as a poetic genius or romantic dreamer but as selfish and isolated (just like the rest of us), and he does not let us forget for a moment that he and we share the unpleasantest of characteristics: we surround ourselves with people and fill ourselves with alcohol in order to avoid thinking about our inevitable ends. Our pretensions that we drink and socialize for positive reasons rather than the starker truth – that we do so out of pure (and perhaps subconscious) fear – implicates readers in a brand of negativity that we would prefer to notice in others and ignore in ourselves.

The simplicity of this poem, then, is not mere straightforwardness but a necessary, and misleading, simplicity that creates a simultaneously intimate and discomfiting relationship with the reader. As in 'Lines on a Young Lady's Photograph Album,' the speaker draws the reader into the poem through his use of pronouns almost to strong-arm the reader into admitting – or, at least, seeming to admit – that he, for example, finds religious arguments specious. Whether or not the reader actually feels this way, the poem seems to establish the speaker's opinions as similarly natural to the reader who, in his implied complicity, temporarily adopts a perspective that may not be his own. In order to create such intimacy, the language of the poem must be conversational and, to some extent, simple, but that does not mean that the poem itself suffers from oversimplification. And it is a poem that, beyond its subject matter, highlights Larkin's ability and desire to connect to readers, to move consciously outside of himself and his speakers' admittedly personal concerns in an effort to raise questions of the reader's role in the poem and to manipulate earlier sub-genres – the aubade, the sonnet lamenting one's own impending death – but without the internal addressee familiar to readers of those poetic styles, an absence which forces the reader to inhabit a position he is generally accustomed only to observing.

We can see clearly that audience is a primary concern in the early poems, but 'Aubade,' for one, demonstrates that Larkin does not abandon that intent in the later poems. Swarbrick and others claim that the poems of *High Windows* show 'a move away from integration and reconciliation' and towards cruelty and 'disturbing intensity.' The poems also, according to Swarbrick, 'suggest a deepening anxiety about the relationship between self and community.'[35] While Larkin's attention does seem to become somewhat more self-focused in the later poems, even while he writes about death and its accompanying fears that same connection to the audience that is evident in many of the more youthful poems appears in the poems of *High Windows*. Noticing Larkin's use of pronouns, rather than merely his subject matter, helps us to focus on the depth behind the poems and the important relationship with audience that lies at the center of the poetic experience. As Mikhail Bakhtin explains in 'The Problem of Speech Genres,' 'when the listener perceives and understands the meaning of speech, he simultaneously takes an active, responsive attitude toward it. He either agrees or disagrees with it (completely or partially), augments it, applies it, prepares for its execution, and so on.'[36] The active nature of the listener (or, in the case of 'complex' speech genres like poetry, the reader) has an influence, however, not only on the listener himself but also, necessarily, on the speaker (or, in this case, writer), who 'is oriented precisely toward such an actively responsive understanding. He does not expect passive understanding that, so to speak, only duplicates his own idea in someone else's mind.'[37] Bakhtin's language is particularly interesting here because it so accurately echoes one of Larkin's stated objectives: to recreate an experience or emotion in the reader's mind. And yet, Bakhtin argues, no writer – no casual speaker, even – could really expect such passive reception of a speech act, let alone a poem. In other words, Bakhtin explains, 'the listener who understands passively, who is depicted as the speaker's partner in the schematic diagrams of general linguistics, does not correspond to the real participant in speech communication.' While Larkin likely did not think in precisely these terms, Bakhtin usefully outlines the layers of audience of which Larkin demonstrates an implicit awareness.

The audience he describes in his prose writings – an audience that might be described as passive 'loiterers' or as simple and 'pleasure-seeking' or even as 'Larkinesque' in the sense that the audience members resemble Larkin-like characters themselves – is decidedly not the only audience in Larkin's work although it is the one most frequently and clearly articulated in the poet's writings and interviews. But Larkin also leaves space for an audience that doubts and questions the Larkinesque speakers as well as for audiences that stand in the positions of the characters – the dancers in 'Reasons for Attendance,' the brides and their families in 'The Whitsun Weddings,' Jake Balokowsky in 'Posterity' – of whom he is critical and for whom he is empathetic.

Often, because the later poems are so dark, critics tend to notice primarily their subject matter and Larkin's pervasive fear of death. But that is only one aspect of the poems, and in fact the loneliness that readers often associate – understandably – with Larkin's fear of death is less obvious when we also note the strong connection Larkin feels with his reader and the connection he attempts to prompt the reader to feel with his speakers. The sense of loneliness is undermined by regular attempts to connect with the reader's emotions and experiences, and this undermining is evident even in the later poems – those most often accused of insularity – if one is able to look past the surface morbidity of the poems' subjects.

John Osborne wisely notes that many of Larkin's poems have been read as gendered despite the fact that they include no gender designations. He notes that 'Counting,' for instance, uses no gendered pronouns and yet Tom Paulin uses it to assert that Larkin's 'poems are often skeptical assertions of male autonomy' and that 'one of his deepest prejudices was against women.' In other words, Osborne explains, 'in order to accuse the poem of sexism, Paulin first had to sex it.'[38] Paulin's criticism is likely influenced by what he knows, or believes, about Larkin's personal life and relationships with women and takes into account some of Larkin's criticisms of women from his private letters, but he personalizes the poem extra-textually; his gendered presumptions are not in the poem but, at best questionably, in the life. I argue that Larkin's audience is similarly falsely personalized by critics, who take at face value Larkin's statements about his own modest intellectual pursuits and assume, wrongly, that the poems' intended (and perhaps actual) readers are similarly unintellectual. In parallel ways, the popularity of Larkin's poetry is often attributed to a national parochialism, thus assigning to Larkin's readers the characteristics that have come to define Larkin, even if his poems do not stand up to such analyses.

'Sunny Prestatyn' is one such misread poem, often used to highlight Larkin's personal flaws and said to 'trick' the sympathetic reader into a pessimism and misogyny parallel to Larkin's own. The poem, written in 1962 and published in *The Whitsun Weddings*, is another of these tributes to the truth of experience and the subsequent translation of that truth to the reader. The 'yes, that's how it is' of this poem lies in its juxtaposition of beauty and ugliness. The absolute violence of Larkin's description of the defacing of the poster could be read in multiple ways. Is it, as Janice Rossen claims, a displaced demonstration of the violence that Larkin himself (or, presumably, his speaker) would like to perform on the beautiful woman? Rossen questions, quite harshly, 'how much complicity the poet shares in the act' of the poster's defacement, or, as she calls it, 'rape,' noting that 'the scene is recounted not in especially satirical terms.'[39] Or is it, as Terry Whalen argues, a poem that praises the defacement of the poster by 'attacking such fraudulence' as the depiction of a scene so falsely perfect as that shown in the advertisement? Is it a reflection of Larkin's own frustrations, as Swarbrick suggests when he writes that the defacement of the girl is 'an expression of vengeance on everything that is tantalisingly unattainable'?[40] Clearly the poem lends itself to divergent readings, with James Booth claiming that, in it, 'irony wins an easy victory over hope' and 'its conclusion is one of sad despair rather than consolation'[41] at the same time that Jeffrey Gray asserts that it is 'a poem about the victory of the reality principle.' Of course, Gray goes on to note the 'human failure, the inability to believe in sunny Prestatyn, to believe in getting it all and getting away from it all, and the inconsolability for the loss of what we might have had' in the poem as well. The irony both Booth and Gray comment on in the poem highlights its dual meanings: '[The woman's] defilement and finally her eradication can be seen as a victory for those who would be "less deceived," and for those who would reject illusion... and yet these can be read also as a failure of faith.'[42] Clearly this poem divides its readers among those who find a brutal commentary on modernity and those who read it as everything wrong with Larkin's own inner life. And yet, again, rather than analyzing the poem primarily as a means to discovering Larkin's views on women or advertising, one can use this poem, with its complicated layering of audiences, to illustrate the relationship Larkin creates with his readers, showing how that 'fundamental nexus' functions and how central it is to his writings.

In 'Sunny Prestatyn' we see Larkin's attention to audience especially starkly. He begins with a description of the advertising poster itself. A laughing woman kneels on the sand in a tight white bathing costume, imploring her viewers to join her in 'sunny Prestatyn.' But we soon find out that the poster was defaced in explicitly sexual ways and that 'someone' had stabbed the poster and drawn a moustache on the smiling woman and had signed this handiwork 'Titch Thomas'. A short time later, the defaced poster is torn: 'a great transverse tear/ Left only a hand and some blue'. While Janice Rossen concludes from this series of events that 'a large part of Larkin's depiction of women has directly to do with a violence against them, and [that] he seems to speak powerfully both for a corporate group of men and *from* a deep subconscious level,'[43] I believe that the poem has much less to do with Larkin's subconscious feelings about women than with his conscious feelings about his readers and their place in the hierarchy of the poem's audiences.

In fact, Larkin sets up a multiplicity of audiences in this poem, beginning with the defacers – Titch Thomas as well as the far less commented upon person who has torn the poster, leaving 'only a hand and some blue' – as primary audiences who react strongly enough to the poster to act upon it. The speaker of the poem is merely a secondary audience, who observes, rather than directly approving of or condemning, the poster's chronologized developments. The speaker is a reporter rather than an actor, caught between the results of the action he observes (he does not see the defacement taking place but notes carefully its details) and the poem's reader to whom he conveys his seemingly dispassionate observations. The reader then becomes the third audience, even farther removed from the scene than the speaker himself, for if the speaker is merely an observer, the reader of the poem is an observer who only 'sees' the scene through the eyes of this passive passer-by. Rossen's analysis of Larkin's misogyny in this poem overlooks the layers of audience he presents and assumes a congruity between Larkin and the poem's action that is not present in the text. The poem distracts readers from its audience awareness because of its vulgarity and violence, but if we can, for a moment, leave the powerful imagery aside, we can see the ways that Larkin establishes a hierarchy of audiences that speaks importantly to his overall vision of what poetry should – indeed must – do.

Analyses of 'Sunny Prestatyn' generally discuss only Titch Thomas as the poster's defacer, but, in some ways, the second defacer is more interesting, particularly since, as Bradford points out, Titch Thomas is a traditional name for 'an inexperienced, over-confident young man with a penis much smaller than advertised.'[44] The motivations of such a character are fairly clear: this is an immature child, a hooligan, not to be taken seriously, not respected, and certainly not sharing the attitude of the speaker of the poem. Why would a speaker circumspect enough to observe so carefully the degenerative process of the poster, not to mention report it to a broader audience, affiliate himself with the childish – and perhaps emasculated – thug who would enact such a ridiculous barbarity? The second defacer offers much more ambiguous motivations, and he is, interestingly, a more passive participant in the poem. In fact, while the person to scrawl obscenities on the poster is called 'Someone' and offers his own signature on the poster, the second defacer does not actually appear in the poem at all: the 'great transverse tear' is presented passively, as something that has simply appeared one day. Who caused this great tear? Well, presumably not Titch Thomas, who seemed satisfied with his initial work. This second defacer could have been acting from one of two opposing motivations: he could have felt even more strongly than Titch Thomas that the poster, and particularly the woman, deserved destruction and therefore taken Thomas' act one step farther by destroying the entirety of the poster. Or the second defacer could have been acting not against the woman but against Thomas' defacing of her. So disgusted was this viewer by Titch Thomas' graffiti that he tore the poster away from the wall so that she would not have to suffer the indignities visited upon her by Thomas.

Given that the passive description of the tear follows immediately upon the speaker's note that 'She was too good for this life,' it is not unreasonable to suspect that the speaker of the poem is not as passive as one might initially assume. Might the speaker have created that tear, given his seeming sympathies for the woman? We cannot go so far as to say that the speaker definitely tore the poster away from the wall, but such an action is at least suggested by the order of the lines. If 'she was too good for this life' is read using this interpretation, then the poem expresses the opposite of Rossen's view and in fact shows tremendous empathy for the woman's body and disapproval of her degradation. Interestingly, though, the solution to the violence enacted upon her is only further violence – violence that puts her out of her misery, as it were, but violence nonetheless – because the damage done by Titch Thomas is irreparable. At least through the tearing of the poster, though, her humiliation is no longer visible to the world.

The final line of the poem, 'Now *Fight Cancer* is there' can be read, as Gray reads it, as coming 'close to the punchline shocker, of which Larkin was perhaps too fond' but it also comments significantly on the content of the rest of the poem. Is the metaphorical fight against cancer literally a fight against the cancer of faithlessness, as Gray implies? Or is it the fight against ugliness and, by extension, the cruelty of Titch Thomases? Or perhaps it is the fight against the poster's deceptive promise of beauty that Whalen believes is the central motif of the poem. The resignation of the line's tone suggests a passivity on the part of the speaker, but that tone is, like much of the poem, a false lead. The word 'fight' could be read as a command rather than a mere observation of the new poster's injunction. And, if we read the speaker as an actor in the previous poster's destruction rather than a passive observer, the replacement of the defaced poster with a new and, in any case, more inspirational message with less likelihood of violent action – comprised as it is of words rather than images – hints at an optimism and solution generally not regarded as part of Larkin's oeuvre.

Titch Thomas is the first audience of the poster, who acts out the conventional immature violence of the hooligan; the second defacer – whether this is the speaker or another viewer – is the second audience of the poster, but his view is compounded by what Thomas has done. The second viewer sees not just the poster but the poster with its violent sexual emendations. The speaker of the poem is then either the second defacer or a third audience, watching but not participating in the actions of the first two and offering no commentary other than 'She was too good for this life,' which might be read straightforwardly or cynically. This hierarchy then establishes the reader of the poem as a fourth audience, left to analyze and interpret the actions and responses of the others in an attempt to make some conclusions about the meaning of this entire weeks-long episode. Ultimately, though, whether the reader decides that this poem is a misogynistic artistic expression of the violence women deserve or a defense of women and criticism of the arrogant violence done to them or even a poem not about women but about perfection and disbelief, this poem concerns the nature of viewership, what it means to be an audience member, and how audiences interact with one another. 'Sunny Prestatyn' is thus as much a poem about levels of participation in and separation from life than it is about Larkin's views of women or the violence enacted upon them. It speaks to issues of how we view art and life and how we respond to the role of viewer: do we interact with the art? Do we speak about it? Do we passively condone what we see or do we tear at it in frustration? Are we proud of our creations or do we only hint at our own participation? Larkin challenges his readers in this poem to affiliate with one of the several audiences he presents in the poem and to take a stand ourselves, to reconsider the role of audience member, just as he does.[45]

From late in Larkin's career, one of the great death poems from *High Windows*, 'The Old Fools,' may strike readers initially as yet another example of Larkin's emphasis on loneliness and isolation. Swarbrick calls it 'unremittingly harsh' and says that 'although there is fascination, there is no compassion.'[46] The poem may indeed lack compassion for its anonymous subjects, but we must also note the ways in which the poem connects the speaker to the reader and moves itself, however briefly, out of its isolation and into a kind of compassion that, while never entirely unselfish, includes and embraces others nonetheless. Simon Petch, in his commentary on the poem, does not comment on the shifting affiliations with readers throughout the poem nor the significance of the various relationships Larkin sets up among himself, his speaker, his subjects, and his readers, instead focusing entirely on the speaker's relationship to his subjects and to himself.[47] Petch remarks that 'the poem makes clear that the dislocation old people experience between past and present is constantly with us in human life, always ready to disrupt our sense of life's continuity.'[48] Petch's emphasis here is on the poem's subject matter and the way that Larkin fits himself and his own fears into his observation of the old people. But by using 'us' and 'our' he also adopts Larkin's own inclusiveness, recognizing without stating it explicitly, that the poem creates a connection not with its subjects but with its fellow observers.

The poem begins in the third person plural, speaking from a distance about age and the disgrace that the speaker finds in aging. As in 'Reasons for Attendance,' the speaker watches from outside, not experiencing the action of the poem himself but imagining the experience and guessing at the motivations and thoughts of the actors' behavior. 'What do they think has happened, the old fools,/ To make them like this?' He questions whether they consciously drool and soil themselves and whether they consider themselves more adult for having lost their minds. The cruelty of these opening lines is evident, both in their graphic depictions of people ordinarily thought to deserve society's greatest respect and in the elitist distancing of the speaker from his subjects' behavior. The reader of the poem is doubly distanced from the old people because our view of them is restricted by the speaker's lens. We see them as he sees them, but rather than being the primary viewers, we see them as viewers of the speaker's viewing.

The second stanza, though, disassembles the distanced relationship of the first stanza. The double distance of the poem's subject from the poem's readers is immediately erased in the second stanza when Larkin writes, 'At death, you break up ...' turning his earlier observations into accusations. The speaker prods his readers to see their self-delusion in having separated themselves from the 'old fools' and braces them for their own eventual oblivion. No longer is the subject these distant, senile people but the readers themselves. The readers become the old fools, nearing the point at which 'the bits that were you/ Start speeding away from each other for ever ...'. The poem becomes instantly less comfortable for the reader, who is implicated in the inevitable future that seems so distant and unrelated to the reader in the first stanza. The relationship between subject and reader is collapsed by the speaker, who forces the reader's recognition of himself in those old fools of the first stanza. James Booth notes these shifting pronouns, stating that 'in the second stanza his jeering shifts to pensiveness as the third person of the poem's opening gives way to a second person which embraces both reader and poet.'[49] As Booth points out, the tone of the poem does change, and that change is dependent not only on a greater pensiveness on the part of the speaker but also on his inclusion of and move towards the readers as he takes their emotions into account and softens the blow of his earlier insularity on their behalf. It is not yet entirely clear, however, that the speaker includes himself (or the poet, for that matter) in this depiction; instead, the second-person voice provides a different sort of distancing than the first-person did, with an alignment between the reader and the subjects that, at least grammatically, excludes the speaker.

Throughout the rest of poem, the speaker remains a distanced figure. He initially acknowledges the disgraceful lives of the old fools and later conflates the reader with them, through his change in pronouns from 'they' to 'you.' Yet he remains himself outside the action of the poem, observing 'them' and observing 'you.' The first time the speaker mentions himself is halfway through the final stanza, and even there he presents himself as separate from the lives of the old fools and even separate from the inevitable end of the readers: 'The peak that stays in view wherever we go/ For them is rising ground.' This isn't a 'we' that groups the speaker with the old fools but one that separates him from them; it presents the 'we' as separate from and superior to the 'them' by positing the two groups against each other. He seems to be leading himself to a state of total denial, maintaining his complete separation from the subjects. Only in the all-important final line of the poem do we find what he knew all along: wondering just what people approaching death know, he states matter-of-factly, 'Well,/ We shall find out.' That final 'we' is the turning point of the poem, and coming as it does just as the poem ends, the speaker seems barely able to admit what he has known since his earliest observations in the poem: that this is not a poem about 'them' or about 'you' but about him. Of course, even in the final admission of that awareness, he does not stand alone. The difference between 'Well, I shall find out' and 'Well, we shall find out' is the chill-factor induced in the reader but also the necessary connection created, as the poem ends, between him and us and the collapse of the speaker's initial self-conscious distance from the elderly. Even in the approach to death, in this poem, the speaker is not alone. *We* shall find out, a collective statement of unity in our approach to the end. At this point of the poem, a separation from the reader seems almost too much to bear, and therefore the end – nothing could be more lonely – is presented not as a journey alone but as one we will enter together.

This relationship with the reader is highlighted by the distance the speaker puts between himself and the reader initially in 'The Old Fools'. The connection he creates at the end of the poem is enhanced both by the obvious loneliness of the subject and by the speaker's initial hesitation to include himself in the pronouns of the poem. That final 'we' is not a change in manner from the earlier parts of the poem, but an admission of what has been in the poem from the beginning: a deep and meaningful relationship between the speaker and his readers and a pervasive sense that we are all in this together and will be until the end. Petch remarks that 'at the end of the poem we are chillingly reminded that old age may come as a 'hideous inverted childhood' to all who live long enough' and that 'the poem's treatment of age and death reflects upon all of human life,' but what is particularly striking and chilling about the end of the poem is not just the reminder that death comes to everyone or that it affects people in these singular and childlike ways, but that the poet can look through that 'fourth wall' of the poem and see our fears as well as he sees his own. It is, in fact, the development of pronouns, and especially that final 'we,' – not just its discussion of inevitable death – that causes the poem's deep impact. Booth proclaims that the end of the poem 'snatches the poignant shadow of consolation from the grim plight of gaga bewilderment,'[50] highlighting not just the chill of the poem but also its essential beauty and even hopefulness. Booth's focus is on the aesthetics of the phrase 'watching light move,' which he calls 'beautiful, ... with all the resonance of a poetic epiphany.' And while that line is indeed beautiful, I believe the glimpse of hope at the end comes, instead, from the human connection the speaker makes with his reader. The poem attempts to speak a fundamental truth, but it does not do so at a comfortable remove from the reader; instead, it does so with a final inclusion of the reader that makes the truth resonate that much more.

In some ways, the ignoring of the audience's role in Larkin's poetry is an understandable manipulation of interpretation in order to make the post-Letters image of the man accord with the image of the speaker. Therefore, just as Larkin is often described as a recluse, readers regularly find his speaker's positioning as far from the action – as a removed observer of others' lives – to fit with that manufactured persona. What necessarily accompanies a poem with such remove from life's action, though, is a placement of the poem's reader either with the action of life or with the speaker who stands aside and watches. Clearly, when reading Larkin's poetry, the readers are not with the laughing couples who stand at each train station but with the distanced speaker who rides away; the readers are not aligned with the dancers in the dance hall who whirl endlessly looking for love but with the figure pressed to the window outside.

The pervasive sense of Larkin's poetry is that he argues, again and again, that he is alone. The world seems to happen around him, and he stands solitary at the center, reporting on, as he says, the true experiences he observes; the experience he means to preserve is the experience of observation rather than of action. But he is not alone. His readers are with him. We are not the dancers or the lovers, but Larkin seems to recognize implicitly that most people are, in fact, not the dancers and the lovers, and so the real theme of Larkin's poetry may be that we are all in this together.[51] Again and again, as we read his verse, we find that idea reinforced. We are all in this together.

And yet Larkin is gentle in his inclusion of the reader: so gentle, perhaps, that readers may avoid noticing their inclusion altogether. Larkin never evades discussing his speaker's own discomfort – both physical and emotional – or attempting to deal with it directly, but he seems to recognize the reader's instinctual hesitation to face his fears so unflinchingly. Therefore, in so many of Larkin's poems, we find the reader aligned with the speaker, whether talking about the discomforts of death or of sex or of work or of politics, and yet the speakers remain willing throughout to bear the brunt of reality themselves. That is, Larkin's implication of the reader is so mild and kind as to allow the reader to find his own place in the poem, but only when he feels ready to do so. And, as we learn from reading the volumes discussing Larkin's verse, few readers do seem ready. They are perfectly willing to note Larkin's fears, his insecurities, and his self-doubt, but they seldom if ever note the subtle but clearly present ways in which Larkin's speakers assign them similar characteristics. Larkin, kindly, allows this comfortable remove to continue on the part of the readers by making his arguments about them consistently subtle, never brutalizing them with their own (mis)reading. But they are in the poems nonetheless, and when they are ready to move away from their view of Larkin as an insecure loner and see him as part of a community – people who, in their love of poetry and their desire to read it and write about it, necessarily separate themselves from others, at least for a time – they will be able to understand more accurately and less critically the speaker of Larkin's poetry not as an unusual specimen of isolation but as a poetry reader: as one of us.

2
Larkin's Voices

Again and again, we find that the most fundamental arguments about Larkin's verse come down to questions of Larkin's identity and that attempts to interpret the poems seem almost entirely predicated on how readers approach Larkin's life. Those readers predisposed to a generally critical view of Larkin – those like Lisa Jardine, Tom Paulin, and Bryan Appleyard – do indeed find in the poems the kind of small-mindedness reflected in many of the letters. Similarly, Janice Rossen, dismayed by Larkin's misogyny in the letters, has no trouble finding a similar attitude in the poems. Those, on the other hand, more inclined to sympathize with Larkin have plenty of support in the poems as well, since many of the poems offer at least glimpses of sensitivity and concern for others. A few critics, like Stephen Cooper, have gone even farther and argued that, in fact, all the negative qualities attributed to Larkin are actually subversive attempts to undermine those very negativities. His apparent misogyny, then, is really an attempt to uncover and dismantle misogyny, and so on. In nearly every case, though, the poetry is held up as a lens through which the life may be viewed. This approach poses as its ultimate question, explicitly or not, whether Larkin was a 'bad' person, variously defined as racist, misogynist, classist, misanthropist, parochial, perverted, philistine, closed-minded, old-fashioned, anti-Modern, anti-innovation, or anti-intellectual, and it mines the poetry to find answers to these questions. Looking to the poetry for explanations of his personality not only undermines the poems as independent – and independently valuable – works but also necessarily forces readings on them that are not fully textually supportable. By beginning with the assumption that Larkin can be discovered through the poems, we do not allow the poems to demonstrate their own impenetrability, nor can we examine the complicated and self-conscious artistry that is far more present and important in the poems than his biography is.

As Andrew Motion half-apologetically explains in the *Observer*, after the publication of *A Writer's Life* and the ensuing backlash against Larkin, 'It's intensely disappointing to read literary commentators who write as if they don't understand that art exists at a crucial distance from its creator.' Motion, for all his earlier undermining of this same idea by, in effect, writing as though he doesn't understand that art exists at a crucial distance from its creator, is absolutely correct in his assertion that the poems do not merely reflect the biography; for Larkin in particular, the poems are far from autobiographical verse. While Richard Bradford does present some compelling conclusions about the links between particular romantic incidents and the writing of certain poems, to mine the poems for biographical detail is to misunderstand the independent significance and profundity of the verse and, more importantly, to misread and discount the depth of Larkin's creation of personas.

A significant part of the problem with the seemingly irreconcilable biographical interpretations of the poems is that, just as the poems often have more than one addressee, the voices of the poems are often readable in several ways. In fact a recognition of the poems' multiple and contradictory voices, perspectives, and intonations is fundamental to understanding them. Accepting this premise may be difficult because if we cannot trust our interpretations of the poet's expression, even through the space of a single short poem, we have very little anchor for our reading. In many cases, the attitudes and opinions of Larkin's speakers often change midway through a poem, and while the final assertions or questions are logically given the 'last word' on a poem's argument, what we find from looking closely at the poems' endings is that the supposed resolution of the various opinions presented in a text is hardly a resolution. Similarly, poems that seem to express clear opinions can be found, upon closer examination, not to express those opinions so clearly or at all. Larkin's manipulation of the voices in the poems argues against a biographical or a simplistic interpretation of his poems and in favor of an argument for his remarkable ability to enact, subtly but unmistakably, precisely the kinds of poetic innovations that he is often accused of dismissing or underappreciating.

Larkin's direct inclusion of his readers in his poems, both by addressing us explicitly and by articulating multiple layers of audience, is only one of the ways we see his interest in audience playing out in the poems. Another way, and the way that this chapter will explore, is his use of modulating, dialogic, confrontational, and developmental voices and personas that both ask his readers to take sides and destabilize the audience's position, thus forcing a reconsideration of the audience's role in reading. By recognizing that the multiple tonalities of the poems preclude these texts from being used as historical assessments of the poet's life, and by examining not just the speakers' self-alienation but the poems' deliberately audience-destabilizing moves, we can appreciate both the poems' ambiguities and Larkin's innovations. Larkin's use of transforming (and transformational) voices is often read as a flaw on the speaker's (or poet's) part; I argue, however, that this destabilizing move is part of Larkin's interest in audienceship and his effort to make readers hyperconscious of their own poses and assumptions. As the poems' speakers undermine and contradict and rethink their attitudes, audiences are asked, similarly, to reconsider themselves.

Quite a number of critics have commented on the 'two voices' in Larkin's work. Andrew Swarbrick discusses in detail Larkin's 'pose of philistinism'[1] while also noting that 'Larkin's poetry is the pursuit of difference, the thing just out of reach, the being different from yourself. [The poems] pay tribute to the universality of uniqueness, expressing a tender regard for the other individual selves in relation to which his own self is defined.'[2] Swarbrick further observes that the ' "I" should be regarded as another subjective presence, another "voice," rather than an unproblematic author.'[3] Nicholas Marsh sagely comments on Anthony Thwaite's remark 'that in [1946] Larkin wrote "the earliest poems which strike his characteristic note and carry his own voice," writing that 'We will investigate this "characteristic note" and search for "his own voice" in the present chapter, discovering that matters of tone and voice in Larkin's poems are a great deal more elusive than Thwaite's comment implies.'[4] Marsh recognizes that the phrase 'his own voice' in reference to Larkin's poems is deeply problematic: even in the poems that bear the most hallmarks of Larkin's famous style, the 'voice' (or, really, voices) is varied and inconsistent. Clive James takes the presence of two Larkins as a necessary quality of Larkin's poetry, and one that is not particularly confusing: in discussing 'High Windows,' James argues that 'strong language in Larkin is put in not to shock the reader but to define the narrator's personality. ... It should be obvious at long last... that the diction describes the speaker. When the speaker is close to representing Larkin himself, the diction defines which Larkin it is – what mood he's in.'[5] In the greatest complication of the 'multiple voices' conversation, John Carey discusses 'The Two Philip Larkins,' not as characters or personas who appear in different poems but as gendered characters who repeatedly appear within the same poems. Focusing primarily on 'This Be the

Verse,' Carey notes that the poem includes 'the offensive Larkin who infuriates critics like Tom Paulin with his right-wing, racist views' and 'puts across a plain man's common-sense view of literature and poetry' as well as 'the sensitive, educated... worshipful, tender voice – the artist kneeling in his heart.'[6]

Certainly Larkin is not the only post-Romantic poet to employ developmental or dialogic voices, but his voices are unique in that they are neither self-evidently shifting (as in Eliot's early poems) nor obviously personae (as in Browning's dramatic monologues). While Swarbrick and Richard Bradford, among others, tend to focus on Larkin's own different voices in the various genres of his writing – the voice of the poems posited against the voice of the interviews or the voice of the letters – and Marsh focuses on the voices that differ among the poems, specifically examining 'Wedding-Wind,' 'Poetry of Departures,' and 'Next, Please' as speaking in different voices, Carey most substantively notes how fundamental the multiplicity of voices is within individual poems. Carey uses his observations about the two voices he identifies to comment on gender: 'the feminine aspect of Larkin's personality.'[7] But, to take a different angle on Carey's observations, we might also call the two voices within a single text the sensitive and the crass, or the longing and the satisfied, or the questioning and the confident. While gender might play a role here, or serve as a useful interpretive tool, the import of Carey's argument lies primarily in his recognition of the competing, and profoundly differing, voices that exist within a single poem. The mere fact of these voices within each individual poem creates a sense of the speaker's personal displacement, especially since the voices are not always dialogic but more often parallel or competing. These two unreconciled voices show the speaker's – but not the poet's – estrangement from himself and his complicated, fractured identity. Noting the dual (or dueling) voices allows us to see the poems less as autobiography and more as narrative. But the voices also actively engage multiple audiences and put readers into unexpected and confusing places. Speakers who are simultaneously self-assured and internally contradictory unsettle readers who are, as the previous chapter demonstrated, implicated in the opinions and actions of the poems.

For example, we see that the poem 'The Whitsun Weddings' has been and can legitimately be interpreted in disparate and sometimes contradictory ways that confound readers' expectations. Simon Petch asserts that 'There is nothing condescending' about the speaker's observations of weddings: 'beneath smutty jokes and jewellery substitutes lies an event of genuine communal significance.'[8] Andrew Motion similarly notes the multiple tones within the poem, saying that 'it strews the path to its extraordinary climax with deliberately ordinary sights and sounds. ... It achieves a tone which is both awe-struck and sharply conscious of absurdity. ... It is bound to the here-and-now while longing for transcendent release.'[9] Anthony Easthope, on the other hand, claims that the speaker's 'uncertainty soon develops into full-blown class anxiety when the train fills with representatives of the post-1950s' newly-rich working class wearing 'parodies of fashion' and 'jewellery substitutes' and, further, that the poem expresses Larkin's 'vehement and traditionally English empiricism.'[10] These interpretations, and many others, alternately find the poem hopeful, pessimistic, classist, socially equalizing, spiritual, and material. What they all, assume, though, is a settled opinion of one thing or another: Petch reads the judgmentalism as merely a cover for the speaker's own deep emotions; Motion finds the contradictions inherent in the poem symbolic of the speaker's 'longing for transcendent release;' while Easthope sees the speaker's class anxieties as primary and only resolved by a kind of cheap, anti-Modernist final reconciliation.

One of the things readers seem to seek from this poem, as, perhaps, from all poems, is a grounded opinion with a clear 'message,' but the poem does not offer exactly that despite all our attempts to force it. Instead, it offers options and possibilities, but none of them is fully realized in the poem. The poem includes arguments for condescension and separateness as well as empathy and a feeling of borderline envy for the same characters who are mocked earlier in the poem, and so readers are unclear if the speaker's mind has simply changed over the course of the poem or if something more complicated is happening; and the final stanza of the poem, where we look for a clear indication of which voice 'won' is as unhelpful on this account as any final stanza could be.

The poem begins with neutral observations about the speaker's train journey and the weddings taking place at every stop along the way, but soon the scenes that the speaker observes through the train's window become weighted and take on a distinctly condescending and superior tone:

> The fathers with broad belts under their suits
> And seamy foreheads; mothers loud and fat;
> An uncle shouting smut; and then the perms...

And yet, as the poem progresses, 'The Whitsun Weddings' presents a very touching and empathetic view of the couples and families the speaker observes from the train window, lacking all sense of condescension.

This development is common in Larkin's poems, including 'Reasons for Attendance,' which, as we have seen, begins with criticism of others and moves towards an interrogation of the speaker's own attitudes and beliefs; 'Church Going,' which, as we will see, begins with a tone of measured cynicism and ends with a thoughtful, if ambiguous, sympathy for religious believers; and 'Faith Healing,' which begins with bitter condescension and ends with a melding of the speaker and his subjects.

Here, though, the speaker's tone changes most notably when he redirects his observation from a literal and materialistic consideration of the subjects' appearances to an imagining of their thought processes. He pictures what they must be seeing and imagines what they must be thinking, realizing that their reflections differ from his own: '– and none/ Thought of the others they would never meet...'. Considering their thoughts humanizes them for the speaker and adjusts the tone back to something neutral, if not positive. While the speaker of these lines remains separate from the action, and even his thoughts are shown as distinctly separate from the thoughts of the weddings' participants, this stanza shows a kind of consideration for the people not demonstrated earlier. While one might still read these lines as condescending – 'these idiots haven't thought about things as I have, and they go through their lives oblivious to the import of moments like these' – they also contain an unmistakable wistfulness. The speaker seems almost to wish for the same level of oblivion that his subjects possess; he wishes to escape the confines of constant poetic introspection and just *live*, even if that living involves the sordid and dirty facts of fat mothers and obscene uncles.

This change, from the condescension towards the 'fathers with broad belts under their suits' to, as Janice Rossen calls it, the 'affection for the groups of onlookers,'[11] is most often highlighted in analyses of the poem, but another, earlier change of tone takes place after the speaker observes the girls waving goodbye:

> Struck, I leant
> More promptly out next time, more curiously,
> And saw it all again in different terms:

What causes this revisioning on the speaker's part? Why does he initially see the brides as both interesting and quaint, noticing them 'all posed resolutely, watching us go' and then see the whole scene all again in different, more judgmental terms? The thing that strikes him seems to be the way that the girls watch the train depart the station, and their watching, 'As if out on the end of an event/ Waving goodbye/

To something that survived it,' makes him reconsider his own looking. Recognizing that they are watching him (or, as the poem puts it,
'watching us') makes him watch them in a more superficial and more
judgmental way. And when he returns to the subject of their watching, the tone of speaker's voice changes again: 'Free at last/ And loaded
with the sum of all they saw,/ We hurried towards London, shuffling
gouts of steam.' From this point on, the poem is more thoughtful and
the tone is more similar to the tone at the poem's start. The sum of
what *they* saw has now joined with the train's progress, and while the
poem seems mostly to focus on what the speaker sees, what makes him
most thoughtful, and what alters his way of viewing most, is thinking
about what they saw. What the poem offers us, then, is not merely the
perspective of an anxious, superior traveler and, later, a more mature,
developed, reconciled alternative; we are offered, instead, at least three
distinct impressions of the scene, all of which are predicated on which
characters are watching and which are being watched. In each case, the
awareness of audienceship, and the resultant change in tone, is pointed
out explicitly. The speaker tells us, 'here is the same scene again "in different terms" ' and then says that 'now' the scene around him has changed.
He is self-aware, but he is also transformed by being observed, and his
awareness of being watched influences the way he watches. This attention to viewership does not suggest that one segment of the poem is more
true than the others, or that one of them could 'trump' the others' opinions, but that the changing subject position, from being the observer
to being the observed, informs the speaker's analysis, making him first
less and later more sensitive to the pressures on the poems' human
subjects.

The multiple voices in this poem – the early descriptive voice, the
condescending voice of the middle stanzas, and the later voice of appreciation for the scene – could be read as showing development on the
speaker's part but might also be read as an attempt to include readers
in his analyses. The persistent 'we' of the poem suggests that readers
are present with the speaker and are able to choose their position with
him: do we notice the young brides in 'parodies of fashion' or are we
more attentive to the possibilities of their inner lives? The use of first-
person plural pronouns throughout the poem places readers alongside
the speaker on the train, but as the train becomes freighted with 'all
they saw,' the straightforward subject-positioning of the earlier stanzas
becomes complicated by the conflation of the new, and newly married,
passengers with the old. After the train is freighted with this new seeing, in fact, the pronouns change for a full stanza, from the 'we' of

earlier stanzas, and of the final stanza, to a pronounced but temporary 'they' and 'I.' Their having seen, and then joining the speaker's traveling position, temporarily fragments the 'us' of the poem, but it is shortly restored. Similarly, the shabbiness and tackiness of the people in the earlier stanzas are replaced by a more universal and productive vision of the world through the windows of the train. The early desolate images of canals filled with pollutants and towns littered with useless automobile parts are replaced by similarly industrial images that offer a sense of productivity rather than waste: 'Now fields were building-plots, and poplars cast/ Long shadows over major roads.' These adjustments, of which the speaker is fully aware, based on his own references to the 'different terms' of his viewing and the sense that 'now' what he sees out the windows is markedly different from what he saw before, also place the reader in a position of constant readjustment to the scene. We necessarily see what he sees, since he is our window (as it were) onto the scene, but we are also asked to recognize that the objects out the window have not changed so much as the speaker himself has. Since we are included with him, we are asked to see differently as well, and to recognize that the experience of being watched has opened the speaker, and therefore us, to new possibilities of seeing.[12]

The reader faces a kind of rhetorical dilemma here, as James Phelan would put it, being unable to align himself fully with the characters described, even when the speaker begins to consider their thoughts rather than their externalities, because they have already been offered to us as common and tacky. But the speaker's efforts, in the penultimate stanza, to connect with them, and his recognition of 'how their lives would all contain this hour,' unsettles the earlier judgments he, and we, have made of them. There is no precise place for the reader in this poem because of its speaker's fracturing, and so we may choose to focus on one or the other voices but have trouble reaching a fully comfortable reconciliation without privileging one voice above the others. Many readers look to the final stanza for an answer to the question of the reader's alignment with the speaker's voices, and while the tone of the final stanzas offers a kind of lovely genuflection to the scene and not at all the snarky, crotchety criticism of happiness that can be found in the third and fourth stanzas, the beauty of the composition in those final stanzas belies the uncertainty of their language. The 'mothers loud and fat' and the 'success so huge and wholly farcical' of the poem's middle-third makes way for a respectful, nearly religious distance in the final third of the poem. And yet this final circumspection, so often read as a resolution of the poem's vocal tensions, is far from it.

The poem's ending leaves behind entirely the speaker's self-satisfied superiority in favor of what Easthope calls 'an apparent reconciliation, the disturbing other recuperated into a significant experience.'[13] While it is true that the poem ends on a hopeful note, the images of the final stanza are only of potential, not of recuperation: the speaker describes a scene of movement and anticipation, but, importantly, the train does not reach its destination within the text. The words and phrases for getting there – 'came close,' 'nearly done,' 'stood ready' 'a sense of falling,' – are not of reconciliation but of possibility. But the possibility is vague and unfinished. While 'somewhere' the power of change has an effect, here the train is slowing and the brakes are taking hold. The language of the final stanza cleverly reads as a resolution, with its suggestions of the journey's ending, its use of resolving words like 'close' and 'done,' and its wide-angled view of the scene, a movement away from the poem's earlier close-ups. It is certainly a good distance in tone from the materialism of the earlier stanzas, but it does not resolve the poem's tensions so much as offer a tension that continues unabated after the poem is finished. The poem ends, but the speaker does not seem to have settled on any one of these three voices as giving a true finale. Indeed, had he written another stanza, he might have offered another vision and revision. The beauty of the images disguises their lack of resolve, but the slowing, the swelling, and the fact that the action takes place 'out of sight' all suggest that this is hardly the final word on the scene.

The changing vocalizations here speak to the role of the reader in nearly all of Larkin's poems. The unsettled feeling readers have in approaching a Larkin poem – the often-cited unease these poems elicit, and the multiple readings they allow despite their being perceived as 'simple' and 'straightforward' – is a secondary effect of the speaker's multiplicity. Because the speaker is hard to pin down, and because we might assign him the characteristics of this line or that line or say that the initial voice is the 'real' one or the final voice shows the 'truth' of the poem, readers are implicated in this poetry in a particularly complicated way. They are asked, first of all, to separate tone from content, as in the final stanza of 'The Whitsun Weddings,' which offers, confusingly, both a sense of reconciliation and a meaning that prolongs the poem's earlier uncertainties. Readers are also asked to consider their own positioning in ways that change frequently and with only the subtlest warnings.

'The Whitsun Weddings' cleverly presents itself, both in the poem and in the commentaries Larkin has offered on it, as a straightforward retelling of an observed incident, but it is no such thing, and so it continually pushes and pulls its readers, disallowing the stability that we expect from lyric poetry in its use not only of standard forms, rhythms and rhyme schemes but also in its reliance on a stable speaker with a fixed perception. Larkin himself promotes a simplistic interpretation, saying that 'It was a wonderful, a marvellous afternoon. It only needed writing down. Anybody could have done it.'[14] Any number of critics, Easthope included, have taken him at his word, but, as Booth points out, these lines were almost certainly spoken in jest: 'Larkin knew perfectly well that 'anybody' certainly could not have done it... he is actually boasting, to those who can hear, about his unique verbal skill.'[15] Larkin knew both how complicated and how playful this poem was, and his assertion that the poem acts merely as a simple snapshot of an afternoon is necessarily disingenuous.

Larkin's approach to the poet/speaker relationship is complicated – and more innovative – than either creating a complete and obvious persona or using himself and his own life as the central subject of his poetry. Instead, his poetry demonstrates a conscious drawing on his own life and specific experiences – both the personal, as in 'Wild Oats' and the merely observational, as in 'The Whitsun Weddings' – and manipulates the truth of his own place in those episodes and the very idea of such truths. Larkin's prose serves as a counterpoint to his poems, so that when he says to John Haffenden that 'anybody could have done it,' he deliberately underplays the poet's effort, both as a kind of role playing to bolster the perception of himself as an ordinary, not particularly gifted or special man of the people, and to suggest that the poem is a perfect, neutral snapshot of an experience rather than the highly subjective poem that it is.[16] Nothing about the poem itself indicates that it could have been written by 'anybody,' not just because it took unique talent but also because it is noticeably personal; the experience is not simply described but heavily interpreted and analyzed. And yet by talking about the poem in the way he does with Haffenden, Larkin leads readers to find what they are already most comfortable finding: an autobiographical moment from an ordinary guy.

It is almost nonsensical to read 'The Whitsun Weddings' as something that 'only needed writing down,' since everything about it is so stylized. Perhaps 'anybody' could have noted that the train pulled out at 1:20 and that it was only one-quarter full, but does Larkin think that 'anybody' would have remarked that 'The women shared/ The secret like a happy funeral;/ While girls, gripping their handbags tighter, stared/ At a religious wounding'? And surely 'anybody' could have noticed that 'We slowed again,' but it seems unlikely that 'anybody' would then have said,

'And as the tightened brakes took hold, there swelled/ A sense of falling, like an arrow-shower/ Sent out of sight, somewhere becoming rain.'
Why Larkin should wish to mislead readers in this entirely obvious way is a good question although I find even more interesting how willing readers are to be misled. Larkin seems to be playing an entertaining game, challenging readers to look beyond the obviously false answers of the interviews to really read the poems. The truths he presents – that he uses no allusion, that his poems are easily interpreted on a first reading, that anybody could have written 'The Whitsun Weddings,' that he hates Modernism – are frequently used by readers in their attempts to understand the poems but are ultimately disproved by the poems themselves. The speaker of the interviews is also a speaker, and not a particularly reliable one. The interviews often suggest two different Larkins, a glib one who answers definitively but not in very provable ways, and a more sincere one who does mean what he says when he says it. As John Shakespeare writes of his early interview with Larkin, to which Larkin made substantial changes, 'Is it too fanciful to see, in his long letter and enclosures of June 29, Larkin labouring to create his own version of his life and work almost as if he were structuring a poem?' The poems also often present dual speakers' voices, both in poems where the speaker changes drastically between the beginning of the poem and the end, and poems where one speaker seems to comment on another's actions and statements. And the interviews are similarly manipulated, always anticipating how readers will react, not only to the verse but to the man behind it: as he tells Shakespeare, 'You may say on this point that that is how I presented myself to you! Well, it isn't how I want to present myself to your readers... I am especially anxious that this article should present me in a reasonably serious light, as so far nobody knows much about me.'[17] And, given the editorial changes he makes to Shakespeare's interview, he ensures that people will continue not to know much, or, at least, only to know what he wants them to know.

Larkin's speaker is consciously placed outside the voice of the poet, and so every 'autobiographical' poem has two 'I's' in it. Bradford, for all his interest in the biographical connections of the poems, notes this separation between Larkin and his speakers: in his poetry, 'he was able to borrow features from the separate dimensions of his protean, real existence and reposition them as a hybrid, recognizably [sic] Larkin to all who knew him but not exactly the one they knew.'[18] The idea of a hybrid Larkin is one that Larkin himself plays with through the poems, drawing on the experiences of his own past but creating a speaker outside himself through whom he can analyze those experiences and speak to his readers. In 'Wild Oats,' as we will see in Chapter 3, we have a speaker who can sarcastically say, 'Well, useful to get that learnt' about his own negative qualities in which he does not fully believe, followed by an admission that he continues to carry photographs of a girl he barely knew and with whom he had no meaningful relationship. Larkin could hardly be writing a confession here; this is instead a character study that presents contradictory levels of self-awareness.

Larkin knows that readers will look to his biography to attempt to find out more about his speakers, and indeed readers have done so; but the biography does not fully accord with the poems' speakers and many of the poems, through their internal dialogues, their use of layered audiences, their inclusion of the readers, and their overall sense of self-awareness, call out for a reading that moves beyond biography. And yet the movement beyond biography is hampered by the constant return to the similarities between Larkin and his speaker – in profession, in attitude, in lifestyle – in this game of personas. As Swarbrick argues in his final chapter, Larkin explores 'fundamental questions about individual identity' and he does this 'through a vocabulary of separateness, of exclusion and difference, establishing a kind of negative self-definition.'[19] While the powerful negations of the poems are no doubt present and do often create this effect, they also, as Swarbrick writes a few pages later, define 'the self not in terms in separateness, but in its sensitiveness to others.'[20] This divide, between the negated self and the self in relation to others, is not merely one of an aesthetic or philistine Larkin, although Swarbrick argues convincingly for those designations. It is also the difference between Larkin the poet, who looms over all the poems, and the Larkinesque speakers who invoke but do not mimic the poet.

If one of Larkin's overriding qualities in the poetry is his use of persona – in other words, the inability for readers to reach the 'true' Larkin through the verse – then a significant obstacle to our understanding the poems is the belief that they are expressing something distillable about the subject they address rather than something more profound about the slipperiness of words and meaning (particularly given that Larkin famously disliked 'poems about poetry'). Larkin's subtlety is such that the poems disguise their own metatextuality by appearing to be straightforward, with easily understood subject positioning. And yet in order to read many of his poems this way, we must ignore certain aspects of the poems. In some cases, we read over their shifting pronouns; in others, like 'The Whitsun Weddings,' we mistake the sound of resolution for real resolution; in some, we believe that the final voice is the true voice, overlooking the ways that the poems draw attention to their own self-questioning; and in others, we take the sound of debate as a marker of real dialogue, misreading the polarities that a poem seems to present. This last type of misreading is most pronounced in 'Poetry of Departures,' in which Larkin plays explicitly with the presentation of an apparent dialogue but that includes, in its own simple and subtle way, undercuttings and circular arguments that manipulate the reader into taking sides in an argument that is not really an argument. This poem, which features multiple speakers, doubles back on itself in several ways. It begins with a confident and opinionated speaker telling 'you' about a similarly confident and opinionated speaker who tells a story 'you've' sometimes heard about someone who impulsively deserts his current existence. 'And always the voice will sound/ Certain you approve...'. The first speaker, despite his self-assurance that 'you've' had this same experience, seems critical of this overzealous gossip who is 'certain you approve' and leaves no room for you to express your real opinion. From the first words of the poem, the reader is told both that he has had this experience and that the speaker of the epitaph has, perhaps unfairly, attributed to the reader an opinion. Complicating the speaker's criticism of this pushy epitaph-sharer, in stanza two, the speaker imposes on 'you' a similarly presumptive assertion of his opinion that eclipses yours: 'We all hate home/ And having to be there.' Certainly on some level this speaker must know, or at least suspect, that we do not all hate home, yet he foists this personal view on all of us, despite having just presented a vague complaint that some fifth-hand voice has overbearingly assigned 'you' an opinion you may or may not share.

The 'you' of this poem is often interpreted as a place-holder for a first- or third-person pronoun, serving a distancing function rather than performing a literal address of an audience. Irene Kacandes explores the various levels of this sort of deixis, identifying as part of interactive talk 'narrative apostrophe,' which draws attention 'to the mechanisms of orientation to exchange by putting into question the issue of who is involved: a speaker addresses someone who is (seemingly) being addressed to provoke response in someone else.'[21] Larkin's use of 'you' might be mere colloquialism, but it also raises – consciously or not – issues of addressee; is the 'you' of 'Poetry of Departures' the literal 'you' of the reader, is it a character within the poem whose interaction with the speaker the reader merely observes (in the vein of Kacandes' 'apostrophe'), or is it a meaningless figure of speech that does not actually 'mean' 'you' at all? While the language is indeed colloquial, it also has meaning beyond its common (and perhaps 'meaningless') use in ordinary conversation. The refusal to take personal responsibility for these statements, which could be accomplished through use of the first-person voice, or to universalize the experiences he describes, through third-person use, suggests a greater significance than mere colloquialism, as do the layers of tone and meaning buried in this poem.

Lurking not far beneath the initial pushiness of the first stanza is a tone of indecision, which is at the heart of the poem's second level of manipulation. The speaker proclaims himself 'flushed and stirred' at the possibility of someone's leaving and asks, 'Surely I can, if he did?' The argument of the poem is presented as a clear binary and an obvious choice – to stay or to go – and the poem invites the reader to contribute to this debate, but the poem also posits, at the same time that it appears to ask questions, that these are false choices and therefore manipulates the reader into participating in a decision-making that is really not a decision-making at all. The indecisiveness of this poem, the inability of the speaker to settle on whether an abrupt departure from one's current life is an 'audacious, purifying,/ Elemental move' or 'Such a deliberate step backwards,' is a way of opening the poem's false questions to the audience. The double-layered confidence with the which the poem begins – the first speaker who knows about an experience 'you' have had and how 'you' feel about home and the second speaker who is certain of 'your' (and the first speaker's) approval – is undermined by the rest of the poem's uncertainty. The speaker is 'stirred' by the idea of leaving his current life behind, but he finds doing so 'artificial.' And, in fact, he would not be leaving a bad life behind but a good one: he claims to detest his room, and yet the ordinary things in it – books and a bed – are described as both 'good' and as 'specially-chosen.' Part of what he seems to hate is the perfection and order of the life he lives now. And for what would he leave? Well, for something that sounds awfully familiar to his current existence: 'Books; china; a life/ Reprehensibly perfect.' So, in fact, the artificial life to which the speaker does not wish to go is almost identical – swapping a bed for china – to the one he currently lives. The parallels between these two types of lives, presented rhetorically as binaries, are stark: both are described as 'good' in that the current life has 'good books' and a 'good bed' while the imagined life sees the speaker 'stubbly with goodness;' both lives are described as 'perfect' too, the real one in 'perfect order' but detested and the imaginary one 'reprehensibly perfect;' and both are seen as unpleasantly tied to material things, the current life with its 'specially-chosen junk' and the imagined one an artificial attempt 'to create an object.'

'Poetry of Departures,' written with such apparent confidence and such overt opinions, is actually a poem with confused opinions that offers a false binary. All lives, the one that stays or the one that departs and begins again, are approximately the same, the poem says, at the same time that it says that staying may ultimately be preferable to going while going is more exhilarating than staying. These confident voices are further undermined by the clichéd and mocking voices embedded in the poem. The speaker offers comparable clichés for this kind of departure, 'Like *Then she undid her dress/* Or *Take that you bastard.*' And then he speaks himself in the voice of cliché: 'Yes, swagger the nut-strewn roads,/Crouch in the fo'c'sle...'. So as the reader is manipulated by the opening voices of the poem and by language that offers polar positions, his invitation to participate is unsettled by the self-consciously affected registers of the rest of the poem. As the reader is invited to join in a debate that offers no choices and speaks in borrowed voices, he is also asked to notice that the content of the argument does not support its tone. The reader is simultaneously manipulated into believing, as the speaker may believe, that the two lives described are somehow opposite and challenged to share in the (un)debate of the poem by looking beyond its strong rhetoric to its contradictory and self-undermining content.

The speaker, who knows not only how he feels but how 'you' feel as well, does not actually have a clear sense of his argument at all, and so he bullies 'you' a bit, but the poem also invites 'you' to participate by escaping from the opinion 'you' are initially assigned and noticing the speaker's misplaced confidence. While the speaker of this poem, like so many of Larkin's others, is assumed by many readers to be Larkin himself, the poet actually presents a noticeable contrast between himself, necessarily aware of the disconnection between the poem's tone and content, and the speaker, who may or may not be aware of his false binary.[22]

Nicholas Marsh notes that 'Poetry of Departures' is built on stereotypes and that 'the poem sets up a choice between conventional and adventurous lives' but that 'the main, ostensible argument of the poem cancels out that impression: there is no choice between stereotypes, which are both dead. Then, this argument is mocked because the speaker has not grown out of his adolescent response to pornography and violence, and his ethics are still couched in schoolroom terms.'[23] Marsh importantly recognizes that this is not a poem of Larkin's life but a poem with distinct speakers' voices, and a separate poet's voice critiquing the speakers. The reader is engaged in the poem by being asked (and often failing) to uncover, as Marsh rightly explains, the disconnection between the speaker and the poet; the reader is initially ensnared by the speakers' authoritative voices and their apparent surety, but he is also expected – because of the parallels between the two lives; the uncertainty and immaturity of the primary voice; that voice's borrowing of other voices; and the rhetorical stance that is not supported by the words' meanings – to look beyond the opening's false confidence and play at the speaker's own game.[24]

Everyone who writes thoughtfully about Larkin at some point confronts this conflict of his voices. Those few readers who feel certain that they know who Larkin is – confident enough to make proclamations about 'the sewer under the national monument Larkin became' – discount the sensitivity that is absolutely evident in the poems in favor of the conservatism, racism, misogyny and other hateful qualities that appear primarily in the letters. They not only assume that the speaker of the poems is necessarily Larkin but also that the author of the letters and interviews expresses, unfiltered, Larkin's own beliefs. Of course, enough scholars have noted the contradictions and untruths evident in the interviews to call them into some question, but the very genre of the letters – regardless of their style – inhibits readers from seeing them as constructions similar to the constructions of his poems or to recognize that Larkin's poetic voices are present in the letters as well. Even the best Larkin readers have trouble discerning which of his statements to take at face value and which to discount as part of that 'vast private joke' Rossen claims is central to Larkin's 'pose to intrigue the public to whom he professed indifference.'[25] James Booth, for instance, who knows Larkin's work as well as anyone, makes questionable guesses on this account. In trying to prove that 'Larkin was very scrupulous about what he published' and that 'the sequencing of the poems is as finely devised as that of the words and phrases within each poem,' he writes this:

> Asked in an interview, "Do you take great care in ordering the poems in a collection?" he answered, "Yes, great care," adding with an affectation of casualness: "I treat them like a music-hall bill: you know, contrast, difference in length, the comic, the Irish tenor, bring on the girls."[26]

While it may be that Booth's assessment of tone here is correct – that is, that the first response is genuine and the second has an 'affectation of casualness,' it is entirely possible that the first response ('Yes, great care.') is equally disingenuous. Because so much of Larkin's voice is created to serve its audience and to cultivate the 'Larkin character,' particularly in the interviews, we cannot be as sure as Booth is here that we know which answer is the 'real' one and which answer is the one he thinks the interviewer or the audience would like to hear.

Clive James also falls into this trap, writing that 'what's open to doubt is whether the narrator believes what he's saying, or, given that he does, whether Larkin (wheels within wheels) believes the narrator'[27] and then following this comment one paragraph later with the observation, based on the poetry, that 'Larkin can't help believing that sex and love ought by rights to have been easier things for his generation, and far easier for him personally. The feeling of having missed out on something is one of his preoccupations.' These statements, taken in conjunction, raise the obvious question of how we know what Larkin 'can't help believing' given that we do not know if his narrator believes what he is saying or if Larkin believes his narrator. James simultaneously recognizes the folly of those who decide that the speaker of Larkin's poems is Larkin himself[28] and seems to believe every word of the interviews. He says that Larkin is a 'self-proclaimed stranger to a good half, *the* good half, of life' and that critics 'seem to think that just because the poet is (self-admittedly) emotionally wounded, the poetry is wounded too.'[29]

Stephen Cooper shows an implicit trust for the Larkin of the interviews while questioning the straightforwardness of the speakers in the novels and poems, writing, for instance, that 'Larkin wanted to be a novelist rather than a poet and he confided in the *Paris Review* that he 'didn't choose poetry: poetry chose [him].'[30] While Larkin did indeed tell the *Paris Review* that he thought he would be a novelist, the idea that this was a confidence, a secret shared from his depths, shows a misreading of the interviews. Larkin is a far more slippery character than Cooper allows, and readers should not assume that the interviews are necessarily any more true than his other writings or that the character in them is any less a persona than the speaker of the letters or poems. All of these comments clearly mean to defend Larkin, and they do, but they also assume that the speaker of the interviews is not a persona and that the interviews do not employ the same careful constructions of speaker that the poems do. And yet, based on what we know of Larkin's complexity and ability to construct characters, we must suspect that every Larkin speaker, regardless of genre, is a persona.

Like readers of the interviews, readers of Larkin's letters often read them selectively and assume, because of both the tone and the genre, that they are trustworthy as guides to the 'true' Larkin, and use them, like the poems, either to defend or castigate Larkin for his sensitive or unpalatable views. The letters can, however, reinforce our understanding of Larkin's complicated voices and demonstrate, as 'Poetry of Departures' does, how Larkin manipulates his readers, undercuts his own arguments, and maintains a constant self-awareness that informs both his personal correspondence and his poetry. What readers often discover from reading

Larkin's letters is a disturbing kind of 'truth' about his beliefs, but if they are read with more attention to their rhetorical poses rather than purely to a highlighted version of their stated opinions, we might notice that they state and undermine their own opinions in much the same way as the poems. If we keep in mind Larkin's heightened concern for audience as well as his regular inclusion of himself as a central member of the audience, we find that we must read the letters more sympathetically, as Martin Amis explains in his thoughtful *New Yorker* essay.[31] 'Words are not deeds. In published poems (we think first of Eliot's Jew), words edge closer to deeds. In Celine's anti-Semitic textbooks, words get as close to deeds as words can well get. Blood libels scrawled on front doors *are* deeds. In a correspondence, words are hardly even words. They are soundless cries and whispers; "gouts of bile," as Larkin characterized his political opinions; ways of saying "Gloomy old sod, aren't I?" or, more simply, "Grrr." Correspondences are self-dramatizations.' Just as poems are self-dramatizations rather than perfect biographical documents, Amis recognizes that the letters are not an absolute declaration of belief. Instead, as he points out, Larkin repeatedly recreates himself for his reader; for instance, 'Colin Gunner, an old school friend, brings out the worst in him.'[32] But even when Larkin is at his worst, he is self-consciously so. That is, he continues to recognize – and explicitly to attempt to make his readers, who are personal friends, in the case of the letters, aware – that he knows he is being publicly unacceptable but that he is choosing to do so for the entertainment of his reader and the perpetuation of his persona.

The letters, particularly the offensive ones, self-consciously include Larkin himself as a reader. Interestingly, even in his defense of Larkin, Richard Bradford quotes selectively from the letters, leaving out context that dramatically changes the tone and style of the most offensive passages. For example, Bradford quotes a letter of 1979 to Kingsley Amis, 'I mean like WATCHING SCHOOLGIRLS SUCK EACH OTHER OFF WHILE YOU WHIP THEM,' prefacing that charming quote with this: 'For recreation he apparently found time for pornography, preferably with a hint of sado-masochism.'[33] By quoting that line out of context and prefacing it with an accusation, Bradford entirely erases its contextual humor as well as the ironic sense of audience that exists in the sentences surrounding the capitalized line. The section of the letter – about Larkin's disinterest in the programs appearing on his newly acquired television set – in which that line appears reads thus:

And your son Martin, going on about porn in the shops: let him come up to Hull and find some. All been stamped out by police with nothing better to do. It's like this permissive society they talk about: never permitted me anything as far as I recall. I mean like WATCHING SCHOOLGIRLS SUCK EACH OTHER OFF WHILE YOU WHIP THEM, or

You know the trouble with old Phil is that he's never really grown up – just goes on along the same old lines. Bit of a bore really.[34]

What we see is not the apparent straightforward desire for hardcore kiddie porn that Bradford presents by quoting only the capitalized section but instead a really funny (if extremely vulgar) self-deprecation meant to humor Amis, who appreciated Larkin's self-effacing sensibility.

The lines preceding the quotation, about the unavailability of pornography in Hull, speak to Larkin's self-imposed isolation from the worldliness of London. His kidding about the permissive society and his own exclusion from it highlight again his sense of humor about himself. More importantly, the line that follows the capitalization shows the way in which that vulgarity was intended. Larkin is not saying that this is what he does, as Bradford suggests, or even what he truly wants to do, but instead that he is a dirty old man and, consequently, a bore. He is so acutely self-aware in this section that his vulgarity is a pure joke. We don't know if the scene Larkin describes is something he would actually like to view, but, even if it is, this letter is not about Larkin sharing with Amis his dirtiest deeds or his basest thoughts but about creating a 'dirty old Larkin' character for Amis' amusement, just as he might have in his college days and as a kind of trick of polyphony. As we learn from Bradford's book and from Larkin's own occasional remarks, impressing Amis was rather important to him, and undoubtedly Larkin believed that Amis would be impressed by sexual language and adolescent vulgarity, but he also seems to be having a bit of literary fun as well, changing voices mid-text, as he does in 'Poetry of Departures,' to shake up readers and to highlight the ways that different voices function within a single text. Bradford's analysis is that Larkin's and Amis' letters to each other 'often read as if produced by men subjected to a radical truth drug which allowed them to maintain deft stylistic control while emptying their minds of everything from their most recently purchased jazz record... to thoughts on the state of contemporary verse.'[35] In other words, Larkin and Amis share absolutely everything with each other.[36]

But I think instead that Larkin is highly conscious of his audience in Amis and does not, in fact, share everything but creates for himself a persona that he thinks will be to Amis' liking. The 'you' of the letters to Amis – or to Conquest or Gunner – is a discomfitingly different 'you' from the 'you' of the poems, which at least leaves a space for the general reader even in the situations when it doesn't address him directly. The poems' casual use of pronouns suggests an appealing intimacy with the reader, but the letters demonstrate how much more intimate that voice might become when addressed to an individual rather than the collective. If, as Bradford states, 'Larkin's presentation of himself to Amis as a lecherous bon viveur was one feature of a letter-writing style that had evolved between them since the war,' then Larkin was indeed creating a character to please his specific letter-reading audience. Little did he know how wide that audience would become after his death, and the readers most stunned by the letters seem unwilling to recognize that what distinguishes them from the poems is not simply the 'I' but also the 'you' of them. In any case, Bradford cannot have it both ways: either Larkin was consciously creating a persona of himself for Amis, or he was confessing all as though he was under the influence of a truth serum. Based on a wide cross-section of Larkin's writings, one can conclude that Larkin's concern was for his audience of the moment, not for a more universal truth-telling. Thus when Amis learns after Larkin's death about his relationship with Maeve, Amis' comment that 'He didn't half keep his life in compartments' suggests a surprise and dismay at finding that Larkin did not come even close to sharing everything with him despite the superficially confessional qualities of his letters.

Other letters demonstrate a comparable sensibility and self-awareness. For example, he writes to Amis on 28 October 1979, again about television, 'Why don't they show NAKED WOMEN, or PROS AND CONS OF CORPORAL PUNISHMENT IN GIRLS' SCHOOLS oh for God's sake Phil can't you NO I CAN'T,' again demonstrating a recognition of his own tiresome pornographic references. This self-awareness is intrinsic to Larkin's poems as well, and, as we saw in the previous chapter, is part of the same attention to audience and viewership and levels of identity that comprise the fundamental tension Larkin values so highly. We see him using a tone of winking self-awareness in poems ranging from 'A Study of Reading Habits,' with its famous conclusion that 'Books are a load of crap,' to 'Posterity,' which imagines the speaker's reluctant biographer, to 'Naturally the Foundation will Bear Your Expenses,' whose title indicates the cynicism with which the poem is written. In these, and many other cases, the poems make serious points but also play with the audience's expectations both of the biographical nature of the poems and the tone with which we should be reading seemingly straightforward but obviously also self-undermining statements.

And, of course, contradictions abound in the body of Larkin's writing. Not only has John Osborne shown how much Larkin was influenced by Modernism despite his many anti-Modern statements, but we can find multiple places where Larkin demonstrates, for instance, a more-than-usual sensitivity to the plight of women. At the same time that he wrote his vulgar and offensive comments to his friends about pornography, we find a review from 1979 that shows a surprising awareness of contemporary attitudes towards women and a sympathy for them. Larkin accuses Henry de Motherlant, author of *Les Jeunes Filles*, of using his themes to 'mount a colossal barrage against women' and that 'daily quotations for a Misogynist's Calendar appear on every page.' Larkin goes on to explain to the readers of his review that de Motherlant's many anti-woman one-liners have 'good sturdy lineage, akin to music-hall jokes and seaside postcards, but as in the case of Butler and Shaw [they have] been somewhat overtaken by events.' In other words, Larkin recognizes that the perception of the difference between the sexes has changed and, although he doesn't go so far as to agree with the changes, he shows a surprising awareness and sensitivity to the fact that "Mysterious Eve,' that fag-end of the courtly love tradition, is no longer peddled even in romantic novels,' and that 'the element in marriage that frightens Costals [the narrator] most – its permanence – is hardly likely to frighten anyone today.'[37] The fact that Larkin himself may have been scared of exactly that aspect of marriage does not discount his sympathy for the changing fates of women in the late twentieth century, and his conclusion to the review, that this 'satire of women... is also an exposure of men' presents a much more enlightened view than Larkin is generally given credit for. This is not to suggest that he didn't also make anti-woman statements but that he offered opinions calculated to meet the needs of his audiences and that, given their contextual self-mocking, the letters cannot be read as any more true of Larkin's 'real' beliefs than any one of his other writings, taken in isolation.

In addition to mocking his own sexual perversity in the letters, he seems also to recognize that his racial views are unpalatable, and he uses that disconnection between what he writes in his letters and how that might make him seem to the public as a kind of joke to Gunner: 'Prison for strikers,/ Bring back the cat,/ Kick out the niggers – / How about that? Ooh, Larkin, I'm sorry to find you holding these views.'[38] That last comment is an apt precursor to what happened when the public actually did become aware of the letters' content, but, again, readers of the letters seemed largely unable to read the context and instead read a kind of highlighted version of the letters, noticing the racism but not the self-mocking for and self-awareness of the racism. We should thus begin to recognize the important subtleties in his unacceptable comments – not in the philistinism, as Swarbrick often calls it, but in the intelligence and social commentary behind them.

His racist sentiments are again evident in letters to Amis, in which he writes, for instance, 'Bob sent m some adverst yktw [sic] for indecent cinemas in San Francisco that nearly had me buying my ticket ('Female Athletes in Bondage' ah go wash your mouth out) but I know I'd be mugged by young blacks as I came out, or went in more likely. Don't read anything, except old tec yarns. Pity old Larkin's gone to seed...'. Of course, this stereotype of young African-Americans as muggers is offensive, but what many outraged readers of the letters seem not to notice is that this passage is not a deepest confession of Larkin's heart but a thorough self-mocking. He makes fun, quite noticeably here, of his predilection for pornography, his anti-intellectualism, and his provincialism. Why, then, should we read the racist passage as fully serious when the context of the passage demonstrates so clearly that Larkin is not revealing what he really believes but exaggerating his conservatism as a form of self mockery? Again, he may indeed believe these things 'in his heart,' but his self-awareness of the unacceptability – the wrongness, even the ridiculousness – of those beliefs is evident in the self-conscious posturing that surrounds these offensive statements.

And, of course, as we see from the many, many polite and tactful letters written not to his college buddy but to other friends and associates, he knows what is appropriate and what is not. He is hardly Ezra Pound, yelling about his racism – broadcasting it, literally – but someone who thinks his provincialism is amusing in an almost embarrassing way and therefore uses it to amuse his closest friends. Neil Roberts correctly notes that 'For a man who, at least in his later years, is supposed to have been a cauldron of rage and prejudice – and who gives vent to much rage and prejudice in the letters – there is not a single wounding word for the receiver.'[39] As Bradford says, there is 'evidence to suggest that Larkin was engaged in a bizarre process of self-scrutiny; he was watching himself.'[40] Bradford makes this remark about Larkin's early years, but the letters – with their regular self-references – indicate that this process was a lifelong one.

Many of the letters to Conquest, Amis, and Gunner also show a kind of strained effort at being 'one of the guys,' as with his excessive use of cursing (for example, calling people 'stupid fuckers' in his letters to Conquest), his self-consciously pathetic attempts at making himself seem highly sexual ('I see strip-tease has been made illegal in US – no point in going now.'[41]) and his admiration for the others' sexual prowess, as in his somewhat jealous accusations of Amis' having young girls regularly chasing after him. Bradford makes much of the tension between them, writing that 'What Larkin would like Amis to notice, or at least consider, is the ways in which their respective literary careers have interfaced with their lives. Just as Amis had made his life and his fiction enviably inter-changeable and interdependent, so Larkin's poetry had become a kind of testament to his dismal retinue or disappointments with women.'[42] Although I disagree with Bradford's biographical approach to Larkin's poems here, in conjunction with Larkin's own self-consciousness and self-proclaimed nerdiness, Bradford's assessment of Larkin's relationship with Amis shows a man trying to prove himself worthy of the friendship of his more popular, hipper, ladykiller friends. Bradford emphasizes the competitive spirit between Amis and Larkin, noting that 'Amis had... kept him regularly informed of his prodigious sex life' and that Larkin was frustrated by the fact that 'while he felt sexually attracted to [women] he did not have Amis's enviable combination of charm, wit and looks.'[43] The letters may be an attempt at reconciling that frustration with his friendship with Amis, and they reflect a lack of self-confidence alongside an effort to entertain a particular audience. Cooper notes that Larkin's early stories (notably *Trouble at Willow Gables*) share this quality with the letters, pointing out that '[John] Carey suggests that the stories "are clearly written to produce male sexual arousal, and... seem to have been partly for the entertainment of Larkin's male friends." '[44]

Similarly, Larkin's fondness for pornography might also be seen as growing out of the patterns of social relationships developed during his college years. Cooper attributes Larkin's approach to photography (not necessarily pornographic in nature) to his shared philosophy with The Movement, whose writers 'argued that mass culture can also be art,' and Larkin does express interest in the power and artistry of photography.[45] But his pornographic interest in particular seems largely rooted to a dual sense of viewership. Laura Mulvey explains the idea of the active male gaze on the passive female in her writings on film theory, and it applies very well to a study of photographic pornography as well. She posits that 'traditionally, the woman displayed has functioned on two levels: as erotic object for the characters within the screen story, and as erotic object for the spectator within the auditorium, with a shifting tension between the looks on either side of the screen.'[46] These relationships also exist in a single narrative photograph, like the ones Larkin enjoyed, including the 'schoolgirl' pictures he often mentions in his letters to Con-quest and Amis. That is, the schoolgirl is the erotic object of the imagined male figures in the school – instructors, presumably – and also of the outside viewer of the photograph, in this case Larkin. Mulvey goes on to state that the male figure on screen (present or imagined) 'cannot bear the burden of sexual objectification' and his characteristics 'are thus not those of the erotic object of the gaze, but those of the more perfect, more complete, more powerful ideal ego conceived in the original moment of recognition in front of the mirror.' That is, the woman is objectified and the man is projected, three-dimensionally, as an ideal male figure rather than the pathetic one living vicariously through images.

If we apply these ideas to Larkin's pornographic interests, which have so captured and altered readers' views of Larkin's verse, we find that we must add one additional dimension of relationship, because a significant part of Larkin's love of pornography seems to include the connection it creates between himself and his friends. Despite the fact that he remains, throughout his life, the occasional butt of their jokes, he seems to want both to impress and to entertain them, as though he is back at Oxford.[47] Therefore, his desire for pornography is about the relationship between the schoolgirl and her imagined tutor, between the schoolgirl and himself, and, importantly, between himself and his friends, with whom he discusses in surprising detail the pornography sent to him and whom he must imagine viewing it as he sees himself viewing it. When he writes to Conquest that he 'admired the painstaking realism of it – I mean, the teacher really did look like a teacher, & I greatly appreciated the school-like bell on the wall,' he is playing, in an obviously light-hearted way, not only with the image of the photograph but with his own image as presented to his friend.[48] This additional layer of suppressed erotic relationship does not change the fact that Larkin likes to look at pornography, but it does perhaps change the way we see his interest. By continuing to communicate with friends from college about pornography and endeavoring to entertain them as he had in his early twenties, he ends up seeming like the dirtiest in the bunch. If we consider his love of pornography in light of his concern for audience, though, we see that much of the complicated desire implicit in his viewing of pornography could be read as a desire to satisfy an audience, not just himself but his friends as well. Thus the pornography is not an end in itself; it must be followed with a conversation with Conquest – an attempt to please and amuse his friend – and so the pornography becomes a conduit for something else: another outlet to connect with a reading audience.

Larkin has his audience in mind during his writing, but not necessarily just to please them; his writing also destabilizes and complicates his relationship with audience in order to foreground it and to create a thoughtfulness about poetry reading. As with the letters, its self-referentiality is one way in which it highlights the audience's role in the reading of a poem. Although Larkin seldom writes poems about writing poetry (except in places where such ideas are read onto poems, as in 'Reasons for Attendance,' where many critics assume that the 'art' the speaker refers to must be the art of poetry, although the poem never says such a thing), the poems that obliquely show their own artifice further involve the reader by pointing out what the current poem is not doing while also doing it. 'Sad Steps,' for example, powerfully expresses the collision of voices as well as the unsettling of the reader's position through poetic self-reference. From the first stanza we can hear the contrasting voices of the speaker:

> Groping back to bed after a piss
> I part thick curtains, and am startled by
> The rapid clouds, the moon's cleanliness.

The crudeness of 'groping back to bed after a piss' is juxtaposed with the lovely, sensitive observation of the beauty of a natural moment, 'the moon's cleanliness.' Here we see a speaker, aware of his own base physicality and the world's lofty beauty – similar to the imagery of the physical body versus the endless sky in 'High Windows' – but who can't let those two separate realms stand as equally worthy or real. Instead, he moves on to mock the natural image, almost to reduce it to the level of his crass self-perception: 'High and preposterous and separate – / Lonzenge of love! Medallion of art!'

He calls the moon's movement 'laughable,' and yet the description he offers for it – 'high and preposterous and separate' – plainly describes not merely the moon but also the speaker himself; the choice of words suggests something much more personal than simply the moon, and the rest of the poem certainly implies that those three adjectives adequately describe the speaker. His self-disdain is evident here, as is the sense that self-awareness, and the separateness is engenders, is a kind of necessity, a permanent state of being rather than a choice. One protection against that separateness is mockery, and the height of the poem's mocking tone occurs in the poem's middle, when the speaker exclaims generically about love, art, and memory with falsely formal verse and exaggerated punctuation, ridiculing his own startled observation, his initial impulse to immortalize the vision in verse, and versification in general. But, of course, even through his self-disgust, he does immortalize the experience. No longer does he offer the personal involvement and tangible physicality of 'I part thick curtains;' now, the speaker has moved, as Larkin's speakers so often do, to the third person singular: 'One shivers slightly, looking up there'. The use of 'one' encompasses the reader's experience in addition to the speaker's – I could be 'one' just as well as the speaker of the poem could be – but also points to the speaker's acceptance of multiple presences other than his own. Both the inclusion of the reader – and even of other non-readers – through the third-person pronouns and the reference to 'others' reminds us how external this seemingly internal poem is.

Following this change in point of view, the speaker observes that the moon's distance reminds him of fleeting youth – its simultaneous pain and strength – and that while one's own youth may be gone, someone else continues to experience it. The primary dilemma of this poem is not at all the speaker's self-absorption, although on the surface that might seem to be the case, but actually quite the opposite: a near-obsession with otherness, with the experience of being other than he is. He refers poignantly not simply to his own remembered youth but to the enviable and difficult youths of people he does not even know. The poem highlights a separation that the speaker has already begun to enact and that he longs for: skyward, youthward, anywhere but in an aging body that has no choice but to disobey him.

'Sad Steps,' for all its solipsism, is, of course, also linking itself with a long literary tradition through its obvious allusions to Philip Sidney's sonnet. Larkin, who was named for Sidney, invokes Sidney's poem, absorbing Sidney's image of the moon's sad steps into the speaker's own steps, and mimicking Sidney's formal language ('Then ev'n of fellowship, O Moon, tell me/ Is constant love deem'd there but want of wit?'). The sonnet, which presents Astrophil lamenting women's love of being loved and their simultaneous – and hypocritical – scorn for their lovers, is reversed in Larkin's poem, which laments the very existence of young lovers. Both poems offer solitary and self-absorbed speakers whose thoughts are prompted by the moon, but Larkin builds on Sidney's poem by partially appropriating its voice while also criticizing Astrophil, who remains unaware of the fleetingness of 'the strength and pain/ Of being young.' The lofty language of Sidney's poem, which itself mocks the caricatured and histrionic Astrophil, is both appropriated and mocked by Larkin, who uses 'Sad Steps' not only to present a twentieth-century speaker but also to invoke Sidney's explicit creation of a character who is decidedly not the poet.

The audience is unsettled by this destabilized speaker and not allowed to maintain a single attitude or emotion through the course of the short poem but dragged from one subject position to another. Is the moon something to be adored or something to be mocked? Is our physicality lamentable or glorious, or both? Is the very act of writing a poem, or of reading one, admirable or ridiculous? Are we aligned with Larkin's speaker or with Sidney's? The poem raises many questions but offers clear answers to none of them. And yet, even 'Sad Steps,' with its statements and undermining of those statements, with its mockery for its own form, and with its alternating inward and outward focuses, retains continuity in its sense of place and speaker's identity. Other poems, though, confront even more unsettlingly the assumptions of poetry readers. By changing speakers from stanza to stanza without other obvious hallmarks of Modern poetry, poems like 'Places, Loved Ones' confound readers, who are unsure of how many speakers the poem has, whether these speakers reinforce or contradict the opinions of the others stanzas, and, especially, where readers fit into the poems' conversations.

For the most part, 'Places, Loved Ones,' like so many of Larkin's poems, is read biographically, but because of the changing voices of the speaker(s), critics most often consider only the first stanza and, at least implicitly, overlook the second and third. The first stanza is written entirely in first person while the second and third stanzas are entirely in second person, with no reappearance of the first-person voice. Both Booth and Motion use the first stanza of 'Places, Loved Ones' to demonstrate that Larkin 'refused to identify himself with the city' and that his ' "here" is wherever or whenever he happens to find himself.'[49] Rossen writes, again using only the first stanza of the poem, that Larkin himself has a 'preference for detachment' and that 'this elusive *"proper ground"* continues to withhold itself throughout Larkin's work, in poems about places and journeys to or beyond them.'[50] The interviewer for *Paris Review* similarly reads the poem as resting entirely on its first stanza, presumably with the second and third stanzas repeating, from a different perspective, the views of the opening speaker. The interviewer asks Larkin, 'Is Hull a place where you are likely to stay put? If so, have you as a person changed since the writing of the poem "Places, Loved Ones" – or is the speaker a persona?' Larkin chooses, wisely, not to answer this last question but to speak instead about a party he had for his anniversary at Hull. All of these commentators, then, see the opening speaker as Larkin himself and ignore the second and third stanzas, presumably reading them as a second-person presentation of the same speaker who uses a barely-disguised voice of mild detachment.

But a more complete reading of this poem opens up several interpretive possibilities, particularly because of its complex use of pronouns and, therefore, the vivid suggestion on the part of the poet that the poem is not merely a straightforward presentation of argument about places and loved ones. The poem begins, as so many of Larkin's poems do, with a strong statement of argument in a personal, confessional-sounding voice:

> No, I have never found
> The place where I could say
> This is my proper ground...

The speaker here expresses himself quite simply and directly, but when the poem then switches to a second-person voice, the effects, and the possibilities, are multifold. One option, and the one assumed by the critics cited above, is that the second voice is as personal as the first but the change in perspective offers the speaker some emotional remove. Using a 'first-person "you" ' thus allows the speaker to reveal more about himself without the discomfort of purely confessional language. It also enacts, rhetorically, the same detachment that is the subject of the poem; not only does this speaker lack a person and a place, but, after the first stanza, he lacks an individual voice as well. Most critical attention to the poem uses this interpretation of the 'you,' and finds it a not-very-subtle disguising of the first stanza's voice. Such readers approach the whole poem as spoken by a single speaker who chooses, because of his own neuroses and an unwillingness to confront them fully, to speak entirely personally but to use second-person pronouns to create emotional distance from the uncomfortable subject matter.

This reading is, of course, not the only possibility for the second-person voice.

> To find such seems to prove
> You want no choice in where
> To build, or whom to love;

In addition to being a second-person representation of the same character offered in the first stanza, this second stanza may be read as a response to the first stanza. In this interpretation, the poem is dialogic, not exclusively stating something about Larkin or his speaker but stating it and then offering a response, whether the respondent is a second internal voice or an external speaker. In this reading, the second speaker attempts to dissuade the first speaker from what is expressed, albeit obliquely, as a desire that the second speaker finds less than desirable. If we see the poem as embodying two speakers rather than a single speaker who chooses varying pronouns, the second-person stanzas act not as a personal justification of the poet's choices but as an argument supporting the detachment that the first stanza laments. The second and third stanzas might speak against the guarded wistfulness of the first stanza, which is often read as a proud proclamation of separation but need not be seen as such.

While the pronouns of the poem lean toward this second reading more than the first monologic and purely personal interpretation, the punctuation of the poem leads to a third reading: a poem with three separate voices. The first stanza and second, while separated noticeably by a change in perspective, are connected to one another by a semi-colon rather than the more logical full stop, which suggests that the first and second stanzas may be two voices of the same individual, one directed inward and the other directed outward, and the third stanza, which is separated from the rest of the poem by a full stop, offers a completely separate voice joining the conversation with a contradicting 'yet' while also addressing a 'you.' The third stanza suggests that people who have not found their permanent partner or home must pretend that these lacks are oppressive, whether that is actually the case. This stanza emphasizes the necessity of putting on an act on the part of the addressed 'you' at the same time that it questions whether these missing pieces in a life should continue to be sought. The identity of this third-stanza 'you' becomes part of the dilemma as well, when we consider that, in addition to being a stand-in for the first-person speaker, as it is often assumed to be, it might also be directed at the general reader. Particularly in the second stanza, the 'you' does not address the first-person speaker's apparent concern at not having found a person or place and instead speaks directly to the person who has, or believes he has, found those things. In other words, the second stanza could be read either as a justification of the first speaker's present state or as an unveiled criticism of the reader for having abdicated the personal responsibility that the first speaker values. If the 'you' of the poem addresses the reading audience, then the poem becomes an accusation on the part of the first speaker, who does not need to justify his own choices to himself but wishes to point out an individual and communal flaw in his audience. The individual accusation is that people who find permanence in another person or in a place have abandoned their responsibility to self; and the societal accusation is that we insist, wrongly, on one's attaching oneself to a person or place and, if one chooses not to do so, there is a communal expectation that he assume an air of desperation and misery at his detachment.

The multiple possibilities in 'Places, Loved Ones,' and the complicated layering of speakers and audiences, should, at the very least, prevent readers from finding in it a purely autobiographical statement of Larkin's own relationships. But they should also highlight the complexity of Larkin's voices and the way that he consciously destabilizes the assumptions of poetry reading and audienceship through his play with perspectives. The most common way to approach this poem as an argument about places and loved ones is to focus on the first stanza as the poem's central argument and assume that the following stanzas echo the first stanza's sentiments. But the poem begs for a reading that is not only about places and loved ones but about conversation, about poetry, and about audienceship. Swarbrick writes that 'it is hard to know how seriously to take the speaker of the poem, which seems to be grappling with something unresolved,' and indeed it is; but part of the reason for this difficulty is not merely the moving arguments of the poem but the assumption that it is spoken by a single speaker to a single audience. The poem does not clarify its multiplicity, nor does it deny it, but it plays with the very idea of singularity by choosing a notably personal subject and expanding it beyond the personal to make an argument about the first-person speaker, about the second-person speaker(s) and, most uncomfortably, about you.

The poem asks readers, no less than Eliot's or Pound's poetry does, to decipher the speakers and their motivations and alterations, just as it places the reader in multiple and changing positions. We can see, even from an often underread poem like 'Places, Loved Ones,' how wrong Anthony Easthope is in his assertion that Larkin 'aligns himself with exactly that notion of experience found in Locke and Wordsworth' and that the voice of Larkin's poem is 'detached, critical, not selfdeceived, confident of submitting the world to a controlling gaze; in other words, very much the poised, individualized, empiricist subject whose voice has been represented as speaking in English poetry for over two centuries.'[51] The speaker in Larkin's poems only feigns those characteristics, but apparently with some effectiveness. Instead, in 'Places, Loved Ones,' as in many of Larkin's poems, the speaker is part of the audience and is himself multiple; the poem has one voice, or two, or three, and one audience, or two, or more. Larkin straddles the complications of resembling the first speaker – very consciously knowing that the *Paris Review* interviewer is not the only one reading his life onto the poem – and being spoken to by the second and third while also intoning those lines.

Although scholars have noted his audience awareness, generally the analysis of that sensibility is applied only to various individual situations rather than to Larkin's complete aesthetic and artistic philosophy. While Bradford too often takes Larkin at his word, he also recognizes that nearly all of Larkin's most 'offensive' statements (the sexual and racist ones, generally) are made to only two correspondents – Kingsley Amis and Colin Gunner (although Neil Roberts and Andrew Swarbrick rightly add a third: Robert Conquest[52]) – as a means of defending Larkin against his harshest critics who dismiss him on the basis of those comments.[53] This defense essentially argues, without saying so explicitly, that Larkin was not a racist or pervert through and through but only in certain situations and with certain people, thus suggesting that our readings of the letters should be tempered by Larkin's audience awareness. Richard Palmer argues as much when he writes that Larkin made 'incautious and frankly disagreeable comments' about race in his private papers but that he wasn't 'a true racist' because he also made sensitive comments about Black musicians and the degradation of African-Americans in his public writings.[54] Motion and Bradford, among others, have also commented on Larkin's consciousness of audience when he talks obliquely about his father's love of Germany; rather than mentioning the elder Larkin's explicit admiration of Hitler, complete with the novelty statuette on the family mantle, Larkin insinuates in his interview with *The Paris Review* that his father's interest grew out of a study of German 'office methods' and leaves it at that, believing (accurately, no doubt) that such an explanation would be far more palatable to the magazine's readership. Again, Motion does not explicitly discuss the significance of this 'reinterpretation' of Larkin's childhood, but Bradford hints at it by suggesting that Larkin has used his audience's likely knowledge of his father's Teutonism to fashion himself as someone who consequently hates travel. More explicitly, Bradford argues that, in 'relationships throughout his adult life' Larkin's 'concerns were as much for the other person as himself; he might argue, disagree, even appear obtuse, but within the controlling ground rules of a game played only by the two of them, if knowingly only by him.'[55] I believe, though, that these moments of audience awareness in both the letters and the autobiographical presentation (interviews and prose writings) are carried over to the poems and even heightened there. The multiple voices we so clearly see Larkin use in his letters are more subtly a part of his poems as well, and they necessitate a reconsideration of his reputation for simplicity as well as a thorough rereading of the poems with the reader's discomfort and displacement in mind.

This chapter has demonstrated some of the ways in which Larkin's poems complicate and destabilize readers' notions of what poetry can do and what Larkin's poetry, in particular, does. There is significant evidence throughout the poems that Larkin is constantly aware of and acutely interested in the reactions and positioning of his audience, and his use of multiple voices and tonalities highlights a primary way in which Larkin manipulates and engages readers. It also confirms the errors of finding Larkin's work simplistic rather than merely superficially simple; common rather than striking a pose of commonness; and provincial rather than mocking provinciality. The next three chapters will examine specific subjects about which Larkin writes – personal history, music and religion – and explore the ways that his attention to audience, his use of multiple voices, and his subtle but unmistakable rhetorical game-playing influence three areas that are of elementary importance to a full understanding of his work.

3
Memory and Change

Two of the few areas in which Larkin seems not to play with readers or manipulate them are in his apparently genuine attachment to things past and his terror of future death. His language and feelings about these subjects are entirely consistent throughout his adult prose writings and interviews. Many of his closest friends remained his old college friends, and his letters to those friends never lost the childishness that was a hallmark of his college years. Motion discusses repeatedly Larkin's immaturity among his college friends, particularly Amis and Montgomery, and notes that he never outgrew the habit of signing his letters 'bum,' even until his death, and of his basic childishness, even when he took his first job, since he had 'never cooked a meal, never washed his own clothes, never had to pay a bill.'[1] Bradford similarly makes much of Larkin's resistance to marriage or long-term commitment, suggesting that he never managed to reach an ordinary level of emotional maturity. Bradford's chapters on Larkin's relationships with Maeve Brennan and Monica Jones particularly highlight a kind of emotional stuntedness on Larkin's part that was never resolved.

Larkin's tastes in literature, music, and entertainment also seem not to have developed much beyond their college levels, which is particularly interesting considering how often his poems rehearse 'development' in attitude and thought. He kept his continuing interest in erotic materials to himself, with the exception of letters to a few close friends, but he was vocal and well published on his opinions about the terrible changes in the arts that occurred after his time at Oxford (or that he became aware of after that time). Early in his life his artistic tastes – D. H. Lawrence, primarily – were largely influenced by his father, but he remained open to new things as a youth, particularly jazz. After college, however, he no longer seemed to feel the need to search for newness and in fact seemed almost frightened by things that differed from his positive college experiences with alcohol, masturbation, certain poetry, certain jazz, and certain male friendships. Larkin's feelings about the developments in jazz music, while not always expressed with perfect gravity, suggest that his music preferences were very much tied up with his memories of childhood and those earliest jazz experiences. As he writes in 'The Rummagers,' 'If I were to frame Larkin's Law of Reissues, it would say that anything you haven't got already probably isn't worth bothering about... if they were any good, you'd have heard of them at school, as you did King Oliver, and have laid out your earliest pocket money on them.'[2] Even in something as innovative and relatively new as jazz, Larkin hesitated to accept change. In writing about new LPs, he says, 'When the long-playing record was introduced in the middle Fifties, I was suspicious of it: it seemed a package deal, forcing you to buy bad tracks along with good at an unwontedly-high price.'[3]

The areas in which we see Larkin's distrust of change range from those as significant as his fundamental beliefs to those as prosaic as co-education or recording technology. When asked about co-education he replies, 'I suppose I'm a little suspicious of it: one's always suspicious of change.'[4] Similarly, he says with trepidation and some disgust that he cannot imagine how much longer the Oxford that he knew will last, given, for example, that 'left-wing agitation' aims to mobilize students into an anti-university 'political force' that would vocally express its hostility toward the ideals of the Oxford of old' and, furthermore, that 'legislation by a succession of socialist or quasi-socialist governments' has impeded the university's ability to earn money from its investments and that other financial considerations suggest the imminent demise of the sort of university experience he encountered.[5] His proclaimed attachment to conservative politics was rooted in similar tendencies to value 'preservation,' and his reminiscences about his early work experiences also demonstrate longing for a better past. When writing about his first job in a college library, he laments that 'the College as a whole was changing: it was becoming larger, less personal, full of scaffolding and piles of bricks.' His sadness at that change is further evident when he writes, 'It certainly did not occur to me that I had belonged to an academic community of a kind soon to be superseded but with virtues that in time would come to seem precious.'[6]

All of this idealization of the past – in his friendships, in the arts, in technology, in education – has led to a widespread belief in Larkin's backwards-looking philosophy. Colin Falck's 1964 review of *The Whitsun Weddings* argues that all of Larkin's subjects 'are bathed in the same general wistfulness,'[7] while John Bayley comments that Larkin, like Keats, focuses on 'an elsewhere conjured up by the soberly precise insistence on the banality of the here and now.[8] Lisa Jardine posits that Larkin's work encourages readers to 'dig in with nostalgic memories of a "great" Britain that (perhaps) once was, and to spend the fading years of British imperial glory trying to persuade our children that everything of value lies behind us.' Larkin's ostensible attitude towards the innovations of Modernism, as he details it in *All What Jazz*, heighten that sense of a staid, old-fashioned, and hopelessly nostalgic outlook that, according to many readers, pervades the poems. Bruce Martin writes that Larkin believes 'that a poem is better based on something from "unsorted" experience than on another poem or other art'[9] while Peter King argues that Larkin's work is 'a poetry of disappointment, of the destruction of romantic illusions, of man's defeat by time and his own inadequacies.'[10] Janice Rossen comments that Larkin's poems 'become elegies for England which range from regret and tenderness to anger and fatalism,' and that 'he continues to write in a romantic vein where a tender sense of loss and melancholy infuses his view of England.'[11] Indeed, he explicitly perpetuates the sense of his own attachment to the past with his oft-quoted statement to D.J. Enright. As discussed in Chapter 1, Larkin wrote to Enright in 1955, in a statement that he was apparently surprised to find published as the preface to his work in Enright's *Poets of the 1950s*, that 'I want to preserve things I have seen/ thought/ felt (if I may so indicate a composite and complex experience) both for myself and for others, though I feel that my prime responsibility is to the experience itself, which I am trying to keep from oblivion for its own sake. Why I should do this I have no idea, but I think the impulse to preserve lies at the bottom of all art.' This approach to poetry, expressed here and repeated elsewhere, is rooted in the idea of preservation, which he articulates for Enright as a kind of universal truth, almost as a human reflex: it 'lies at the bottom of all art.'

Such a definitive tone understandably prompts readers to find that sort of preservation in the poems. The poems, however, display a more subtle and nuanced view of personal history than this 'Statement' indicates. What the poems show us that the prose, quite pointedly, does not is that these poems are not, in fact, preservations of things in a standard sense. Straightforward, unanalyzed experiences are almost never present in the poems, and the belief in Larkin's tendency towards 'preservation' in its most literal sense is compromised by the poems' complicated attitudes towards the past.

Larkin's use of the idea of preservation in his answer to Enright suggests the standard definition of 'to preserve': 'to maintain in unaltered condition.' And yet any close consideration of Larkin's poetry demonstrates not only that experiences are not preservable but that perfect preservation is undesirable and, furthermore, that 'preservation' has multiple, and sometimes contradictory, definitions. Larkin's poetry shows a perhaps surprisingly intricate relationship with the past and even with the idea of the past, melding nostalgia and bitterness with a self-awareness of the past's malleability and the easy corruption of memory. From the poetry we see not a poet mired in an idealized past nor distrusting the new but one who plays with ideas of past and truth and who asks readers to think about the power and failure of memory.

'Wild Oats,' as much as any of Larkin's poems, demonstrates his complicated notions of an individual's past and of the idea of the past. Bradford has made much of the poem's historical accuracy and highlights the ways in which the poem perfectly parallels Larkin's own life and experiences.[12] He writes that 'while one might be tempted to treat ['Wild Oats'] as insensitive, confessional would be more apt' and further asserts that in other poems of the same period 'there is a confidential openness interweaved with mundane, sometimes embarrassing, personal detail.'[13] Indeed the poem may have been sparked by an early experience with Ruth Bowman, and yet to reduce the whole poem to a diary entry in verse is to ignore its insight into Larkin's larger aesthetic and particular self-awareness in regard to his personal past and to the general past. Bradford writes that 'the dynamic between secrecy and quiet disclosure that fed his addiction to the diaries and notebooks – and in an adjusted way his exchanges with Amis – would become an equally important feature of his best verse.'[14] And while we might consider the verse as mere reflection of the life's experiences, to do so is to read the verse as illuminating the life and not as simply illuminating.

Larkin's 'personal history' poems, including 'Wild Oats,' 'I Remember, I Remember,' and 'Maiden Name,' among others, are not the work of someone living in the past so much as the work of someone considering the intrusion of the past on the present and the present's manipulation of the past. 'Wild Oats' shows not just a single incident in Larkin's life and serves not merely as a versified form of a youthful experience, but demonstrates some of the larger themes that preoccupied Larkin throughout his poetry. In particular, it plays with the relationship between speaker and poet that is central to almost all of Larkin's 'autobiographical' poems, and it questions the validity of memory and the confidence with which one relies on his memory.

The speaker's chronological remove from the experience he describes, and its apparent emotional rawness in spite of the casual and self-deprecating tone, may make the poem seem more personal, but the enumeration of the poem's various nouns highlight both its artistry and its ambiguous relationship with the experience it describes. 'Wild Oats' presents a superficially self-assured character with plenty of answers to the questions of his life, which opens him to being judged, as Rossen does, saying that 'the very egocentrism, anger and frustration which Larkin articulates form the heart of his argument against women throughout his work,' a mischaracterization that conflates poet with speaker and that suggests surety on Larkin's part, despite textual evidence to the contrary.[15] Instead of highlighting Larkin's clear feelings about women, or about any single issue, the personal history poems raise more questions than they provide answers, and they show a speaker who is unsure of the superiority of the past or how it should impact one's present.

The poem casually and, apparently straightforwardly, presents a story that recounts a seemingly simple past experience. Two girls entered the speaker's workplace two decades ago; one was a conventional beauty and the other wore glasses and was more approachable. It goes on to explain that for the next seven years, the speaker and the girl 'in specs' corresponded, got engaged, and met multiple times in various places around the country. And, finally, the relationship ends: after multiple break-ups, the couple terminates their engagement with the 'agreement' that the speaker had too many faults to continue in a meaningful relationship: 'I was too selfish, withdrawn/And easily bored to love.'

The speaker begins the poem by coldly and superficially judging the two young women of the poem based on their appearances, and although he eventually gets engaged to the less physically attractive of the two, he remains in thrall of 'bosomy rose,' of whom he keeps two photographs in his wallet, even twenty years later. It is understandable, then, why readers – particularly those who, after the publication of the letters, might be predisposed to find Larkin insensitive to women – would find this poem swaggering, misogynistic, and offensive.

The speaker's swagger, though, is a ruse: his insecurity is written everywhere. The first words of the poem, 'about twenty years ago,' already offer a hint to the imprecision of the memory recounted here and this history's place in the speaker's current existence. The rest of the short poem is riddled with language that questions the historical accuracy of the memory: the speaker 'doubts' if another's face was as beautiful as the girl's; the notable use of numbers in the poem is surprisingly imprecise for things that should be quantifiable, including modifiers like '*over* four hundred letters,' '*numerous* cathedral cities' and '*about* five rehearsals;' the speaker merely 'believes' that he 'met beautiful twice' rather than knowing it; and he parenthetically questions whether 'she was trying/ Both times (so I thought) not to laugh.' While Larkin's prose presents his relationship with the past as fixed and opinionated, his poetry – even those poems whose surface tone seems nostalgic or regretful – presents the past as moveable and uncertain, filled with the same doubts and insecurities as the present and the future. Perhaps it is the case, as I will argue in the concluding chapter, that Larkin is simply better able to express nuance and sophistication of concept in verse than in prose; but it is also possible that he uses his prose to obscure rather than illuminate the poems.

The final assertion of the poem leaves readers with one last uncertainty: 'Unlucky charms, perhaps.' This poem does not merely question the speaker's motivations or the nature of romantic relationships but the more fundamental belief in memory. The speaker remembers approximately when something happened and is able simultaneously to doubt and believe details about the experience; he remembers what he thought but does not know if it was true; and he wonders, ultimately, how the photographs of 'bosomy rose' that he continues to carry with him have affected him in the intervening years. Have they indeed been unlucky charms? And, if so, were they unlucky by themselves or, as the word 'perhaps' suggests, because of the speaker's inability to move beyond this early and poorly-handled experience? The poem begins with 'about' and ends with 'perhaps' and is filled, in between, with 'belief' and 'doubt,' but not with much certainty or definition. The questioning, though, is not merely of the truth of memory but also of the speaker's responsibility for the events described.

The poem presents a speaker half unwilling to recognize his own faults and his own living in the past, but it hardly presents such a poet. The poem's placement in the relatively distant past acts as a recognition on the speaker's part that he has not been able to move beyond an experience that should have been, as the poem suggests, learned from and moved beyond. But those two photographs still in the speaker's wallet – and presumably there until the time of his lonely death – prevent him from moving forward in a way of which Larkin is very well aware. The speaker's idea of unlucky charms is that they have prevented his further luck in love for these two decades, but the implication of the poem is not merely that they have led to bad fortune in some predestined way but that the speaker's own inability to clearly view his own situation has promised him years of loneliness based on his own romantic blindness. The poet possesses an awareness of the speaker's bind, and he presents that awareness, with an evident dramatic irony, to an audience he knows has clearer vision than the speaker has.

All these years later, the speaker still does not fully acknowledge or take responsibility for his own selfishness or withdrawal, about which he claims to have come to an 'agreement' with the 'friend in specs,' and his agreement now seems much more cynical than genuine. In addition, the speaker's memory of the bosomy friend having, according to this poem at least, a significance equal to or even greater than to that of the woman with whom he had a lasting and committed relationship does indeed indicate a selfishness and superficiality of which Larkin himself has been accused. What this reading overlooks, however, is the disconnection between 'Well, useful to get that learnt' and 'In my wallet are still two snaps/ Of bosomy rose with fur gloves on.' These lines, the latter of which immediately follows the former, show the poet's awareness of what the speaker has actually 'learned' from the experience. The speaker's negative qualities – 'I was too selfish, withdrawn,/ And easily bored' – about which he seems not to have fully been fully in 'agreement,' despite his tongue-in-cheek statement to the contrary, continue in his attachment, all these years later, to the two photographs. Keeping those pictures in his wallet demonstrates withdrawal, from reality if nothing else, and selfishness in his continued obsession with a woman who apparently never cared for him at all, perhaps at the expense of the woman who tried to form a real relationship with him. The continued exhibition of those qualities is something that the speaker does not acknowledge but that the poet certainly does.

The mere fact that this poem begins with the phrase 'About twenty years ago' suggests how strongly Larkin's poetry connects to the past and how large past experiences continue to loom in the imagination. The poem's emphasis on how long ago these experiences occurred clashes noticeably with the poem's casual tone and the fact that the speaker seems not to take very seriously either relationship – the one that involved a 'ten-guinea ring' or the one that involved only unre-quited infatuation and, apparently, had a greater impact on him. The tone of 'Well, useful to get that learnt' shows a lack of commitment to a seven-year relationship that most people would consider a signifi-cant life experience, but the fact that the speaker not only remembers but recounts it twenty years later – thirteen years after the relationship ended – contradicts the poem's almost lighthearted tone. Attention to the time frame of the experience, so distantly remembered, highlights

Larkin's poetry's complex relationship with personal history. He creates a speaker who lives in the past and for whom the past is a kind of impossible weight, but he simultaneously illustrates the folly of that sort of bondage to the past and the imprecision of the speaker's memory.

A connection to the past here, in this case to physical relics of the past, is presented as fundamental to the speaker's life-long problems. As in 'Home is So Sad,' 'Love Songs in Age,' and 'Lines on a Young Lady's Photograph Album,' the attachment to relics of the past leads to sadness and to error. In these poems, Larkin thoughtfully considers ways of confronting the past while in his prose writings he simplifies them. And while the speaker may be unable to move beyond his past experiences, even if he does say he has 'learned' something from this particular experience, the poet is acutely aware of the problems with stasis and acts not as a mirror of the speaker but as a judge. The speaker's refusal to move past the photographs is separate from the poet's, and the poet aligns himself with the audience in judging the speaker. 'Wild Oats' mimics 'Lines on a Young Lady's Photograph Album' in its prurient interest in holding on to old photographs of young women and in its recognition that photography is both 'faithful and disappointing,' condensing 'a past that no one now can share.' The two photographs are real and concrete, but, like the photographs in 'Lines on a Young Lady's Photograph Album,' they are illusory, looking 'empirically true' but ultimately depicting not reality but 'just *the past.*' 'Wild Oats' also models 'Lines on a Young Lady's Photograph Album' in its divided speaker and its implicit expectation that the audience will read the speaker differently than he reads himself. The poet aligns himself with the reader in his ability to know how the reader will watch and judge the speaker; the author of the poems stands aside, watching the first-person speaker as the reader does, and acknowledging that the speaker is partially blind to his own situation despite his confident tone of self-awareness.

'Wild Oats' creates a separation between poet and speaker through chronological remove, and that separation underscores the multiple ways that the past is considered in the poem: with fondness, with bitterness, as an ideal, and as an impediment to forward progress. In other history-focused poems, though, the entire concept of personal memory is undermined. 'I Remember, I Remember' is one such poem. It is more explicit about its subject matter, the nature of memory and the romanticization of the past, than 'Wild Oats.' While 'Wild Oats' claims only to tell a story – albeit a story that constantly questions itself through the language of doubt and approximation – 'I Remember, I Remember' explicitly questions the nature of memory and the way that storytelling alters and shapes memory. This poem could be seen as a self-indulgent poem of anti-nostalgia in the vein of 'Annus Mirabilis,' but it could also – I believe more accurately – be read as a poem that has much more to do with readerly expectations imposed on the poet than with the speaker's own defeated expectations. That is, 'I Remember, I Remember' speaks as much to the reader's relationship to memory as it does to the speaker's (and the writer's).

The list of things that never happened to the speaker in Coventry illustrates the literary rhetoric into which the speaker buys. His problem with the place itself is not that nothing of particular interest happened there but that the kinds of things he – and more pointedly his audience – expected to have happened in the early life of an author or literary character never happened. Unlike most people, who upon seeing a familiar place recall what happened there, the speaker of 'I Remember, I Remember' 'recalls' the many things that didn't happen: his creativity did not blossom in the garden, he did not run to his family to fulfill emotional needs, he did not lose his virginity in a thicket of shrubs. The generic items of pastoral life – a garden, the family, the bracken – may have existed, but not with the uses one might imagine. In each case, the speaker claims to be able to show readers the real places where various things did not occur, confusing the readers' expectations for a remembered experience.

The irony of the poem's approach to history is accentuated by the title: 'I Remember, I Remember ' But what, exactly, is remembered here? The actual remembering is painfully imprecise: as he pulls into the train station, the speaker remarks, 'I wasn't even clear/ Which side was which.' And what he does 'remember' is not only a fiction but a negation of a fiction. The use of the title from Thomas Hood's poem provides the additional counterpoint of a poem in which things are concretely remembered, and fondly so, and the speaker feels himself now 'farther off from heaven' than he had been as a child. The speaker of Larkin's poem certainly does not seem to feel that his childhood had been closer to heaven than his adult life although we don't hear much about his current life in the poem. Nonetheless, when read in conjunction with Hood's poem, Larkin's has a rather hopeful and optimistic tone, lacking the regret for lost childhood that Hood's emphasizes. Hood remembers 'the roses red and white' and 'where I was used to swing' and the way the fir trees' 'slender tops/ Were close against the sky,' but he also writes, 'My spirit flew in feathers then/ That is so heavy now' and, more starkly, 'Now, I often wish the night/ Had borne my breath away.' Larkin's lack of true remembering, and the imprecision of memory, is posited against Hood's poem of remembering in which childhood is the apex of the speaker's life: 'But now 'tis little joy/ To know I'm farther off from Heaven/ Than when I was a boy.' Larkin's poem not only argues against such idealization of childhood but also questions the very nature of such remembering and, consequently, the emotions that accompany it. By presenting an un-memory, based on the clichés and popular tropes of youthful memory, Larkin offers not so much a complaint about his own uneventful childhood but an argument against imposed autobiographical interpretation, which is almost necessarily fictionalized.

The biographical approach to this poem, offered by Rossen, who notes that in this poem 'Larkin is angry... because he did not have the idyllic childhood which Coleridge wished for all mankind;' Bradford, who points out that, on the occasion described in the poem, Larkin 'was alone on the journey to Liverpool, Monica having, customarily, not accompanied him to Swansea;' and Booth, who explains that 'the poet finds his train passing through Coventry;' among many others, obscures what the poem actually does and the explicit relationship between speaker and audience created by the poem. By reading the poem as a retelling of Larkin's own childhood (or un-retelling) readers can ignore the ways that they are both included and implicated in the poem: they are presented as imposing false expectations on writers' lives (presuming that someone who wrote 'doggerel' as a child indeed grew up to be a writer, which is not even made clear in the poem) and as associating, as Hood does, childhood with idealism.

Furthermore, readers are aligned most closely with the 'friend' of the poem, who is often assumed to interpret accurately the look on the speaker's face but whom the poem presents as potentially misreading that look. The friend first appears in the third stanza, after the speaker has recognized Coventry, and he asks, "Was that... where you 'have your roots'?" This question sets the speaker on his flight of anti-remembrance, and then the friend reappears at the poem's end:

"You look as if you wished the place in Hell,"
My friend said, "judging from your face." "Oh well,
I suppose it's not the place's fault," I said.

"Nothing, like something, happens anywhere."

This poem presents layers of audience, and the 'friend' of the poem reads and interprets the speaker's face for the poem's readers. The friend clearly cannot know the direction in which the speaker's thoughts go between the friend's first statement – 'Was that where you 'have your roots'?' – and his final observation that 'You look as if you wished the place in Hell, judging from your face.' But, as readers know from having followed the speaker's intervening thoughts, the disgust apparently registering on the face of the speaker may be directed towards the place itself, as his friend obviously imagines, or towards the absence of the mythology of childhood, or towards the mythology itself. Readers often unquestioningly accept the friend's analysis, both trusting his interpretation of the look on the speaker's face and assuming that the look is indeed in response to the place. Swarbrick writes that 'the fellow passenger's observation ("You look as if you wished the place in Hell") makes the speaker's seething resentment look just a little absurd.'[16] John Osborne similarly assumes that the friend's comment can be fully trusted and that the friend's interpretation of the speaker's look is accurate, despite the reader's having more information than the friend has: 'Its initial negative sense, that the narrator did not spend the happy childhood enjoyed by others, may be used to explain the feelings of grievance he apparently still harbours towards Coventry ("You look as if you wished the place in Hell").'[17] The audience's absorption into the poem this way, and our implicit alignment with the speaker's friend, allows us to overlook the possibility that the friend has offered a misinterpretation. His line is an assumption, and readers are often too quick to take the friend's assumption as truth, in spite of the fact that we have had the advantage of knowing the speaker's thoughts. Does he wish the place in hell? Perhaps, but he has not indicated any such thing in the course of the poem, and his thoughts about the place run not towards hatred but towards a kind of bitterness about the false expectations for what *should* have happened there. True memory is not the problem in this poem, but imaginary memory is, and the poem speaks broadly to the nature of storytelling in its stark creation of an un-past.

The implicit criticism of this poem is not for the childhood that lacks 'technicolor,' as Larkin remarks about his own life. Instead, it is for the writers – and their audiences – who prefer these kinds of fictions and maintain them at the expense of the more realistic but perhaps less appealing truth. Just because the speaker might look as though he 'wished the place in Hell' does not mean that his friend has read his facial expression accurately; his ambiguous response leaves open the possibility that his expression of disgust was not for the place at all but for these biographical fictions. In this case, the 'friend' of the poem is something less than a true friend, which adds to the speaker's sense of remove from his circumstances. We could take the speaker at his word in calling his traveling companion a 'friend,' but his pointed reaction to the friend's smiling question in stanza three ('No, only where my childhood was unspent,/ I wanted to retort...') demonstrates an important disconnection between the speaker and the friend that opens the poem to the possibility that the friend misunderstands the speaker throughout the poem. In fact, the poem acknowledges that the place could not possibly live up to the expectations the speaker imagines it might have fulfilled in popular imagination by using mocking, exaggerated language to describe these false reminiscences.

Like many readers of this poem, Nicholas Marsh reads the final line – 'Nothing, like something, happens anywhere' – as a demonstration of 'the emptiness of [Larkin's] own early years:' 'Larkin consistently portrayed his childhood as boring, his family as unhappy and himself as isolated from an early age.'[18] But the mocking of Lawrentian clichés need not be posited directly against autobiography. Although the poem's final line suggests that the speaker's childhood was really as uneventful as Larkin claims his own to have been, in fact we have no indication from the rest of the poem that nothing happened nor that the speaker of the poem is the poet, despite their sharing a home town. On the contrary, what we are told is that certain embellished, highly stereotyped conventions of the Perfect Childhood never happened there. Larkin highlights the potentially biographical nature of this poem by titling an ostensibly biographical essay about his childhood with a line from 'I Remember, I Remember,' calling the essay 'Not the Place's Fault' and apparently using the poem as a jumping-off point for autobiographical exploration – an exploration that he said, on several occasions, failed. He told Blake Morrison that the essay 'is written as a kind of commentary on the original poem, but this does not come through and in consequence it seems rather rambling' and that 'I should prefer it to remain in obscurity.'[19] He wrote to Anthony Thwaite that the essay 'gives me small inexplicable shudders.'[20]

In any case, the poem does not actually lament the absence of the unnatural 'writer's life' so much as lampoon it and the readerly expectations that perpetuate it. The disappointment is present, though, only if one believes that the speaker actually longs (or longed) for the absent experiences he describes in the poem. And while the images described as not having happened are ideal in some ways, they are so over-idealized as to be nearly ridiculous: the child inventing 'blinding theologies of flowers and fruits,' the family with 'the boys all biceps and the girls all chest,' the first sexual experience (so ludicrously idealized that even Larkin can't help but put quotation marks around 'all became a burning mist'), and the early praise and recognition from a 'distinguished cousin of the mayor.' Indeed, the final line of the poem may suggest that the speaker might have wanted these things to happen, but the things themselves are not presented in a tone of longing so much as a tone of ridicule. The mere idea, for instance, that the speaker could really 'be himself' somewhere is offered not so much as something he wished for but as something he sees as utterly absurd. The quotation marks around the phrase 'really myself' indicate disappointment not with the speaker's particular childhood but with the fictions of childhood, or the fictions of selfhood, in general. The poem does not argue that Larkin sees these idealized memories as any less than other authors' autobiographical flourishes that attract and retain readers who prefer the beautiful life to the beautiful line. And it does not indicate anything in particular about Larkin's own life, other than what might be read onto it through readers' knowledge of 'Not the Place's Fault,' an essay Larkin explicitly and repeatedly disowns.

The approach to issues of history and memory in 'I Remember, I Remember' highlights Larkin's self-effacing recognition of his own relationship with the past. By mocking the stereotypes of biographies, novels, and poems, he undermines his own well-documented attachment to the past, showing that we all have our own preconceptions of what a perfect past should be. The famous and relatively eventful lives of the young T.S. Eliot, or of Dylan Thomas, or of the young characters in D.H. Lawrence's novels and Wordsworth's poems are thus posited against the intentionally underplayed life of a Larkinesque character to show that all are fictions of their own kind. And while one of the fictions is more appealing to its audience and fits more readily with readers' expectations, it is no more a fully truthful history than the other. That is, many writers' attachments to their pasts or the pasts of their characters are actually attachments to a fictionalized past, and Larkin here sends up that fictionalization by demonstrating how easily imagined it is. He claims, in an interview with Neil Powell, that 'I Remember, I Remember' is not a 'negative poem, I think it is a very funny poem' and that it began 'as a satire on novels like *Sons and Lovers* – the kind of wonderful childhoods that people do seem to have. ... It wasn't denying that other people did have these experiences, though they did tend to sound rather cliché...'.[21] And yet, unlike other writers, Larkin's speaker here refuses to whitewash his own history and instead highlights the ordinariness of his own childhood by positing it against a different kind of ordinariness: that of the 'ideal' biography. Thus, his conclusion that 'it's not the place's fault' is more true than one initially realizes: the fault is instead of the people who believe that the 'successful' childhood looks a certain way or of the writers and biographers who perpetuate these mythologies.

So while 'Wild Oats' presents personal history as lacking precision and as being open to multiple kinds of remembering, 'I Remember, I Remember' presents the larger flaws of personal history as needing, impossibly, to meet both personal and public expectations. These are not, however, Larkin's only poems that problematize and directly confront the notion of memory and its place in our current existences. 'Maiden Name,' on first reading, might be seen as the straightforward preservation of an experience or emotion in the vein of Larkin's 'Statement.' Taken as something purely biographical – an absolute preservation of experience, a simple letter to Winifred Arnott – it expresses regret and nostalgia for an honest remembered experience. As Bradford says of the poem, 'when we read it accompanied by the knowledge that the maiden name is Winifred Arnott the strange tension between cordiality and part-restrained bitterness tells us something more about its writer.'[22] Larkin reinforces the biographical reading by writing to Arnott that 'Maiden Name' 'was about you...'.[23] John Haffenden picks up on 'Maiden Name' as a poem that fulfills Larkin's 'Statement,' saying that the poem 'is about a sense of preservation from time.'[24] The poem itself, though, beyond its possible biographical resonances, speaks to the nature of memory, not as a longing for the past but with a recognition of the past's changeability. It explores the power of memory to select, to change, and to reinvent the past.

Regardless of what Larkin says about his motivations for writing poetry and what he tells Arnott about her role in the poem, the poem itself does not preserve an experience so much as describe the impossibility of true preservation. Instead of favoring the experiences of either the past or the present, the poem favors a remembered past, which offers its own distinct experience. In this case, the maiden name triggers, and 'shelters,' a pleasant memory, but the poem acknowledges that the remembered past is preferable to the real one and accepts that memory has improved the past rather than merely preserving it. Because the addressee's maiden name is no longer her name, it does not refer to her current face, her current voice, or any of her other contemporary characteristics. Instead, it recalls only a person who no longer exists:

> For since you were so thankfully confused
> By law with someone else, you cannot be
> Semantically the same as that young beauty...

'Semantically,' the first stanza says, the woman addressed by the poem cannot be 'the same as that young beauty' the speaker remembers. Neither, though, does the name preserve an absolute truth of the past; rather, as the third stanza has it, 'It means what we feel now about you then.' The speaker recognizes that memory creates an amalgam of past and present, not an honest past or the sadder present but an idealized past as viewed through the lens of current knowledge and experience.

Larkin speaks of this poem as a kind of reaching out, his having always wondered what it would be like to lose one's name. Maiden names, he tells Haffenden, 'are very powerful things. I often wonder how women survive the transition: if you're called something, you can't be called something else.'[25] But the poem is at least as much a commentary on what that loss means to the people around the woman whose name has changed. The name recreates a relationship that no longer exists, and so while the poem's first two stanzas are completely focused on the 'you' of the poem, the third stanza moves to a 'we' that the speaker suggests only existed most perfectly in 'those first few days'. 'So your old name shelters our faithfulness...'. The woman's name contains not only her identity but her identity as it existed alongside the speaker's. The memory allows those 'unfingermarked' days to have a life of their own and a prominence that only a few days would not otherwise have. The name is thus not about semantics, exactly, nor really about the identity of the addressee – despite Larkin's assertion of his curiosity about women's surviving the semantic switch and Swarbrick's suggestion that the poem implicitly says that 'in changing her name she had in some fundamental way changed her identity'[26] – but about recalling the undepreciated opening days of a relationship, perhaps even burnishing them.

William Pritchard explains that 'it is the difference between now and then that moves [Larkin] and animates a poem.'[27] We can see in 'Maiden Name' a not uncomplicated relationship to both personal history and general history. This is not a pure longing for the past or even an idealization of the past beyond a brief moment. It offers, instead, a fully self-conscious view of the power and appeal of memory not for a precisely accurate past but for the life that can only be created through a merging of yesterday's world and today's perspective. 'What we feel now about you then' is not a preservation of experience but an old experience viewed through a new lens. It is not, as the speaker argues, 'untruthful,' but it does not offer full truth either. Time does depreciate people's value, according to the poem, but the value of memory is greater than the value of either the real past experience or the real present. Like photography in 'Lines on a Young Lady's Photograph Album,' which makes things both 'smaller and clearer as the years go by,' words (in this case, a name) also clarify and lessen the full truth, which is unavoidably malleable. The idea, also expressed to Enright, that a poem is its own newly created universe is thus true in 'Maiden Name,' a poem that seems to be almost entirely stuck in the past, because it recognizes that the new universe of the poem is in the unique feelings of now about then. Nicholas Marsh calls this 'the process by which life is turned into art,' but it also the process by which the past is turned into something other than itself, when an impulse towards preservation becomes an act of creation.[28]

The preservationist tendency we see in a much later poem, 'Going, Going,' suggests an additional level of complication in Larkin's approach to the past. The history in this poem is not personal so much as communal, and specifically national, but it is, perhaps strangely, a *present* history for which the speaker longs. He laments what he believes will soon be 'England gone' and notes that, for the first time, he believes that he himself may outlast the country – and particularly the countryside – he knows. Unlike the previous poems we have considered in this chapter, 'Going, Going' does not look back to the past from the present, as 'Wild Oats' and 'Maiden Name' do, but it looks back to the present from an imagined future. As 'I Remember, I Remember' considers an imagined past from the real present, in 'Going, Going' the present is tangible and real but painfully fleeting. The imagined future, unlike the ridiculous imagined past of 'I Remember, I Remember,' is looming and terrifying. Without the tone of mocking and humor of 'I Remember, I Remember,' 'Going, Going' highlights the future's possibilities for loss and destruction.

One might easily think that the fear of the future is rooted in the future's uncertainty while nostalgia for the past is rooted in the past's knowability. And yet 'Going, Going' seems to suggest that the future is known much more than 'I Remember, I Remember' suggests that the past is. In fact, the past is an absolute enigma in that poem of supposed memory, but in this poem of an imagined future, the speaker is quite confident: 'I just think it will happen, soon.' The speaker's self-awareness here, his ability to place himself in a fleeting present and look back at the present in which he currently lives as a relic of something almost gone, makes the act of remembering into a kind of game. What he remembers in this poem is what he currently sees around him; and while he observes changes that might lead, eventually, to the wasteland he envisions, his nostalgia is for the existent present. He projects himself into the position of rememberer, just as so many of the earlier poems are written in the voice of that rememberer. The speaker does dread the future in 'Going,

Going,' although that dread is for the natural world and specifically for England rather than for his personal state, but he does not idealize the past so much as recognize that even in the past people wanted change. That move towards destruction, which the poem implies has been happening for ages, is prompted by the 'young:' 'Their kids are screaming for more – / More houses, more parking allowed,/ More caravan sites, more pay.' The speaker's reluctant preservationist tendencies here are not for pristine wilderness but for a slower sameness, for industrialization and development that does not completely overtake the fields and farms and trees:

> I knew there'd be false alarms
>
> In the papers about old streets
> And split-level shopping, but some
> Have always been left so far.

The sense of nostalgia within the preservationism is palpable, and yet it is not for a perfect past but for an imperfect present. The speaker certainly does not seem overly attached to the past and, in fact, mildly mocks those who aim for extreme preservation. Thus 'Going, Going,' like Larkin's other poems of 'preservation,' moves well beyond the simplicity of the 'Statement' to Enright – and certainly beyond Jardine's accusations that, for Larkin, 'everything of value lies behind us' – and instead presents one of various ways of confronting the past and questioning one's feelings about it.

Because Larkin's personal life is so inextricably connected, in the public imagination at least, to an almost pathological desire for an England past, his well-articulated dislike of Modernism is often read as a mere symptom of his wide-ranging nostalgia. In the Introduction to *All What Jazz*, Larkin outlines his criticisms of Modernism most starkly, and perhaps most aggressively, saying that his 'essential criticism of modernism, whether perpetrated by Parker, Pound or Picasso' is that works by these artists 'are irresponsible exploitations of technique in contradiction of human life as we know it' and that they help us 'neither to enjoy nor endure' and have no 'lasting power.'[29] These harsh criticisms of the movement reinforce the belief that Larkin's poetry is antithetical to Modernism and, consequently, that it is simple and old-fashioned, an analysis that Larkin himself cultivates in his interviews.

Both Leggett and Osborne have proven, however, that Larkin's poetry relies on a (perhaps surprising) amount of allusion along with other Modernist techniques. As Osborne writes, 'Larkin is, in a precise sense, a

Postmodern, absorbing and moving on from Modernism – rather than, like Betjeman, pretending it had never happened.'[30] Furthermore, the reason Larkin is 'routinely lauded or damned for a thoroughgoing resistance to twentieth-century ideologies and aesthetic developments' is that

> commentators remark on his use of inherited poetic forms, regular metres and descriptive verisimilitude but not the way in which these traditional elements are eviscerated by ellipses, paronomasia, citationality, negative qualifiers and the four-act structure with closing reversal. They see the empiricist but not the deconstructionist. They see the Realism but not that it is being employed against itself, to undermine rather than endorse "reality".[31]

Of course, Larkin embeds these tendencies more deeply in his texts than do Pound and Eliot, for whom much of this boundary-pushing is the top – and therefore the most impenetrable – layer of the poems, and he uses his own prose and interviews to further disguise his poetic innovations and boundary-pushing. He uses the superficial techniques of pre-Modern poetry – meter and rhyme and regular stanza length and such – but works against pre-Modern subject positioning, characterization, and argument. And, because Pound, particularly, so vocally presented himself as fundamentally innovative, we may have trouble seeing literary innovation as anything other than poetry containing the very obvious Poundian hallmarks of unusual vocabulary, complex constructions, heavy use of allusion, integration of foreign languages, and fractured dialogue and settings. While Larkin did employ some of these techniques, he did so in the service of more traditionally structured, traditionally lyric or narrative verse. Stephen Regan points out that Larkin's poetry employs 'linguistic strangeness, self-conscious literariness, radical self-questioning, sudden shifts of voice and register, complex viewpoints and perspectives, and symbolist intensity.'[32] But those are not the most obvious elements of Larkin's writing.

It is possible, as well, that Larkin might be more closely aligned with the quieter and less abrasive Modernism of some American (rather than expatriate) poets, including Wallace Stevens and William Carlos Williams. Although Larkin does not write explicitly about their work, his railing against Modernism is directed exclusively at the Modernism practiced by Pound and Eliot, whom he frequently names as having primary responsibility for popularizing the kinds of poetic techniques he dislikes: the poetry Larkin enjoys 'has not been Eliot or Pound or anybody who is normally regarded as "modern" ' and he objects to the fact that poetry has been taken over by 'a critical industry which is concerned with culture in the abstract, and this I do rather lay at the door of Eliot and Pound'.[33] Stevens and Williams, on the other hand, are more likely to use the kinds of modernist techniques Larkin himself uses and to be 'people to whom technique seems to matter more than content, people who accept the forms they have inherited but use them to express their own content.'[34] Terry Whalen writes extensively about Larkin's imagism, for instance, a term more often applied to Williams' work, and notes that the 'empirical gaiety' of Williams' poetry 'is an effect which Larkin also manages in "The Whitsun Weddings" and "To the Sea" and it is attributable to his empirical curiosity of mind and his kinship with the Imagists' view of the poem as the act of the mind in close contact with the physical world.'[35] Larkin's frustration with a particular brand of Modernism has often been interpreted – understandably, given Larkin's own equation of Pound to Modernism – as an objection to the whole endeavor rather than merely a preference for particular kinds of poetic innovation with reliance on particular parts of poetic tradition.

Larkin's critical discussions of Modernism's 'myth-kitty' further complicate our understanding of his view of past and future by criticizing Modernism not for its boundary-pushing but for its too-heavy reliance on past works. At the same time that Larkin promotes reliance on inherited forms, he insists on particular kinds of newness. He tells Enright, 'As a guiding principle I believe that every poem must be its own sole freshly created universe, and therefore have no belief in 'tradition' or common myth-kitty or casual allusions to other poems or poets.'[36] This statement, which might seem like just another way to attack a poetry he dislikes and which Larkin claims to have written quickly and with no thought as to its being published, is actually repeated and reinforced throughout Larkin's writing and suggests strong beliefs about the responsibility of the poet to be original and the problems with an over-reliance on others' work. About a decade later, to Ian Hamilton, he explains that he objects to poetry that is 'almost mechanistic, that every poem must include all previous poems.' He sees this sort of work as showy and ineffective: 'you've got somehow to work them in to show that you are working them in...' a technique that allows writers to evade their 'duty to be original.'[37] Although he says in his interview with Robert Phillips that 'I've never had any "ideas" about poetry,' he expresses the same 'idea' in 1982 that he had expressed in 1955: allusions 'are not a property to be dragged into a new poem as a substitute for securing the effect that is desired... I am not going to fall on my face every time someone uses words such as Orpheus or Faust or Judas. Writers should work for the effects they want to produce...'.[38] This criticism, then, is not only a dislike of the Modernists' apparent pushing away of their audiences but a more pointed and cerebral attack on what he sees as a sort of intellectual laziness, an unwillingness to work for emotional effect and to rely instead on archetypes and previous works. While Larkin himself often invokes past works in his poems, his criticism of the overuse of this technique is lifelong and something he thought about even before the famous 'Statement.'

In a 1947 letter to J.B. Sutton about Eric Newton's *Stanley Spencer*, a book given to him by Sutton, he writes, 'He tends, though, to give the impression – which is surely a wrong one and only given by accident – that the history of painting is chiefly a history of technique, and that logically what you (for instance) paint is Giotto plus Leonardo plus Monet plus Cezanne plus Picasso. While in a minor sense this may be true, I should think the larger truth is that each painter represents an exhaustion of a particular way of seeing things.'[39] Even this early in his career – and in a context having nothing to do with Modernism – he expresses incredulity about this sort of historical and intellectual approach to artistic creation. He is open to allusion, but primarily the sort that does not build on obviously academic experiences. As Swarbrick writes, 'it could be argued that Larkin's work expresses a private myth-kitty in which elemental presences have an absolute value. What he rejects is the erudite and academic quality of much modern poetry.'[40] His objection seems to be that he is expected to 'fall on his face' at every allusion rather than having allusion serve a larger purpose. So Larkin's problems with Modernism – a movement that was ending as Larkin's career began – was that, in its attempts to break from the past, it relied too heavily on the past, and the apparently anti-Modern bent of Larkin's verse also relied on the past but in a different way from the Modernists (while still using subtly Modern techniques). This web alone should demonstrate how complicated Larkin's relationship to Modernism was and that his anti-Modernist statements do not signal an unwillingness to break from the past but a desire to enact that break differently.

In Larkin's interview with *Paris Review*, Robert Phillips asks, 'Why do you distrust the new?' and Larkin answers, 'It seems to me undeniable that up to this century literature used language in the way we all use it, painting represented what anyone with normal vision sees, and music was an affair of nice noises rather than nasty ones,' and he proclaims that Modernism's goal is precisely the opposite of these aesthetic tendencies.[41] Larkin's oversimplified answer here is a bit disingenuous, perhaps overstated to make a point. It is hard to imagine that Larkin fully believes that poetry before the twentieth century 'used language in the way we all use it' or that 'painting represented what anyone with normal vision sees.' His having discussed art, even casually, with Sutton would have shown him that painting was much more complicated than he admits to here, even in fundamental issues like perspective. And he would almost certainly not have thought that poetic language was conversational or fully unexperimental before the twentieth century. Larkin's primary idea in his answer to Phillips, that art should be pleasant and realistic and should perfectly mimic life, sounds fine and has undoubtedly influenced recent readers of his work to find the simplicity and commonness for which Larkin has become known. But we should note both that the poems do not support these comments and that this interview is also filled with sarcastic and misleading remarks: he tells Phillips that he 'arrive[d] upon the image of a toad for work or labour' through 'sheer genius;' that he 'doesn't read much;' that he's never heard of Jorge Luis Borges; and a number of other statements that are easily undermined or disproved, even by other statements in the same interview. This is not to say that nothing in the interview can be taken seriously but that even serious-sounding comments to Phillips about Larkin's poetry are suspect, particularly when they are not borne out in the poems themselves.

In fact, most of the time Larkin is not as closed to innovation in the arts as one might expect, given Phillips's question and Larkin's apparently conciliatory response. His attachment seems to be not to the past, precisely, but to a kind of aesthetic philosophy that evokes emotion rather than the resistance to emotion and emphasis on formal education he feels is evoked by the Modernists' use of literature 'replacing experience as material' for verse.[42] Larkin's explanation for his dislike of the invoking of past characters and past ideas does correspond with the feelings he expresses about student audiences and the trauma wrought on students by artists who create self-perpetuating self-employment by making their writings impenetrable and then appointing themselves the teachers and critics of their own styles. As James Booth argues of Jake Balokowsky, 'Jake is no champion of this system; he is its victim. His plight is similar to that of the poet himself, both being fouled up by the gulf between their dreams and hard reality.'[43] Booth emphasizes that both Larkin and Balokowsky must work for a living and thus Jake is 'the poet's intimate alter ego,' but they are also both discounted by a system that dismisses 'old-type' poets, and Jake's frustration is directed towards, among other things, the apparent unimportance of an old-type poet.

And so Larkin's poetry is, indeed, more accessible than Pound's *Cantos* or Eliot's *Waste Land*, but it is not exclusively accessible; that is, it also uses allusion but in more subtle and less confrontationally erudite ways. One can read Larkin, miss every one of the allusions, and still 'get' the poem, while *The Cantos* makes its allusions primary and rests on them. Nonetheless, Osborne wonderfully catalogues Larkin's use of allusion in his poetry, with references to Sidney, Shakespeare, Marvell, Keats, Tennyson, Housman and Waugh, not to mention Eliot himself and the many French symbolists Larkin pretended not to have read.

Larkin's interest, then, is not simply in 'language as we all use it' – something he does only on the most superficial level in his poems – but in certain unstated but implicit values, particularly the values of originality, appeal to emotion, and audience awareness – not for the purpose of driving the audience away or making the audience feel inferior but to make the audience share in the poet's self-doubt and self-awareness. His poetry does not indicate a dislike of those who are highly educated but a desire not to speak *exclusively* to them. Thus his mocking, in the prose, of the student audience is unifying for the rest of his audience, which feels protected from the challenges of concordances and footnotes when reading Larkin's poetry but might still, if individual readers are looking for it, find references to other texts, self-awareness, self-interrogation, shifting speakers, and an undermining of the meanings of individual signifiers much in the vein of the Modernists he claims to dislike.

Larkin's attachment to emotion above intellect is expressed in many ways and throughout his life, from his early letters to Sutton to his later prose writings, and his poems defend the position that poetry can be both erudite and emotional; Larkin's choice in interviews and prose writings is to present it as purely emotional, though, and allow the erudition to be uncovered without his explicit help. In a BBC program of 1956 he opens his review of poets published that year by saying, 'I am always very puzzled when I hear a poem condemned as 'mere personal emotion. ... To me, now as at any other time, poetry should begin with emotion in the poet, and end with the same emotion in the reader. The poem is simply the instrument of transference.'[44] Larkin's attachment to these principles is also evident well before he is widely known as a poet and on a more private scale. He writes to Sutton, in 1947, that he appreciates a Cezanne painting *'because* – and this is important – it shows me and helps me realize what a fine piece of creation the man himself is. It's in fact an emotion comparable to what I feel about Morel in *Sons & Lovers*. Now when I look at Picasso *Still Life*... it arouses hardly any emotion in me at all. It's like a poem I can't understand.' After stating these responses to the art, he questions himself (as he suggests, decades later, all students of the arts are made by Modernism to question themselves – 'You've got to work at this: after all, you don't expect to understand anything as important as art straight off, do you?'[45]) and wonders if he is being too devoted to 'human interest,' but then goes on to say, 'I rather fancy that the object in art – at least in painting or writing – could be a worse thing than "a heightened presentation of life".'[46] Thus, it seems, his objection to a certain brand of Modernism is not to the practices of Modernism itself but to the wall it builds around itself and to its exclusivity; what Larkin manages to do, 'in the way that 'The Whitsun Weddings' far more than *The Waste Land* or *The Cantos* may be appreciated by those who ken none of its citations,' is use some Modernist techniques but pretend not to, thus allowing the poetry to appeal to a mainstream audience.[47] His prose reinforces the interpretation of the poetry as plain narrative, as anti-intellectual and, ultimately, as stuck in a pre-Modern past despite the more complicated and nuanced expressions of the poems themselves.

One demonstration of Larkin's willingness to push boundaries separate from his conflicted relationship with Modern arts is in his use of vulgarity in his poems. He does so sparingly but to great effect. The use of 'fuck' and 'piss' and 'fart' certainly differs from the language of poets he claims had the greatest influence on his writing – namely Yeats and Hardy – and from the poets he claims to admire, like Betjeman and Dylan Thomas. But those words have a small and immediate effect and capture the subversion that moves beyond mere appeal to the common man. That language causes some shock for readers who think of poetry as a purely high art and who expect a kind of formal and staid literariness from poets. It speaks to the ethos of the poet, who is willing to say that poetry is not separate from the reality of its readers and not above the people for whom it is written; it speaks their language too, and it does not worship poetry as a pure and holy thing.

Joseph Bristow, who writes extensively about Larkin's obscenity, argues that the use of obscenity 'was the one thing that could connect Larkin's intellectual dependence on words with those working-class lives upon which he felt he would unconsciously pass judgment'.[48] This 'judgment-passing' is far more self-aware and nuanced than Bristow allows, however. It shows not only a connection to the common reader but also a willingness to break from tradition in poetry and move towards a hybrid of lofty and base voices and towards a melding of coarse language with formally structured and traditionally aesthetic verse.

As with so many of Larkin's apparent characteristics – his racism, his misogyny, his insularity, his attachment to pre-Modern literature – his public statements about an idealized past are complicated by poems that show exceptional self-awareness and an ability to question the very notions they seem to promote. Their surface simplicity is belied by their complicated arguments, and attempts to read the poems biographically are stymied by their rhetorical tricks and shifting narrators. Larkin's supposed traditionalism, his resistance to Modernism, and his personal inability to develop tastes and proclivities beyond those of his college days are all pushed aside by poems that question their audience's beliefs about the past, that highlight the malleability of memory, and that remind us that our present will soon be past, too. Poems that are often read as self-serving and autobiographical just as often prove to have more to say about their audience's needs and beliefs than about those of their author, and the longing for a simpler past expressed in interviews and prose pieces is utterly undermined by complicated, thoughtful, and metacognitive poems that use, but do not inhabit, the past.

4
Jazz and Audienceship

.

Talking about Larkin without discussing jazz is practically an impossibility, not because Larkin makes it a subject of his poems but because it is a subject of his life. Readers, understandably, find it difficult to separate the oft-discussed interest and early artistic and personal inspiration from the composition of the poems, even if very little in them suggests any overt musical influence, at least in the ways musical influence is generally conceived. Larkin himself frequently discusses jazz in his autobiographical prose as one of the greatest influences on his adolescence and one of his greatest pleasures. As an adult, he wrote jazz reviews for years and published a collected volume of them, featuring a very opinionated introduction outlining his musical preferences and his connection to the genre. This lifelong and well-documented interest must, many readers assume, be reflected in Larkin's poetry, particularly given the many poets of Larkin's generation and the generation preceding his who took advantage of the artistic overlapping of poetry and music. Obviously Larkin was fully aware of Eliot and Pound's high-minded delving into musical form in poetry, not to mention the musical poetics of Wallace Stevens, Louis Zukofsky and other American writers and the crossover interests of artists in other media, such as Piet Mondrian and Henri Matisse. And yet, despite his knowledge and love of jazz, few of Larkin's poems make music their overt subject, and even trying to find music more subtly or implicitly in the poems proves challenging. 'To Sidney Bechet' and 'Reference Back' are two of the only published poems that deal directly with the musical theme and certainly with jazz in particular. A few poems from *The North Ship* do use musical metaphor, but they are hardly 'music' poems in the conventional sense of recreating musical forms in poetry, loosening signifiers from their significations, or privileging sound above meaning; in general, those early poems – like 'The Horns of Morning' and 'Night Music' – instead use musical terms as analogies for nature. Other later poems refer to music, as in 'Reasons for Attendance,' 'Triple Time,' and 'Broadcast,' but these poems are not *about* music so much as they use musical imagery or vocabulary. Because readers are so aware of Larkin's love of jazz and long history with it, they expect it to be more fully evident in his poetry, which in fact it seldom is. While one might find individual moments of jazz in the poems, overall they have other predominant themes and subjects, and music remains a part of Larkin's life that may touch but certainly does not permeate the poetry.

Nonetheless, understanding Larkin's relationship to jazz is essential to understanding Larkin's poetry not because of the literal echoes of improvisational or syncopated music throughout the verse but because of the myriad ways that Larkin's relationship with jazz mirrors his relationship with the other arts, especially poetry. He makes these connections most explicit in his introduction to *All What Jazz*, in which he grouchily explains that the greatest flaws of contemporary jazz can also be found in Modern poetry and Modern art. He approaches the topic with the explicit assumption that bebop began jazz's move toward 'Modernism,' a common argument throughout the 1940s. A later and more convincing argument, however, posits that all of jazz is Modernist and 'unquestionably informed modernism as intellectual challenge, sensory provocation, and social texture.'[1] And, as John Osborne suggests, Larkin uses his comparison to cover for his own adherence to a number of Modernist principles. Regardless of Larkin's part in the equation of bebop with Modern art (and its corollary: pre-bebop with pre-Modern art), his convenient grouping of Parker, Pound and Picasso demonstrates a particular way that he thinks about interactions among the arts. His interest in the arts' relations to one another is evidently philosophical and not merely practical, and the parallels he lays out as criticisms can be examined to find much deeper and more sympathetic interactions between jazz and poetry well beyond the easy Parker/Pound linkage. Although *All What Jazz* is one of the only places Larkin explicitly asserts these ideas, it is far from the only place that these parallels present themselves in his work, and examining Larkin's musical interests in order better to understand his poetic production is my goal here. In this chapter, I will consider Larkin's prose writings as entry points into the poems and examine the poet's parallel attitudes towards jazz and poetry as they reflect and shape each other even outside of the literal resonances readers may expect.

While some critics, notably B.J. Leggett in *Larkin's Blues*, find some literal moments of jazz in the poetry, for the most part these arguments stretch the reasonable interpretations of the poems and feel more as though they *should* be true than that they actually are.[2] Leggett himself acknowledges that 'the traces left by jazz and blues in Larkin's verse are so elusive, so deeply submerged as to be nearly inaccessible or to be retrievable only through more speculative readings.'[3] Leggett, rhetorically, asks, 'Can there be much question that in the traditional sense Larkin's music was an 'influence' on his poetry?' and while this question depends, of course, on how one defines 'influence,' the question deserves our attention. Leggett cites Tolley's belief in the ideal transference of the jazz aesthetic to other art forms and quotes Clive James, who writes of Larkin that 'the same [jazz] aesthetic underlies his literary criticism and everything else he writes. Especially it underlies his poetry.'[4] Interestingly, Leggett argues that 'Larkin's poems frequently achieve the effect of authenticity... not because they have somehow managed to incorporate unmediated reality... but because they have employed conventions and artifices that readers identify with something other than the classical poetic traditions.'[5] This fascinating idea underscores Larkin's awareness of jazz traditions and his clever manipulation of them, and especially of jazz lyrics, in his poetry, which adds to its sense of familiarity and being firmly part of mainstream culture. This use of jazz conventions may also be what leads some critics to call Larkin's poems both lowbrow and clichéd; those critics recognize something both popular and familiar in Larkin's writing, but, as Leggett explains, those qualities represent a conscious effort on Larkin's part towards echoing another art form rather than an inability or unwillingness to write more conventionally 'intellectual' poetry. Of course, interdisciplinarity is its own kind of intellectualism.

There is, indeed, a unique musicality in Larkin's verse, which can be seen not only within an individual poem but in the whole body of work. The elements of Larkin's poetry that parallel the conventions of traditional jazz – the hierarchy of front and back lines and of rhythm and harmony and melody, the back and forth play among the soloists, the anticipatable rhythms, the 'judiciously timed "hot" breaks' that served as 'an appointed (and strictly delineated) place for sowing wild oats'[6] – can certainly be identified in his regular line lengths; the patterns of rhyme, consonance and assonance; the stanzas rather than irregular verse paragraphs; and the standard short poem length. But even more notably, Larkin's poems tend to have hummable melodies, if we can apply such musical terminology to poetry. So much of Larkin's poetry feels familiar to readers, precisely because of his use of 'melody.' We see it within individual poems, with echoing lines like 'And age, and then the only end of age' and 'And saying so to some/ Means nothing; others it leaves/ Nothing to be said.' But there are also 'melodic' connections between poems; for instance, 'Going Going' says, 'Most things are never meant./ This won't be, most likely' while 'Aubade' says, 'Most things may never happen: this one will.' So when a reader is familiar with one of these poems, reading the next offers a kind of familiarity or variation on a theme that resonates in the reader's aural sense. Similarly, the reuse, in a majority of Larkin's poems, of certain words that are common to speech but uncommon in poetry – most notably 'something,' 'nothing,' and 'never' along with the prefix 'un' – serves not merely to mark Larkin's language as uniquely his but also creates a melodic recognition, not just of the author's identity but of a particular sound and, by association, a particular meaning.

That is, the melodic connections among the poems can help readers to find substantive resonances among them as well; the language of 'Going Going' necessarily connects it to 'Aubade,' and then readers can find that the poems are a kind of pair, one about the death of the speaker's external world and the other about the speaker's own literal death. The pairing may be a bit lopsided, in that 'Going, Going' is not particularly highly regarded, while 'Aubade' is considered one of Larkin's greatest works, but their parallels are striking nonetheless. Like 'Toads' and 'Toads Revisited,' 'Going Going' and 'Aubade' serve as a rethinking of the speaker's fundamental point. The speaker's own death seems fairly removed in 'Going Going:' he regards the demise of the natural world, and of the England he knows, as far more imminent and frightening than his own mortality, and more serious as well. The primary concern in 'Going, Going' is not at all the speaker's own demise, the 'Not to be here,/ Not to be anywhere' of 'Aubade,' but the concern of nowhere to be, with 'England gone.' And yet, almost exactly five years later, 'Aubade' presents opposing fears with a heightened intensity, an improved diction, and a sophistication of presentation lacking in the earlier work. The casual tone of 'before I snuff it' is replaced by the palpable fear of 'the dread/ Of dying, and being dead' while the fear for the natural world in 'Going Going' – 'all that remains/ For us will be concrete and tyres' – is pushed aside with a suggestion that England will go on: 'Meanwhile telephones crouch, getting ready to ring...'. While the images in the last stanza of 'Aubade' are not of the natural world, they nonetheless do not suggest in the least that the speaker's greatest fear is any longer for the state of England but has been personalized, for the state of himself. The melodic resonances between these two poems serve as their first connection and then highlight the ways that the later poem rewrites, and improves on, the first.

Leggett asserts that a recognition of the influence of jazz on Larkin's poems is gratifying but ultimately uninteresting: 'so long as it remains at the level of "influence" it cannot be pursued very far or yield anything of consequence. It becomes merely a confirmation of what we already are willing to grant, Larkin's love of traditional jazz in all its forms – blues, swing, popular standards – and the (occasional) presence of these in the poems.'[7] Leggett's solution is to move beyond the level of 'influence' to suggest that adaptations of cliché are fundamental to both popular song and to Larkin's poems, and he argues convincingly for such parallels. According to Leggett, readers run the risk of mistaking 'the guise of art-lessness with the absence of art, of thinking of Larkin – as he thought of himself – as having broken from convention and artifice to arrive at the threshold of the real.'[8] This important aside – how Larkin thought of himself – takes too much at face value the interviews and prose writings, not recognizing the constructed character of 'Larkin' that the man himself so consciously presents in certain public situations. 'He didn't half keep his life in compartments,'[9] Amis bitterly reminds himself, and readers would do well to remember how much of Larkin's public persona was also artistic creation.

And, of course, there are other ways to move beyond 'jazz influence' as well; one of them is to note the specific philosophies of art that Larkin defends and find them used in his poems. In that way we see not just a straightforward influence of one art on another but an all-encompassing idea of art's purpose that transcends genre boundaries. Some critics are able to find simple and direct influence of jazz on the poems, and we see that, following Larkin's own example in the introduction to *All What Jazz*, they find parallels between jazz and Larkin's poems, particularly those that highlight his anti-modernist tendencies. Cedric Watts, for instance, notes that Larkin's poetry speaks directly to its readers, as 'good jazz' does and thus communicates 'itself more readily to readers and hearers than did much of the academically respectable poetry of modern times'.[10] Janice Rossen comments on jazz's 'middlebrow' position, and Andrew Swarbrick argues that Larkin's jazz influence shows a 'rejection of the pieties associated with "highbrow" arts.'[11] While these observations may indeed be true, they offer only a single, and rather limited, possibility for the connection among Larkin's artistic interests. Indeed, though, a number of parallels between Larkin's jazz and his poems can teach us about the poetry itself: his feelings about definition and words retaining their meanings; his love for things that are unpopular or mildly contrarian; his often problematic and complicated views of race; his desire to reach out to an audience and recreate his own sense of belonging through viewing; his belief in emotion as a guiding principle for the creation of art; and his appreciation of literary accessibility and of rules and patterns.

Outside of his critical observations in the introduction to *All What Jazz*, Larkin's discussions of poetry seem largely to compartmentalize music and poems and, unlike many of his contemporaries and poetic predecessors who work explicitly with artistic intersection, he seems not to feel strongly about the connections between these two arts beyond the fact that both of them captivate him. While Larkin does not explicitly deny such connections, he also neglects to present music as a principle poetic influence. Instead, he seems to feel it as a personal influence that is not central to his poetry. He writes about his college days, in the introduction to *Jill*, that 'we devoted to some hundred records that early anatomizing passion normally reserved for the more established arts,' but goes no farther than that in his comparison. In his interview with the *Observer* he slightly expands the relationship, noting that 'I must have learned dozens of dance lyrics simply by listening to dance music. I suppose they were a kind of folk poetry,' adding that 'I often wonder whether my assumption that a poem is something that rhymes and scans didn't come from listening to them.' That comment, while certainly connecting these two interests for Larkin, serves to locate his poetic traditionalism in his love of jazz – a neat trick – but still offers scant insight into the deeper, extra-structural relationship between the arts and consciously bypasses the possibility that his poems are musical beyond their scansion (the most obvious and universal way in which poetry might be musical, regardless of poets' musical knowledge or interest).

Late in his career, he offhandedly mentions, in a review of a Johnny Dankworth record, that he'll leave aside 'the poetry-and-jazz fallacy,' frustratingly not explaining what he means by the phrase.[12] The implication is that the connections people wish to find between those two arts are fallacious, and it seems clear that Larkin would expect readers to impose that phrase onto his own (by this point well-known) verse rather than limiting it to his understanding of Dankworth's music. The phrase does suggest an exasperation with readers who naturally jump to the conclusion that poetry and jazz are inextricably linked when, in fact, they should be considered as fully separate arts, even, apparently, in cases where artists choose to link them, as Dankworth did (since the record under consideration is 'Shakespeare and All That Jazz'). Nonetheless, Larkin himself links jazz and poetry with subtle yet unmistakable parallels between what he loves most in jazz and what he enacts in his poems. If the poems themselves do not contain overt echoes of jazz, they demonstrate concern for the same issues that Larkin cares about in jazz.

Words should 'keep their meanings'

Larkin, for all his fame as a jazz lover, has a very limited definition of jazz, and he is adamant that what many listeners – perhaps even most listeners – term 'jazz' should not be labeled as such. The types of jazz he prefer are blues, Dixieland, swing, and the early-century New Orleans sound, and the musicians he loves – Bix Beiderbecke, Louis Armstrong, Sidney Bechet – are, despite their vast stylistic differences, more melodic and accessible than the jazz greats we might think of from more recent years: Miles Davis, John Coltrane, Thelonius Monk.[13] It's not that Larkin refuses to listen to the later artists but that he (in places, at least) strenuously resists their styles of music and powerfully argues for their being a new category or genre of music: his frustration with the newer styles and rejection of their artistry seems to be both a personal and an aesthetic matter for Larkin, and he aims – explicitly throughout his prose writings and implicitly through his poetry – to prove that accessibility is an artistic necessity and should not be regarded merely as one choice among many.

His presentation of his jazz choices as definitional rather than merely preferential – what he likes *is* jazz and what he doesn't like isn't – lends a credence and a kind of authority to his choices that both emphasizes his sense of self-righteousness and opens him to charges of closed-mindedness and stodginess. He argues that the 'new jazz' 'wasn't like listening to a kind of jazz I didn't care for. ... It wasn't like listening to jazz at all.'[14] Again and again in Larkin's later writings, we find him discussing, with apparent dismay, 'the decline and death of jazz (or its transformation into something utterly unlike itself),'[15] and he argues rather forcefully that 'I don't like fancy time signatures, or want any African or Latin-American or Indian or Caribbean tinges, or bass solos, or New Wave nonsense, or free form fatuity; ... but this is no more than saying I want jazz to be jazz... I can recognize jazz because it makes me tap my foot, grunt affirmative exhortations, or even get up and caper round the room. If it doesn't do this... it isn't jazz.'[16] Larkin's assertions here are especially interesting in his assumptions that the jazz he prefers has no 'African or Latin-American or Indian or Caribbean tinges,' and one cannot help but wonder if this overstated curmudgeonliness was another bit of game-playing or merely an exaggeration to emphasize his definitional point. Certainly he knew enough of jazz to recognize the profound influences of, especially, African drum rhythms on the New Orleans jazz he loved. To suggest no African – or even Caribbean – influence on early-century jazz is to misunderstand the music entirely, and Larkin's body of jazz writings shows a far more thoughtful comprehension of jazz's development than could possibly coexist with such musical xenophobia.

And yet the stakes for the term 'jazz' seem to be both very high and quite personal for Larkin. He states in 'Moment of Truth' that 'this extraordinary and ecstatic musical phenomenon' of jazz 'lasted a mere twenty or thirty years in the first half of the century,'[17] which brazenly discounts the jazz through 1970 when this piece was written, but as he explains in 'Wells or Gibbon?' 'Our difference may be a semantic one. ... The Wellses want to extend terms, to stretch points, to see things change. The Gibbons want words to keep their meanings, to be definite, to see things stay the same.' He goes on to claim, later in the same article, that the music of Parker, Monk and Miles 'isn't jazz.'[18]

To fight an entire genre this way, and to take on the majority of its most knowledgeable and committed proponents, is bold even for someone with opinions as strong as Larkin's. But it also shows a fundamental illogic, of which Larkin himself seems to be at least partially aware but to the reconciling of which he is decidedly resistant. His unwillingness to acknowledge that an art form might change over time – even in ways he dislikes – and still *be* that form is strangely stubborn. Yet he will not expand the *word* 'jazz' to include new styles because it seems to him not merely a descriptor but a value judgment. 'After Coltrane, of course, all was chaos, hatred and absurdity, and one was almost relieved that severance from jazz had become so complete and obvious.'[19] Indeed, many listeners actually consider Coltrane the height of jazz rather than a near total severance from it, but for the Larkin of the *All What Jazz* Introduction, Coltrane's music can exist but should not be affiliated, linguistically, with the music of Armstrong.

In this piece, Larkin's tone of defiance suggests something more profound than simply a dislike of certain contemporary jazz artists or the form that improvisational jazz has begun to adopt; he seems to feel abandoned, even personally injured, by the movement away from his favorite jazz styles, and this perceived attack on his tastes and preferences may help us better understand his attitude towards poetry and the changes in that genre. The sense that words must 'keep their meanings' and 'be definite' has at least as much to do with his approach to poetry as it does with the word 'jazz' itself. The frustration with artistic changes affects Larkin's relationship to jazz, but it touches just as profoundly on his artistic production as well. Losing touch with current art, Larkin says, 'is parallel to losing one's faith in a religious age,' no small claim for

Larkin, who, as we will see later, felt deep ambivalence about his religious disenfranchisement.

This considerable attention to labels and to definitions in Larkin's later prose writings about jazz is also apparent in Larkin's poetry, perhaps most obviously in 'Maiden Name,' which offers a careful consideration of the meanings of words and how those words define their subjects. As we saw in the previous chapter, the speaker's concern with the woman's inability to be 'semantically the same as that young beauty' calls into question the meaning and changeability of labels. Larkin's attention near the end of his writing career to such labeling is evident even in his earlier works and demonstrates not simply anti-Modernism in his dislike of shifting signifiers but a desire to preserve the precision of meaning – although not necessarily in the simplest or least academic way, as is often assumed – as well as a continuity in his beliefs across his career.

Other poems, too, demonstrate Larkin's grappling with words' meanings and with the precision of expression. In 'Love Songs in Age,' the omniscient speaker considers the way that song lyrics mislead and, particularly, how the word 'love' is a kind of lie. The disillusionment in the poem seems to be with the concept of love, but it is expressed as disillusionment with the word itself, much in the same way that Larkin complains about both jazz and 'jazz.' The woman in the poem remembers how the progressive chords of her beloved music had introduced lyrics – 'word after sprawling hyphenated word' – and then, ultimately, how 'that much-mentioned brilliance, love' offered false promises of solving problems and ordering lives. The frustration in the poem is not simply with the promise of love as a concept but its promise as a *word*. Part of love's problem in 'Love Songs in Age' is with its being a word among other 'sprawling hyphenated word[s]' and its being 'much-mentioned,' thus unfairly building up its promise. What the woman in the poem feels about how 'love' has let her down, has not fulfilled its promises, is remarkably similar to the way Larkin discusses his disappointment in 'jazz' and his wish for a linguistic, if not a conceptual, differentiation between his 'jazz' and later 'jazz' to assuage his sadness at the music's alteration.

In 'Talking in Bed,' the speaker's ultimate interest is in the meanings and negations of words, and the poem demonstrates an insight into words' meanings. It is, on its surface, about honest communication:

> Talking in bed ought to be easiest,
> Lying together there goes back so far,
> An emblem of two people being honest.

And yet the poem argues that finding honest language is not so easy, and in its final lines, the poem highlights its own attempts to use language with full honesty.

> It becomes still more difficult to find
> Words at once true and kind,
> Or not untrue and not unkind.

These lines might be read, as they are by Bradford and Motion, to show that Larkin's relationship with Monica was conflicted or that Larkin's 'feelings of guilt and anxiety about his relationships with women continued to gnaw at him.'[20] But they also demonstrate the central premise of the poem, which is about language's tricks and traps. It 'ought to be' easy, but as the final lines demonstrate, the vast semantic difference between 'true and kind' and 'not untrue and not unkind' is profound and deeply meaningful. It is a difference that, superficially, should not much matter, and yet the change in tone between the words 'true' and 'kind' used straightforwardly and used in their double negative forms is at the root of what matters in this poem. The speaker's use of 'not untrue and not unkind' might show a callousness on the speaker's part – an inability to connect meaningfully with another person, even in the most intimate of situations – but it speaks more directly to a linguistic rather than a psychological problem. The idea of words keeping their meanings, of 'jazz' meaning '*that* jazz' and 'true' meaning something importantly different from 'not untrue,' is carried across genres for Larkin. He expresses this concern carefully and with unambiguous articulation in his jazz writings, but it is no less emphasized in his poems.

This attention to linguistic precision is especially telling when one considers the frequency with which Larkin chooses imprecise words, particularly indeterminate pronouns like 'something' and 'nothing,' a diction generally considered unfit for poetry in its lack of specificity and imagery. Consider a few examples from his poems: in 'The Whitsun Weddings,' he writes, 'Waving goodbye/ To something that survived it,' and 'Children frowned/ At something dull.' Again and again we see this use of 'something' to stand in for that missing signifier: 'like something almost being said' ('Trees'); 'something in me starts toppling' ('The Dance'); 'someone had used a knife/ Or something' ('Sunny Prestatyn'); 'something sufficiently toad-like' ('Toads'); 'Nothing, like something, happens anywhere' ('I Remember, I Remember'); 'round something nearly at an end' ('Ambulances'); 'something laughable' ('Sad Steps'); 'And leaves what something hidden from us chose' ('Dockery and Son'); 'She found them, looking for something else' ('Love Songs in Age'); 'Something that bores us, something we don't do well' ('Vers de Société'); 'here to confess that something has gone wrong' ('The Building'); and so on. And nearly the same frequency of 'nothing' can be found throughout the poems, in 'Faith Healing' ('That nothing cures'); 'Nothing To Be Said' (And saying so to some/ Means nothing; others it leaves/ Nothing to be said'); 'Dockery and Son' (For me nothing,/ Nothing with all a son's harsh patronage'); 'Aubade' ('nothing more terrible/ nothing more true' and 'nothing to think with,/ Nothing to love or link with'); 'Talking in Bed' ('Nothing shows why...'); and 'High Windows' ('And beyond it, the deep blue air, that shows/ Nothing') among others. This apparent overuse of imprecise diction might indicate a kind of laziness on the poet's part, but taken in conjunction with what we know about his feelings for words retaining their meanings, we see that 'something' and 'nothing' for Larkin are imageless for reasons: these words open possibilities to their readers, who may fill in the gaps they leave; and they work as powerful counterpoints to the many concrete nouns of the poems, positing themselves against the minute details that situate the poems.

'A fugitive minority interest'

As far as music is concerned, perhaps Larkin simply likes what is unpopular, not that he particularly seeks out the unpopular but that he finds a kind of thrill in the untrodden path. 'In the Thirties it was a fugitive minority interest, a record heard by chance from a foreign station, a chorus between two vocals, one man in an otherwise dull band. No one you knew liked it.'[21] In this proclamation, Larkin demonstrates a kind of pride in his own taste and a thrill in its underground nature. It was not just the music that excited him but the sense of involvement in a secret club whose members had the same experience he did. The use of the second person – 'no one *you* knew liked it' – differs from Larkin's frequent use of the third person voice in describing a personal belief or experience (as in his answer to Robert Phillips' question 'How do you decide whether or not to rhyme?' 'Normally one does rhyme'). The second person in his description of his early experiences with jazz illustrates his sense that there were others like him out there, also listening to obscure radio stations and waiting for a particular song to come on; it puts him into a group of others with the same specialized taste and aesthetic sensibility. And his experience at Oxford of meeting a group of students who did indeed relish the same musical style only confirms for him that he was, as a child, part of this special group that had not yet met but nonetheless shared a meaningful experience with music.

When jazz gained popularity and became part of the wider conversation about music, Larkin began to demonstrate his disillusionment with it. Of course, he presents his unhappiness with jazz in terms that suggest that he genuinely hated everything about the newer style, but his stubborn insistence that jazz is only the music he likes and not this new-fangled experiment also shows how violently he resists the idea of jazz as a popular form. Yes, he wants people to love the music he loves, but at the same time, a little perversely perhaps, he wants to retain that remembered experience of liking something no one else liked. He writes, with apparent sadness, 'I can tell that adolescents don't feel like this about jazz today. ... It has become respectable: there are scholarly books on it, and adult education courses; it's the kind of interest that might well be mentioned on a university entrance form.'[22] He also seems to believe wholeheartedly in his earliest listening experiences. That is, he does not recognize that emotion or sentimentality might color his memories or even his current listening experiences. Instead, he suggests to the readers of his reviews that they not even bother picking up the records of musicians with whom they are unfamiliar: 'if they were any good, you'd have heard them at school... and have laid out your earliest pocket money on them.'[23] Of course, Larkin utters this 'Law of Reissues' with great humor, but he does seem to mean for it to be taken seriously, as his writing in this review is self-deprecating but never reverses or undermines his views. And he frequently expresses a similar belief about his own listening experiences; he had heard everything worth hearing by the time he left Oxford. If he hadn't heard it by then, it obviously wasn't any good.

Larkin undoubtedly also recognized that the 'fugitive minority interest' was not merely on the part of the listener although he, understandably, emphasizes the listener's role in jazz. Speaking of his own experience, he focuses on the unpopularity of jazz for the early audience member. But for the artists as well, jazz represented 'the allure of the renegade, the dissident, the upstart.' The appeal of jazz was in its outsider status as an audience member but also an artist. Jed Rasula points out that, for the Blacks and Jews who largely populated the ranks of great American jazzmen, 'being an outsider was a given,' and so the communality of outsider status connected listeners to the artists, a technique that Larkin certainly exploited successfully in his poetry, fashioning himself as a literary outsider and thus appealing to readers who perceived, accurately or not, their own academic and social disenfranchisement.[24]

Larkin's approving attitude towards unpopularity – towards membership in a small and self-selecting group – is evident throughout his
poems as well, and it is a poetic posture for which he is often criticized. Before having written the introduction to *All What Jazz*, Larkin
expressed almost identical feelings for the unpopularity of poetry that
he later does for the unpopularity of jazz. He tells Miriam Gross of the
Observer that he is not particularly worried that people in the future will
not read poetry but that 'I'm much more worried about poetry becoming official and subsidized. I think we got much better poetry when it
was all regarded as sinful or subversive, and you had to hide it under the
cushion when somebody came in.'[25] This language clearly prefigures his
concerns about jazz's move toward the mainstream and his sense that it
has become, unfortunately, 'respectable.'

We can see throughout the poems speakers who choose unpopular
routes, particularly those who do so in relation to music. In 'Reasons for
Attendance' the speaker makes a point of staying separate from the crowd
and attempts to justify that choice by finding an almost moral superiority
in the decision to do the unpopular thing – and to criticize the popular one. And yet, as in Larkin's discussions of his early jazz experiences,
the speaker of the poem feels a connection to the unknown and invisi-
ble others who share his perspective and his attachments. The speaker's
outsider status in 'Reasons for Attendance' could parallel the 'fugitive
minority interest' of jazz that seems to be part of its appeal for Larkin.
Similarly, the speaker of 'Toads' suggests, in an awfully contrarian manner, that he cannot choose the more popular routes of living on his wits
or living in poverty and thus must continue to work because he follows
the unpopular but questionably superior path. The speaker of 'To Sidney
Bechet' separates himself from other jazz fans who might misunderstand
the music and asserts that 'My Crescent City/ Is where your speech alone
is understood...,' again emphasizing his membership in a select group of
exceptional listeners. In this case, the speaker is almost certainly not
Larkin himself (who, far from being a New Orleans listener, had never
even visited that city), and yet the sense of belonging to a unique and
specially self-selecting group remains even for this anonymous speaker.

'The great coloured pioneers... and their eager white disciples'

So while his choice of jazz is certainly more forward-thinking than the
music one familiar with the popular persona of the stodgy Larkin might

have expected him to choose – more likely Baroque or Romantic-era classical composition or even opera – his attachment to a certain period of
jazz, a kind of 'safe' jazz, underscores his traditionalist tendencies. It
also, as is so often the case with Larkin, confounds the easy lines drawn
between high and low culture of earlier in the century. As Pound so vocif-
erously appreciated both the classical baroque forms of Bach (notably the
canon and fugue) and the obscure avant garde music of Schoenberg and
Antheil, among others, Larkin makes much of his love for the music
of the common man. His highlighting of this music's American origins
as opposed to the continental preferences of the American poets with
British pretensions might suggest merely a dissolving of class and intellectual distinctions on Larkin's part and a snub of the American writers
whose relocation to Europe belies their common roots. But his strong
arguments in favor of certain kinds of jazz and not others shows something more complicated than a mere attempt to undermine social strata
differences. Because, in his advocacy of certain music and certain musicians, he never aligns himself with them but holds himself separate from,
and often above, them he simultaneously underscores and upsets these
differences. Unlike Pound, who fully aligned himself with artists of other
genres whose work he admired – suggesting, for instance, that George
Antheil was his own equivalent in the musical rather than the poetic
genre – Larkin both admired and held himself consciously apart from
the jazz musicians whose work he liked most. This separation is clearly
tied to national and class differences between Larkin and jazz artists,
and it is at least in part a conscious effort on Larkin's part to confound
boundaries, but it is also inevitably tied to racial difference.

In discussing Larkin's views of Black America and the social influences
on the music, we must remember the depth of Larkin's outsider status.
Because of his authoritative written voice, particularly in the jazz reviews,
and because of the ease of mobility between Europe and America, one
might forget how very little Larkin knew of the real America, having
never visited himself. Although he admits to being a homebody, he does
not as readily acknowledge the global ignorance that springs from such
provincialism, and his views of America are deeply rooted in his unfa-
miliarity with the realities of America. Larkin is, to an extent, in good
company here: 'while jazz was unquestionable American, serious attention to it was European.'[26] And, like many of the European artists who
admired jazz, he clearly saw race as emblematic of America. But because
his connection to America is largely through jazz – and, to a lesser extent,
through poetry and some pornography – his oversimplifications of Black
life in America are understandable, if not forgivable.

Larkin's discussions of jazz's Black origins highlight a tension we see in other areas of Larkin's life, with a kind of condescension and egomania that many critics have found profoundly objectionable and a simultaneous sympathy and understanding that have allowed the debates about Larkin's feelings of cultural superiority (or lack thereof) to continue. Obviously many of Larkin's statements about race are problematic, and a few are deeply offensive, and his writings about jazz highlight the tensions in his expressions most clearly. The esteem with which Larkin regards the many Black musicians he admires is offset by troubling paternalistic and provincial tendencies, not to mention a few written instances of outright racism in the letters. And while many of his assessments of the Black oppression that have led to certain jazz styles are astute (if somewhat oversimplified), they are also disturbing in their unsentimental approaches to discussing relatively disturbing topics. The apparent disconnection between the sensitivity of the reviews and the absolute callousness of some of the letters is especially confusing.[27]

Larkin's analysis of the changing reality for Blacks in 1960s America may seem cold-hearted, particularly since readers are aware of his own musical leanings towards the 'Negro... wanting to entertain the white man,'[28] but his understanding of those competing desires is also perfectly clear throughout his jazz writings, and his sympathy for the men who were oppressed in order to create the music he loves is evident. Although he does not implicate himself in that oppression, he has obviously thought extensively about the history and culture out of which his favorite music grew, and although he would be sad to see the music go, he does present the end of jazz as a kind of social progress: 'jazz will become an extinct form of music as the ballad is an extinct form of literature, because the society that produced it has gone.'[29] When he writes of Nat Hentoff's *The Jazz Life*, he notes that jazz recordings earn their performers – regardless of race – very little money, but goes on to say, 'If the musician is a Negro, his lot is much worse. It might be imagined that in the jazz world the reputation of its most celebrated artists... would render the colour problem less acute; but this is not so.'[30] He also sympathizes with the African-American's plight outside of the jazz world, explaining in 1963 that 'despite the dogs, the hosepipes and the burnings, advances have already been made towards giving the Negro his civil rights. ... These advances will doubtless continue. They will end only when the Negro is as well housed, educated and medically cared-for as the white man.'[31] While Larkin's continuation of these thoughts to discuss what might happen to jazz if Black Americans earn true equality might be seen as callous, it is also not lacking in real feeling for Black suffering and a recognition of how such suffering has led to art: 'The Negro did not have the blues because he was naturally melancholy. He had them because he was cheated and bullied and starved. End this, and the blues may end too.' He goes on to explain that American Black musicians are 'caught up by two impulses: the desire to disclaim the old entertainment, down-home, give-the-folks-a-great-big-smile side of his profession that seems today to have humiliating associations with slavery's Congo Square; and the desire for the status of musical literacy, for sophistication, for the techniques and instrumentation of straight music.'[32] All of this effort to understand the African-American experience and to get at the root of what prompts the changes in jazz of which he despairs is made in a surprisingly sensitive manner. It does not tiptoe around racial issues but attempts to understand them from the inside, as much as is possible for someone with no inside experience or direct contact with the people whose minds and emotions he attempts to inhabit.

Leggett quotes Simon Frith, who asks, 'how could a white British audience be other than "entertained" by noises made meaningful only in terms of their black American roots' and then claims that 'the only authentic jazz "was produced by black musicians for black audiences." ' Frith's dismissal of the possibility of Larkin (and his friends) having a 'real' experience with jazz because of his racial and geographical remove from its creation – and perhaps from its intended audience – is hardly in keeping with the words of the jazz musicians themselves or of Larkin's deeply professed love of the music. Larkin's remove from the music's creation is true enough, but his belief that it could be deeply felt in spite of the listener's distance from its origins, and maybe even because of that distance, is more profound and more believable than Frith's connection of race to art and geography to audience. Frith's unwillingness to see that barriers might be broken down by art leads to precisely the kind of easy categorization that Larkin works to overcome.

If we are, as Larkin argues, instinctively drawn to certain types of music, we are instinctively distanced from others, and those artists who do not write with the ambition of touching 'our instinctive musical sympathies' are necessarily uninterested in the desires of the audience, according to Larkin's reasoning. Those artists, like Fats Waller, who see jazz as entertainment and cultivate their inevitable relationship with their audiences – what Larkin at his most tactful phrases as 'the great coloured pioneers and their eager white disciples' – are posited in *All What Jazz* against those artists, like Charles Mingus, who feel that 'the word jazz means discrimination, second-class citizenship, the whole back-of-the-bus bit.'[33] And so adhering to or departing from 'natural' patterns of jazz is tied up inextricably with racial politics. Interesting, then, that in this binary of Black artists and White audiences, Larkin as a poet presents himself most often – and most emotionally – as the artist who aims to please his audience, follow accepted tropes, and adhere to a tradition; in other words, he aligns himself, at least in his self-presentation, with the early apolitical Black jazzman, a rhetorical move that should lead to a questioning and a complicating of Larkin's racist statements in his letters.

John Osborne uses Larkin's poem 'Sympathy in White Major' to illustrate the poet's racial sympathies and the ways that he plays with conventions of race. Osborne argues that the poem features dialogic narrators, one White and one Black, and that the poem's final lines 'drive a wedge between white as a symbol of moral purity and white as a racial signifier... Larkin has dramatized the dissonances within the unisonant discourse of cultural belonging.'[34] In 'For Sidney Bechet,' we find a similar sympathy towards racial difference, if only subtly in the poem's use of a Black central character whom the speaker clearly admires. The poem is one of the few that uses jazz explicitly – even the poems about music seldom assert that the music in question is jazz – and Larkin's choice of a Black musician as the focus of the poem is central to its argument, which parallels ideas expressed in Larkin's prose writings.

Unlike many of the poems from *The Whitsun Weddings*, which feature nameless and placeless characters, 'To Sidney Bechet' uses extreme specificity, including the name of a particular musician and his placement squarely in New Orleans: 'My Crescent City/ Is where your speech alone is understood.' While race is not explicitly mentioned in the poem, the speaker suggests a racial subtext and may even, as Osborne argues of 'Sympathy in White Major,' write from the perspective of a Black listener. The speaker is certainly one who feels that he understands Bechet's music better than the average listener, but for the speaker of the poem, Bechet's music does not conjure a postcard-ideal vision, nor the sexualized world of 'Mute glorious Storyvilles,' and instead it speaks 'the natural noise of good,/ Scattering long-haired grief and scored pity.' The speaker who claims Crescent City for himself is hardly Larkin and therefore could be a character more like Bechet. Certainly he is someone who aligns himself with the musician more than with the other, falsely interpreting admirers.

Even if the speaker of the poem is not Larkin, as I assume him not to be, he coins a phrase that Larkin later appropriates in speaking about his own art. The climax of the poem describes the speaker's reaction to Bechet's music: 'On me your voice falls as they say love should,/ Like an enormous yes.' Twenty-five years later, Larkin tells the *Observer*, 'I really want to hit them, I want readers to feel yes, I've never thought it that way, but that's how it is.'[35] Larkin uses the language of 'For Sidney Bechet,' whether consciously or not, in describing the reaction he would like readers to have to his own works, thus drawing an implicit parallel between the two arts and, specifically, between himself and a Black musician. The reaction he has to Bechet's music is, years later, the identical reaction he hopes to evoke from his readers, indicating both the implicit parallels he finds between music and poetry – or between the emotions they evoke, if not the genres themselves – and the extent to which he identifies his own art with that of the Black jazzmen he so admires.

'The essential nexus between the writer and the reader'

Some critics present the sentiments of the Introduction as inferior to and therefore less true to Larkin's own feelings than the reviews themselves, as Cedric Watts claims.[36] He calls the writer of the Introduction to *All What Jazz* 'frank' and 'sincere' but the author of the jazz reviews 'fair and conscientious.' Partially, at least, this difference may develop from the different audiences Larkin addresses; the individual reviews are directed towards jazz lovers who subscribe to jazz publications while the edited and prefaced collection of reviews is almost certainly more likely to be purchased by Larkin fans who will not be alienated by aggressively stated opinions about various jazz artists. Watts points out that although the Introduction is the best known and most read section of *All What Jazz*, it is not necessarily the best: 'by an obvious literary test – stylistic acuteness – the "conscientious" Larkin seems to be a better and more intelligent critic than the "sincere" Larkin.' Furthermore, 'the discipline of trying to write fairly may actually have liberated more of his intelligence than did the freedom he enjoyed in that Introduction.'[37] But it's ultimately not clear which of these sentiments – or at least which of these tones – is the 'true' Larkin, or if both or neither of them is fully true.

As Larkin makes clear in the introduction to *All What Jazz* as well as in the reviews throughout that volume (and, as I have shown earlier, in writings throughout his life), the art that most appeals to him is that which he believes takes into consideration the desires and reactions of the reading, viewing, or listening audience. More to the point, he appreciates the artists who speak directly to their audience rather than around them or in opposition to their aesthetic desires. He claims to be disgusted by artists – musical or otherwise – who ignore the fundamental tension 'between the artist and his audience' in favor of the 'tension between the artist and his material' because 'in consequence the artist has become over-concerned with his material, and, in isolation, has busied himself with the two principal themes of modernism, mystification and outrage.'[38] He expresses concern that 'subsidies and official support' for the writing of poetry will 'destroy the essential nexus between the writer and the reader' because 'if the writer is being paid to write and the reader is being paid to read, the element of compulsive contact vanishes.'[39] The feelings of abandonment not by people he has known personally but by artists – and, even more broadly, by genres – he has admired colors his writing of poetry and, I argue, helps him simultaneously to create an autonomous work that resists easy interpretation while reaching out to audiences and drawing them in to his work. Again, this is not jazz enacted in poetry, but it is what he wishes jazz would do and what, at its best, jazz does for him. Jazz 'was something we had found for ourselves, that wasn't taught at school... and having found it, we made it bear all the enthusiasm usually directed at more established arts.'[40]

This experience of having been a listener first and never a performer tunes Larkin in to the value of being in an audience. Despite his dabblings in drumming, his position in music is always opposite the performer, and he is most effusive about the performers who seem to have him in mind when they play. That relationship inevitably carries over to his writings where, on the other side of the performance relationship, he observes this Golden Rule of art, treating the reader as he liked to be treated himself by artists. That consideration of how he feels when he hears the music he loves seems to be part of his thinking when writing even his most personal or seemingly autobiographical poems. As he emphasizes again and again in his prose writings, Larkin feels strongly that the audience should be a fundamental – if not the primary – concern of the poet, and that feeling seems to grow from his relationships to jazz musicians, both the symbiotic relationships and those that struck him as – willfully, maliciously – disenfranchising.[41]

We gain some insight into 'common' readers and their proximity to Larkin-as-listener in the introduction to *All What Jazz* when Larkin describes them: 'sullen fleshy inarticulate men, stockbrokers, sellers of goods, living in 30-year-old detached houses among the golf courses of Outer London.' This description is not so vastly different from J.R. Watson's presentation of Larkin himself: 'Philip Larkin is a middle-class Englishman, born and living in the provinces, who works hard for a living, wears a collar and tie, drives a motor-car, and has the same life-style as thousands of his unpoetical contemporaries.'[42] The description is also not dissimilar to Al Alvarez's depiction of the speaker in 'Church

Going,' (although, as James Booth points out, that description is more fanciful than text-based): the speaker is 'shabby and not concerned with his appearance; poor – he has a bike not a car; gauche but full of agnostic piety; underfed, underpaid, overtaxed, hopeless, bored, wry.'[43] A good portion of this portrait could be attached to the readers Larkin describes.

Alongside the illustration of their own hopeless state and their awareness that everything good in their lives is past, the readers of jazz reviews are posited against newer, younger readers of another generation with strange and ultimately backward notions of life and art: the readers are 'fathers of cold-eyed lascivious daughters on the pill... and cannabis-smoking jeans-and-bearded Stuart-haired sons whose oriental contempt for 'bread' is equaled only by their insatiable demand for it.'[44] The disgust that registers in this description veers awfully close to that expressed towards students in several of Larkin's prose pieces, most notably in 'The Pleasure Principle.' In both 'The Pleasure Principle' and the Introduction to *All What Jazz*, the 'good' readers are distinguishable not only by their ordinariness but also by their old-fashioned aesthetic values and their air of pathos; these (inevitably) men 'who drift... into the darkening avenues of age and incapacity' are a poetic embodiment of the old, rather clichéd idea that nothing is as good as it used to be. And they resemble the caricatured Larkin in telling ways; their attachment to jazz is manifested in its connection to their memories of youth more than to their disappointingly average present lives. They are 'men in whom a pile of scratched coverless 78s in the attic can awaken memories of vomiting blindly from small Tudor windows..., or winding up a gramophone in a punt.'[45] And, of course, their overwhelming mortality, these men 'whose first coronary is coming like Christmas,' is as resounding an echo of their Larkinness as anyone could ask for. While these parallels do not indicate that Larkin merely writes for himself, they do show his sense of himself as audience member, highlighting how important – almost lifesaving – it is to remind such readers of 'everything that once made life sweet.'[46]

Larkin presents his belief in artists meeting audience expectations – that is, in adhering to patterns – not merely as one of several possible artistic conventions but as something absolutely fundamental and, furthermore, natural. As he explains in one review, 'Don't Go 'Way Nobody,' jazz's declining popularity has much to do with what Larkin, at least, perceives as a new attitude towards audience expectations: the styles of jazz Larkin prefers mostly anticipate their listeners' expectations but that 'post-Parker' jazz fails its listeners 'because we no longer know what to expect... The extension of the harmonic and rhythmic range of jazz that has taken place since 1940 has inevitably removed it some distance from our instinctive musical sympathies.' The implication here is that desire for rhythmic and melodic patterns and for diatonic scales is not merely a preference but a facet of human nature.[47] In addition, the impetus for meeting audience expectations is placed entirely on the performer. If audience desires are natural, then listeners (or readers) are not expected to have to work against their instinct at all; instead, performers are meant, if they are to follow Larkin's rules for good performance, to meet audience expectations without challenging or pushing the audience's natural inclinations for certain aesthetic principles. As an artist himself, this sense of having to shape his work to meet the needs of the audience is both unusual and profoundly outwardly focused. His sense of responsibility – both for his fellow poets and musicians and for himself – is very serious, and as much as he claims to feel responsibility to the experience, 'responsibility for preserving this remarkable thing by means of a verbal device,' he seems to feel even more responsibility to the audience, for causing 'the same experience in other people.'[48]

Throughout Larkin's poetry we can see what being an audience member means to him. As I have shown in previous chapters, the speakers of his poems are almost invariably positioned as members of a viewing audience. And while this separation between speaker and action is often read as a weakness on Larkin's part and as a mirror of his own social isolation, it might also be seen as enacting in verse what jazz allowed Larkin to do in life. In 'Reasons for Attendance' we see this comparison most starkly, since the poem is literally about listening to music. But in quite a number of other poems as well, we see the importance of being an audience member for the poems' speakers – the clarity and insight such a position offers them – and the way that such conscious structuring engages and reenacts the audience experience for the poems' audience of readers.

'High Windows,' for instance, begins with an experience of 'seeing' and ends with a visual image as well: 'And immediately/ Rather than words comes the thought of high windows.' As the speaker sees, rather than does, the reader is made part of the visual experience and is watching alongside the speaker. 'The Whitsun Weddings' emphasizes visual images similarly, with the speaker positioned behind glass (as he also is in 'Reasons for Attendance,' 'Arrival,' 'Sad Steps,' 'I Remember, I Remember,' and 'Here') and using the train window as a lens onto others' lives. 'Lines on a Young Lady's Photograph Album' uses the literal lens of the camera to present an audience experience. 'Sunny Prestatyn' places its speaker as a viewer of another photographed image, this one impersonal and used for commercial purposes but nonetheless leading to the speaker's placement as an audience member among other audience members. The speaker in 'Faith Healing' watches and judges the preacher as he watches and judges the women who watch the preacher; the women eventually become participants in the preacher's show, though, while the speaker of the poem remains aligned with the readers, outside the action but imagining their own emotional relationship with the participants.

These are not pastoral scenes, observed from afar as in the Romantic tradition; instead they are all scenes that involve other people but with whom the speaker does not directly interact. In Wordsworth's work, on the other hand, the speaker is only separate from scenes of nature or landscape, but in most of his poems that feature people – 'We Are Seven,' for example[49] – the speaker engages in conversation with the people and becomes part of the action of the poem himself. Larkin's speakers, regardless of the types of scene he observes – human or landscape – remain apart and observing, and thus we readers do not watch him, as we watch Wordsworth's speaker converse with the child in 'We Are Seven' or retell a story from his own acquaintance, as in 'Michael,' where the speaker writes, 'I have conversed with more than one who well/ Remember the old Man.' Instead, we watch *with* him, from a position of similar remove, and the regular use of the device of glass and windows reinforces the sense that the speaker and readers remain on the same side of each scene, in the same way that the fourth wall of the theater separates a group of audience members from the performers.

In each of these cases, and many more, the poet's membership in an audience is more significant than his participation as an actor in the poems. What he views always touches him in some way, making him consider something about himself or affecting his mood, and therefore his role as a viewer is not so much a sign of outsider status or social ineptitude as it is a promotion of audienceship as valuable and meaningful. Just as he is changed by watching and being watched in 'The Whitsun Weddings,' the experience of watching in 'Faith Healing' humanizes him, and in 'Reasons for Attendance' it infuses him with self-doubt. His role in jazz is as a viewer – a role he explains as central to his life – and his desire to maintain that position in other, non-musical situations both aligns his jazz interest with his poetic production and brings his own readers into his poetry by recreating their roles, which are naturally exterior to the poems, as interior and explicitly articulated positions. The 'yes' that he wants readers to feel about his poems is the same 'yes' he feels in listening to his favorite jazz, and by articulating his role as audience member, he highlights for readers the necessity and vitality of that position.

David Timms describes the 'parallel between [Larkin's] beliefs about jazz and his poetic practice'. 'He has said that poetry is 'born of the tension between what [the poet] non-verbally feels and what can be got over in common word-usage. ... In common with Dr Johnson, Larkin sees in life "much... to be endured and little to be enjoyed;" and like the blues singer's art, Larkin's poetry mediates between this experience and his audience.'[50] Although Timms overlooks the many things in life that Larkin feels are indeed to be enjoyed as well as the emotional complexity of much blues music, this parallel is precisely the kind of relevance that jazz can have to a reading of Larkin's poetry and to an understanding of Larkin himself. Like jazz, Larkin's poetry serves as an intermediary between an experience and an audience; and although Larkin takes on the role of intermediary in his poetry, he remains a life-long audience member as well because of his love of jazz. Jazz forces him never to forget how important the musical role of intermediary is, which focuses his attention on the enjoyment and inclusion of his audience. Jazz serves to pull him out of his primary artistic role as creator and constantly recreates him as artistic consumer.

'Emotional in nature and theatrical in expression'

What Larkin claims to love in jazz – that little moment of syncopation, that one drummer, a single verse in an otherwise uninteresting song – is evident in his poetry as well, and one has to listen for it, as one might have listened over the radio for that magical moment. He does not admire jazz that upends all musical conventions nor jazz that speaks only to itself nor, especially, jazz that lacks or eschews emotion, and his poetry could be defined almost identically. Larkin's poems are often criticized for being too based in emotion, yet he praises explicit emotionality in poetry and music alike. He explains in 'The Pleasure Principle' that 'poetry is emotional in nature and theatrical in operation, a skilled recreation of emotion in other people'[51] and in 'The Writer in His Age' that 'good writing is largely a matter of finding proper expression for strong feelings'[52] and, about his own writing, that 'the poems I write are very much more naïve – very much more emotional – almost embarrassingly so – than a lot of other people's.'[53] About the music he admires, he uses similar language concerning emotionality and its place in art. In regard to early jazz, Larkin writes that 'all the emphasis was on feeling, emotional communication, sincerity' and that 'for a player to have a better-than-average technique... was thought to be dangerous... or at best a little irrelevant.'[54]

But more subtle instances of the same sentiment are presented throughout Larkin's prose, as in 'The Pleasure Principle,' where he remarks that 'at bottom poetry, like all art, is inextricably bound up with giving pleasure, and if a poet loses his pleasure-seeking audience he has lost the only audience worth having.' While this essay is almost exclusively about poetry and does not mention jazz explicitly at all, Larkin's easy addition of 'like all art' to the statement above about poetry shows how comfortable he feels with a philosophy that transcends genre boundaries and how obvious it is to him that such transcendence exists, or should.[55] This conflation of the arts is also evident in Larkin's interview with *Paris Review*, in which Robert Phillips asks Larkin about the *All What Jazz* introduction and what the 'innovation of 'modernism'' and 'things that seem crazy now, like *Finnegan's Wake* and Picasso' have to do with jazz,' and Larkin answers, 'Everything'. He goes on to explain that jazz is 'dead now, dead as Elizabethan madrigal singing,' and he blames it on Parker's version of modernism, which is, as far as he is concerned in this interview, perfectly parallel with literary Modernism and Modernism in the visual arts.[56] All of this emphasis on Modernism's denial of pleasure and its inability (or unwillingness) to touch the audience emotionally is borne out in Larkin's poetry, which emphasizes emotions, both on the part of the speaker and, by extension, for the readers.

For example, the poems Larkin wrote during 1970 are extremely different in their forms, subjects, and styles but might be said, at their root, all to be poems of emotion. 'The Explosion,' 'The Card Players,' and 'Dublinesque,' all published in *High Windows*, do not seem to have much in common other than their year of origin, but all reflect the interest in emotion as the basis for artistic expression. 'The Explosion' tells the story of miners, childlike on their way to work, chasing rabbits and collecting larks' eggs. And then, 'at noon, there came a tremor;' following the explosion, Larkin moves his attention to the workers' wives, who 'for a second,' saw their husbands

> Larger than in life they managed –
> Gold as on a coin, or walking
> Somehow from the sun towards them...

The obvious emotion of this poem, with its bathos and its refocusing from the men killed to the women left behind, evokes empathy on the part of readers and asks them to feel, with the wives, the loss of these 'Fathers, brothers, nicknames, laughter...'.

'The Card-Players,' written five months later and published in the same volume, is an utterly different poem. Instead of unrhymed three-line stanzas, it is a sonnet. It, too, tells a story, but the characters are as unsympathetic as one could imagine: caricatured figures with vulgar names drink to excess, publicly urinate, belch and stagger and snore. They are, frankly, horrific, a quality made explicit by one's description as having 'his skull face firelit.' The characters in this poem are, like those in 'The Explosion,' archetypal rather than realistic or individual, but they are horrible and disgusting, named to indicate their distastefulness. The poem, in the vein of William Carlos Williams' and W.H. Auden's poems that idolize the work of the Dutch masters ('Musee des Beaux Arts,' 'Peasant Wedding,' 'Landscape with the Fall of Icarus') shares its name with a series of paintings by Cezanne.[57] It mocks these characters but maintains the accessibility and emotional connection of the poem to its readers. It does so through the visceral reaction readers have to the pissing and snoring and farting and spitting of the characters and also through the separated and differently voiced final line: 'Rain, wind and fire! The secret, bestial peace!' That removed line reconnects the readers to the narrator, who does not present this repulsive narrative for its own sake but to analyze and comment on it. Like 'The Explosion,' it remarks on something fundamental in human nature and combines disturbing images with a final image that is at least vaguely redemptive.

The third poem Larkin published from his work of 1970, 'Dublinesque,' is a more personal poem than the other two and describes a funeral parade passing by. This poem recalls the work of Langston Hughes, who describes a similar scene in 'Night Funeral in Harlem,' and it explicitly discusses emotion, noting that 'There is an air of great friendliness. ... And of great sadness also.' These seemingly conflicting emotions and their accompanying behaviors – dancing, clapping, doleful singing – emphasize the ways that an experience one expects will elicit a particular emotion – sadness, or mourning – can, perhaps surprisingly, evoke other, unexpected feelings and behaviors too. Larkin is willing not only to *show* these emotions but to *tell* them as well, to use otherwise bland descriptors like 'sadness.'

In all three of these poems, and in very different ways, Larkin emphasizes emotions, almost telling readers what they might feel. The feelings, in each case, are multiple rather than simple. Thus we are asked to feel grief at the miners' loss and wonder at the almost supernatural reactions of their wives; disgust at the card players and a kinship with nature and humanity in the 'secret, bestial peace;' and the same simultaneous friendliness and sadness that the participants in the funeral feel for the deceased. The emotions are not simple or entirely clear, but they are laid out for us in the poems and presented as coinciding or parallel and as centrally important, just as emotion is to the experience of listening to – or performing – jazz.

'It's all quite clear what it means'

Larkin's poetry is simultaneously praised and dismissed for what is often termed its 'easy accessibility'. Larkin presents his poetry this way himself, telling the *Observer* that 'there isn't much to say about my work. When you've read a poem, that's it, it's all quite clear what it means.'[58] He seems to think of the music he likes best as similarly accessible and presents his tastes as simple and plain. He writes, for example, that he prefers the 'entertainers' of the jazz world to those artists 'who suggest by their demeanor that I am lucky to hear them,' and puts Fats Waller into the former category. While acknowledging that Waller's technique on the piano was 'a baroque triviality,' he nonetheless finds Waller compelling, not least because he attracts listeners ranging from serious jazz collectors to 'housewives' and appeals equally to members of these disparate groups.[59] In a later review, he writes in favor of those musicians who do not 'attempt to push the boundaries of music any farther back, at least for the moment'[60] and that 'readers of this column may rest assured that as long as there is any swinging or Dixieland jazz in straight two or four on recent records they will hear about it.'[61]

A piece like 'Tiger Rag,' which Larkin mentions several times in his prose writing and interviews, and which was performed by many of his favorites jazz artists, including Sidney Bechet, Bix Beiderbecke, and Louis Armstrong, is accessible not only through its use of the diatonic scale and regular time signature but also through its use of predictable patterns and adherence to certain implicit rules of the genre. Armstrong begins his version by growling, 'Look out, boys. That tiger's coming down,' and the 'subject' of the song is fairly clear from there. But the music itself is clear as well. Armstrong's version has a strictly patterned layering of instruments, with drums providing a strong and regular 4/4 beat, trumpet leading the melodic voices, clarinet in the second melodic slot accompanying the trumpet and filling in with occasional and brief breakthrough solos, and short intermittent solos by trombone and drums that are both preceded and followed by the leading trumpet, with the plucked bass taking over the secondary line a couple of times. This is music with rules, and while it does something fun and interesting and catchy, it also very much fulfills expectations and adheres to the conventions of early jazz.

Sidney Bechet's 'Tiger Rag' is a mellower, less frantic number, but it plays by the same rules: organized ensemble work of drums, an oompah trombone, and a perky plucked bass, with clarinet and trumpet lines headlining. (In this case, the clarinet carries more of the melody than in Armstrong's version, for the obvious reason that Armstrong is a trumpeter and Bechet a clarinetist.) The ensemble drops out briefly for clarinet solos, and the clarinet takes a backseat for an extended trombone solo, featuring iconic slides. But everything here is fundamentally hummable, and the foot tapping need never be interrupted by an unexpected drum pattern or a solo that stretches the metrical pattern.

Bix's tempo falls between the other two, and the solos on the cornet (Bix's primary instrument) are slightly rhythmically funkier than Bechet's, but the same rules – Larkin's understanding not of what jazz is capable of but what it *is* – still apply. Just as one who has listened to enough Mozart can guess with relative accuracy how a given passage might end – or at least give about three informed guesses, one of which will be right – so one might hear and correctly anticipate the phrasing and melody of any of these versions of 'Tiger Rag.' Certainly nothing about them particularly surprises, as much as the music might please, the listener.

Listening to John Coltrane or Charlie Parker or Thelonius Monk, on the other hand, is an utterly different kind of musical experience. Larkin explains the difference to Robert Phillips, with slightly feigned musical ignorance, by saying that 'Charlie Parker wrecked jazz – or so they tell me – using the chromatic rather than the diatonic scale. The diatonic scale is what you use if you want to write a national anthem, or a love song, or a lullaby. The chromatic scale is what you use to give the effect of drinking a quinine martini and having an enema simultaneously.'[62] And while the scaling is one difference between Bechet and Parker, the more fundamental difference is based on the observation of patterns and established, or at least expected, rules. The hierarchy of instruments described in 'Tiger Rag' above, regardless of the artist, is undermined by the artists Larkin accuses of killing jazz. One of them, Ornette Coleman, very deliberately manipulates the rules Larkin believes in, and Gary Giddins describes his jazz this way: 'He has usually avoided instruments with fixed pitch, like the piano, and instead has sought bassists and guitarists who, through special tunings or sheer empathy, can harmoniously balance his timbre and intonation... Jazz typically involves soloists improvising over a beat and bass line provided by a rhythm section, but Coleman always demanded greater involvement on the part of his bassists and drummers.'[63] Giddins explains that some of Coleman's most recent music, written and performed after Larkin's death, eliminates the traditional melodic instruments altogether and brings the traditionally rhythmic instruments to the forefront by having them serve simultaneously as rhythm and melody sections, thus blurring the distinction between the front and back lines of the band about which Larkin felt so strongly.

Larkin exclaims about his first experiences witnessing jazz performed live rather than simply hearing it over the radio and the importance of seeing the physical movements that accompanied the patterns of performance: 'I was able actually to see... the different sections rising to play four bars then sitting sharply down again; the shouts of "yeah man," the slapped bass, the drum breaks.'[64] That connection between the patterned music and the *movements* of the musicians matters to Larkin, and his part in it – insisting that 'our tickets were for [the drummer's] side of the house' – highlights the relationship between performers and audience. Coleman's performances, or Parker's or Coltrane's, do not follow such patterns and are more introspective, less obviously performative, events. The audience is permitted to observe what seems, essentially, to be a private musical experience for the performers who seldom acknowledge the audience's presence and certainly don't rise in instrumental unison to clarify the performance's trajectory.

Larkin's strong feelings about the changes in jazz are addressed directly by Ekkehard Jost, who defends the 'free jazz' Larkin so dislikes by undermining Larkin's understanding of the 'rules' of jazz: 'it has become clear to all that Free Jazz does not mean either musical arbitrariness or a break with jazz tradition. The aesthetic standards of tonality and form which it broke away from were not principles inherent in natural law but conventions agreed between men. They were not physical formulae but culture-linked historical phenomena.' In other words, Jost argues, the patterns and rhythms and instrumentations that got Larkin 'hooked on jazz' and that Larkin claims are 'instinctual' are not somehow more true to 'real' jazz than the free and modern styles Larkin dislikes, and Larkin's assertions that jazz was 'wrecked' by Charlie Parker, or, more pointedly 'destroyed by a paranoid drug-addict,' misunderstand jazz's evolution entirely.[65] As Jost explains, modern jazz is not 'an impenetrable enigma' but 'a source of revelation – revelation about aggression and bitterness, but no less about joy, communication and humor. This emotional power establishes it in the jazz tradition more surely than any convention of style.'[66] Jost also posits, in his volume *Free Jazz*, that 'one of the first things that strikes one in traditional jazz is its formal simplicity.' Jost means that melodies – or, as he terms it, 'the musically particular' – could be superimposed over a repeated chord pattern – 'functional harmony' – without any disruption to the general rules of the background. 'In this way, *How High the Moon* could become *Ornithology* without the improviser having to depart one bit from the old familiar chord patterns of the original tune.'[67] Jost argues, quite convincingly, that the functional harmony had been used, in the forties and fifties, as much as it could be and was leading 'more frequently to clichés from which even the most inspired improvisers could not escape.' Jost also states, about early jazz rhythms, that 'the process of breaking up the beat had gone on continuously since the march-inspired music of the New Orleans veterans. But apart from a few exceptional cases on the periphery of jazz, it had never been abandoned.' Ultimately, Jost shows that, in traditional jazz, 'the interpretation of a given piece by two different musicians or groups playing in different stylistic areas of traditional jazz, will differ in the choice of rhythmic, harmonic, melodic and tone-colour resources, but will not differ in principles used.'[68]

According to Jost, then, the definitive split between older and newer styles that so weighs on Larkin is not a split at all but a natural development of the identical emotions at the root of the jazz Larkin loves. At the same time, though, 'The Free Jazz musicians threw overboard a large number of time-honored basic rules and thus provoked a crop of misunderstandings which persisted well into the sixties.'[69] And since Larkin loves both the emotions behind the music and the formulae of the music, this overthrowing of the rules disturbed him, probably more so because the music was so deeply tied to his own emotions and fond early memories and because 'on leaving Oxford I suffered a gap in my jazz life.' As Larkin explains in his introduction to *All What Jazz*, he lived in places that did not welcome record-playing, and 'when I was united with my collection in 1948 and had something to play it on there followed a period when I was content to renew acquaintance with it and to add only what amplified or extended it along existing lines – new records by old favourites, replacements of discs previously abandoned or broken.' His skepticism of newer forms of recording 'deepened my isolation.'[70]

Larkin's love of the 'hot numbers' from jazz bands, particularly the ubiquitous 'Tiger Rag,' speaks precisely to his delicate balance between pushing too many lines and staying too far away from change. The basic dance songs were less than fascinating for young Larkin, who would 'listen to hours of dance music in order to catch [the hot numbers] when they came,' which was 'about every sixth piece.'[71] Finding those hot numbers between ordinary dance songs on regular radio stations was 'that unique private excitement that youth seems to demand.' The hot numbers had a little something special: 'the one or two men in the band who could play jazz would be heard.' What made them special, at least according to the introduction to *All What Jazz*, was some small moment, something subtle for which listeners had to pay attention and which made those attentive listeners part of a club. At the same time, even the hot numbers followed the same basic format, offering something more interesting – much more interesting, for Larkin – than the standard dance numbers but nonetheless maintaining certain patterned musical and performative conventions.

The accessibility of Larkin's poetry is made not only through his appeals to emotion, on various levels, but also through his belief in and adherence to patterns and readerly expectations. With very few exceptions, his poems include both nearly photographic specifics and clearly articulated emotional passages. The order of presentation of these items differs, but the presence of both types of writing, generally sectioned off from each other, is as visible as sections of a band rising to play solos. The poems thus adhere to expectations – a kind of poetic functional harmony – while presenting variations on the form. For instance, 'Love Songs in Age' uses the ordinary and realistic details of aging album covers to make real the failure of music's promise. The precise visual details of the albums and their covers – bleached by the sun, watermarked by a vase, colored by a child – are posited against the vagueness of 'that much-mentioned brilliance, love,' which offers a continuing promise 'to solve, and satisfy,/ And set unchangeably in order' despite its practical, and eternal, inability to do so. In this poem, the precision of the album covers seems to hold a promise that cannot be fulfilled by the emptiness of 'love' itself, which ought to be powerful but actually cannot enact any sort of change, and never has: 'It had not done so then, and could not now.'

Similarly, 'Show Saturday' lists at length the multiple items that comprise the show and disguise the passage of time. Only when the poem ends are we made aware of the meaning behind the lists of 'Bead-stalls, balloon-men, a Bank;' 'four brown eggs, four white eggs,' 'Needlework, knitted caps, baskets.' The show is

> something people do,
> Not noticing how time's rolling smithy-smoke
> Shadows much greater gestures; something they share
> That breaks ancestrally each year into
> Regenerate union.

and the speaker finally, abstractly, entreats, 'Let it always be there.' The poem builds up, through its beautifully phrased but unweighted lists of items, to a lesson that shows where all those lists were headed, to a perhaps surprising idealization of this common scene and the common people who inhabit it. The resolution could as easily have gone another way, perhaps reminding readers that 'Lots of folk live up lanes/ With fires in a bucket,/ Eat windfalls and tinned sardines – ' as 'Toads' does; or that these common people dress 'in parodies of fashion' with 'mothers loud and fat; An uncle shouting smut' as in 'The Whitsun Weddings'; or that the people at the show – 'men with hunters, dog-breeding wool-defined women,/ Children all saddle-swank, mugfaced middleaged wives' – might turn out to be as common as the women 'who leave at dawn low terraced houses/ Timed for factory, yard and site' in 'The Large Cool Store.' The many details of Larkin's poems do not necessarily give away what the vaguer resolution will be, but the poems nonetheless follow this predictable pattern, albeit with sometimes unpredictable outcomes.

Larkin's poems always include such specificity, but never in isolation; the poems either begin with a removed-sounding lesson and move towards specificity or begin with the resoundingly concrete, and end with the less precise, straightforwardly stated emotion. 'Home is So Sad' follows the former patterns, with the devastating final fragment concretizing the vague, strangely banal title. The poem begins with its first line repeating the vague sentence of the title and continues with a similar lack of specificity:

> It stays as it was left,
> Shaped to the comfort of the last to go
> As if to win them back.

As it continues, though, it moves towards an extreme precision that uses concrete objects – without additional commentary – to illustrate the sadness of the title and first line:

> You can see how it was:
> Look at the pictures and the cutlery.
> The music in the piano stool. That vase.

'Money,' however, follows the opposite pattern, beginning with the most material of titles and the first illustrative line, 'Quarterly, is it, money reproaches me' and the reminder that 'I am all you never had of goods and sex./ You could get them still by writing a few cheques,' focusing on material acquisition and the plain materiality of 'goods.' The poem ends, though, with a line that sounds remarkably like the opening of 'Home is

So Sad:' 'It is intensely sad.' With a pronoun instead of a concrete noun, and the word 'so' replaced by the word 'intensely,' it is the same sentence, one that employs the simplest of emotions to make a statement about the concreteness of objects.

Keeping in mind this adherence to pattern as well as the many other parallels between Larkin's feelings about poetry and those about jazz, we can find in Ekkhard Jost's assessment of the demise (or evolution) of early jazz an explanation for the eventual extinction of Larkin's own poetry. Jost claims that early jazz could not continue as it was, the variations on the same functional harmonies having played themselves out. 'Even the most inspired improvisers' could no longer avoid self-repetition and cliché. The drying up of Larkin's poetry may thus be a function of his unwillingness to alter the (very successful) patterns of his poetry, to move beyond his own versions of *Ornithology* and *How High the Moon*. And once those were done, he had nothing more to say, and he had established himself as a writer who would not have another phase, who would not become an Auden, who 'at one stroke lost his key subject and emotion ... and abandoned his audience altogether with their common dialect and concerns.'[72] This criticism of Auden was written at the height of Larkin's poetic power, between the publications of *The Less Deceived* and *The Whitsun Weddings*. But he seems to have felt the sentiment deeply, and revisits the issue numerous times, including in the *Times Literary Supplement* in 1981, when he remarks that 'American Auden,' (as opposed to the earlier, British poet, whom Larkin sees as an unarguably superior writer) 'was a ponderous windbag.'[73] And in a 1983 review of John Haffenden's *W.H. Auden: The Critical Heritage*, Larkin again highlights the change in Auden from his 'blinding explosion' into poetry and 'the fierce ten-year flare' to the later 'flatulent abstractions' and 'protracted guttering twilight.'[74] Rather than risk becoming like the utterly changed poet that he believed Auden became through abandoning his earlier style, or like the innovative, combative modern jazz musician, composing under 'constant pressure to be different,'[75] Larkin chose to maintain the basic poetic values he had long held and patterns he had long used. In the face of that attachment to an unchangeable artistic ethic, though, he was eventually unable to produce any more. As his poetic philosophy throughout his life mirrored his feelings about jazz, so the petering out of his poetic production mirrored the production of jazz he loved. As he tells A.N. Wilson, 'I would sooner not write any poems than write bad poems.' The 'great sorrow' of poetry having 'given [him] up'[76] is expressed in similar terms to the 'astonishment,' 'disbelief' and 'alarm' he feels at finding that 'nearly every characteristic of the music had been neatly inverted.'[77] The need to explain in writing, as late as 1984, that 'in any case, my views haven't changed' shows Larkin's unalterable commitment to his aesthetic values and, also, the way that those values both shaped and paralyzed his output, just as they froze his musical taste. He maintained similar patterns and rules for poetry throughout his career, and that final parallel between his favorite pre-modern jazz and his poetry meant, eventually, that the poetry abandoned him for good.

5
Religion and Empathy

As we have seen thus far, many elements of Larkin's writing point out his perhaps surprising interest in people, in their actions and interactions. Although in the abstract he can be fairly cruel about people, or about specific groups of people, his individual interactions and discussions of specific individuals almost never indicate such levels of vitriol.[1] For a writer popularly called 'misanthropic,' he can be sensitive, insightful, and remarkably inclusive in his writings about people. Within the poems especially, he seems to try to embody others in order to experience their feelings and understand their perspectives. Even poems that seem initially to resist affiliation with the characters described, like 'The Whitsun Weddings,' alternately offer a kind of empathy and even a kindness towards the people who seem, in places, only to evoke condescension.

Many critics have questioned Larkin's widespread popularity and why a poet so inward-looking and so apparently misanthropic should have such wide appeal. Some have concluded that it is because of Larkin's low-brow subject matter and unsophisticated writing. As Gary Kissick explains, Terry Eagleton criticizes Larkin's 'deep fear of human involvement' and life of 'timidity and evasion' and, furthermore, claims that Larkin was popular 'because his plain-speaking verse appealed to English anti-intellectualism and parochialism. ... Somehow, he tricked his readers into joining him in this bleak world.'[2] Anthony Easthope argues that the simplicity of 'The Whitsun Weddings,' for instance, appeals to readers in its invisibility, 'to give the effect of someone 'really' speaking:' 'a plain transcription of reality.'[3] The implication of these critical evaluations is that Larkin retains unwarranted feelings of icy superiority to his readers and, simultaneously, that he dupes them into believing him to be one of them. Both Eagleton and Easthope argue for Larkin's uncomplicatedness and his erasing of the speaker persona in favor of a fully conjoined poet/speaker who is utterly self-absorbed, as well as an audience of literal-minded populists whose own anti-intellectualism is bolstered by Larkin's simplicity.

A less jaundiced view of the poems, though, and one that allows for the possibility of Larkin's self-awareness and of a separation between poet and speaker, shows that the basis of Larkin's ongoing popularity is his genuine attempt to foster a relationship with his audience not through condescension but through an almost novelistic character development. The growth of the speaker during the course of even a short poem highlights a reaching out to the audience that does not condescend so much as it plays with the idea of condescension. In fact, as Tijana Stojkovic has demonstrated, Larkin's poems are accessible for readers precisely because 'their narrative nature manages to activate an "appropriate scenario" and readers perceive the narrative of the poems 'as a truthful and concise expression of things we have witnessed, or heard about, or think possible... the narrative composition facilitates such identification.'[4]

Larkin's tendency towards sympathy with the poems' characters, even when that sympathy includes some level of resistance or separation from the characters described, extends to an even deeper and more consistent sympathy for or understanding of the reader and the reader's expectations. Larkin makes his own claims against simplicity, or against being tricked by apparent simplicity, telling Roy Plomley that 'a poem should be understood at first reading line by line, but I don't think it should be exhausted at that first reading. I hope that what I write gives the reader something when they read it first, enough in fact to make them read it again and so on *ad infinitum*.'[5] But even in arguing against a single reading (and in favor of a fundamentally comprehensible first reading), he has the reaction and perspective of his reader in mind. And although it may be argued that he has in mind a reader too like himself, the frequent turns in his poetry – the willingness or even compulsion to argue both sides of an issue, to present what John Carey and M.W. Rowe both describe as the 'male and female' sides of himself – shows a sensitivity to audience and a willingness, even a compulsion, to consider multiple possibilities. This openness to multiple perspectives also allows him to reach a wide audience by offering something for each reader – a sense that he speaks directly to 'my' concerns and beliefs – and leads to wildly disparate readings of the poems, depending on the reader's emphasis and focus and on which aspects, and which voices, of the poem speak most directly to the reader in question. The blanks in narrative that Wolfgang Iser considers fundamental to the reader's role in interpretation might, for Larkin, be more accurately described as places not merely where the reader can insert his own interpretation but where he can insert *himself*. Iser asserts that the text is the 'hollow form into which the reader is invited to pour his own store of knowledge,' but Larkin's poetry asks less for a store of knowledge than for a broader insertion of the reader both to imagine himself as part of the scene described and to recognize that he is doubly built into the poem, as an observer and a (potential) participant.

This tendency is nowhere more pronounced than in the poems about religion. The subject, which seems so fraught in Larkin's writing and about which he is sometimes called dismissive or even hostile, is one of the places where he demonstrates most astutely his connection to his readership and his openness to alternate views. Andrew Motion, in his 1983 biography, comments on the lack, in Larkin's writing, 'of the most time-honoured absolute of them all: religion... Larkin's dilemma is not whether to believe in God but what to put in God's place.'[6] Richard Hoffpauir writes that Larkin, 'without even [John Betjeman's] tenuous faith, was more disillusioned and resigned. He had a more intense awareness of discontinuity between the spirit with its will to purity and nature as a realm of change, obscure forces, decay, and death.'[7] In 'The Young Mr. Larkin,' his childhood friend Noel Hughes recalls an instance when Larkin passed him a book under the school desk 'and hissed 'get out of that.' I believe the book to have been an early Joad and the paragraph set out the clear illogicality of any belief in God.'[8] D.Z. Phillips reacts most strongly to Larkin's skepticism, arguing that 'What one is able to accept as a reading, what one is able to believe or care about, all depend on what one takes the limits of reality to be. ... Does religion lie outside these limits for Larkin? Obviously, it does.' Furthermore, Phillips continues, for someone who thinks as Larkin does, 'religion will appear, necessarily, to be a delusion.[9] All of these comments reinforce the sense that Larkin's statements of his own atheism are perfectly reflected in his poetry and that the poems present religious belief as delusional and religious practitioners as backwards, illogical, and duped.

There is an obvious logic to the parallels between Larkin's poetry and jazz: he loved jazz and wrote about it in multiple venues and genres. His poems about religion, on the other hand, defy that logic: he claimed to have no attachment to religion, almost never wrote or talked about it except when asked about religiously-themed poems, and occasionally expressed explicit hostility toward the idea that he was secretly sympathetic toward religion. I have no intention of questioning Larkin's lack of religious faith or any reason to believe that his statements of personal atheism were disingenuous, and yet he wrote more poems about religion than about jazz and makes more religious than musical references throughout his verse. The fact that he offers such frequent religious imagery while claiming to live in an age that is no longer religious and to feel no religious pull at all suggests a tension that Larkin does not acknowledge. I argue in this chapter that the poems about religion, even those that approach the topic with cynicism or frustration, show most profoundly Larkin's interest in and attachment to the concerns of his readers, both by undermining their expectations through play with his persona and, in the poems, by adopting shifting religious poses to explore the topic not as an observer but as a participant. Like 'Reasons for Attendance' and 'The Whitsun Weddings,' the religion poems momentarily remove the glass that so often exists between Larkin's speakers and his subjects and highlight a moveable speaker capable of placing himself both inside and outside: the scenes, the characters' minds, and the reader's positions.

The poems most evidently about religion – particularly 'Church Going,' 'Faith Healing,' and 'Water' – demonstrate a fascinating and profound sensitivity to others' beliefs and to the possibility of belief. Larkin's own interests – but not beliefs – in ritual and in the trappings of religion are clear in various ways, as will be explored in this chapter, but his interest extends beyond a curiosity about church buildings and ceremony to a genuine attempt to get inside the heads of religious believers and find what prompts them to believe. And while occasionally his conclusions are not complimentary, the honest attempt not to insult believers or to close off understanding but to understand and, if not sympathize, at least to empathize is present in each of these poems. Despite their first-person perspective and their external emphasis on the speaker's feelings and reactions, they are actually finely attuned to the experiences of others and, in particular, to the appeal of religion both to the poem's characters and to their readers.

Larkin is widely known to be an atheist, and he refers with some frequency to his lack of faith or interest in church or organized religion. As he tells John Haffenden, 'I didn't lose faith. I never had it.' The poems, however, especially 'Church Going' have been read as deeply religious, most notably by J. R. Watson but also by Maeve Brennan and less dramatically by others. Ian Almond remarks on the 'capacity of Larkin to desecularize the particular (ambulances, photographs, hospitals) and glimpse infinity' and on the poems' 'strange, original, disconcerting holiness.'[10] Roger Day calls some of Larkin's poems 'secular hymns' and compares 'Solar' to Psalm 103; he further suggests that 'High Windows' may be a "secular' equivalent' of Psalm 138.[11] In any case, while Larkin's own proclamations of atheism may place him firmly in a particular theological camp, they belie his obvious interest in the trappings of faith and his multifaceted relationship to believers. As James Booth observes, 'despite his dismissal of the large claims of religion, Larkin remains a secular rather than an atheist poet. He is unreligious rather than anti-religious.'[12] Booth notes that 'this is a crucial distinction,' and it is one that could be taken even farther. Larkin is not only not anti-religious, he is, in some ways, pro-religious without actually being religious. That is to say, he is drawn to religion both in its superficialities and in its bigger questions, and he is particularly interested in what makes religion meaningful to others. One could go so far as to say that his poems are supportive of, even subtly envious of, others' religiosity. Larkin's resistance to organized religion or to belief in God does not abate throughout his lifetime, yet his poems are consistently tinged with a kind of religious appreciation that connects him, through his speakers and characters, to the average believer as well as to the non-believer.

Andrew Motion, in response to those critics who see Larkin as 'uniformly depressed,' explains that Larkin's lack of religion forces self-reliance and therefore, in so far as this means that individuals must discover and develop their own internal resources, his poems have an unmistakably affirmative aspect.'[13] While the poems are indeed affirmative in some ways, the affirmation is not exactly in their self-reliance but in their genuine interest in the lives and needs of others. Even the most pessimistic of poems does not exempt itself from this reaching out to others in a secular but not fully individual way. In 'The Building,' for instance, where hospitals are explicitly compared with churches, the necessary self-reliance of 'a touching dream to which we are all lulled/ But wake from separately' is tempered by a recognition of people clutching at one another and an understanding that 'All know they are going to die,' not with an attitude of self-reliance but with a recognition of universality. Similarly, 'Ambulances,' a parallel poem from eleven years earlier, focuses on the self, but in a communal way: '*Poor soul*, they whisper at their own distress.' The individual impulse for self-pity is couched in collective terms, and solitary behavior is presented as both private and universal. One might expect, given Larkin's popular image, that the Larkinesque speaker would be doing this whispering, but Larkin's poetry often revels not in the speaker's own self-absorption but in collective emotions. In some ways, Larkin's lack of religious faith does point him towards faith in people, but not in quite so unabashed a way as Motion suggests: 'the fear of death and the loss of religious belief are counteracted by an ineradicable faith in human and individual potential' is something of an overstatement and leaves aside the conflicting attitudes and postures in Larkin's work. But the poet's interest in and connection to others, sometimes in place of and sometimes in conjunction with religion, is what moves his poems beyond the simple depression and isolation with which he is popularly associated and to a universalizing of emotion – including the emotions that accompany and bolster faith.

In 'Church Going,' by far the most widely-discussed of Larkin's religiously-themed poems, a solitary speaker enters an empty church and offers his thoughts on the building itself – its purpose and contents and uses – and on the people who have various feelings about the building and its purpose. The tone is alternately read as irreverent and respectful, atheistic and religious, hopeless and hopeful. And indeed the tone is the most puzzling part of this poem, with so many undercuttings and changes that it is hard to tell where it finally settles. The poem begins neutrally, if disconcertingly casually, given the subject: the speaker assures himself that a church he has happened upon is empty and enters it, letting the door close behind him. He describes what he sees there: seats, books, old flowers, 'some brass and stuff,' an organ, 'and a tense, musty, unignorable silence'.

As the speaker continues to observe the church, he notes the 'hectoring' verses of the open bible on the lectern. After mildly mocking the place and being mocked in return (I 'pronounce/ 'Here endeth' much more loudly than I'd meant./ The echoes snigger briefly.') the speaker reflects 'the place was not worth stopping for.' As the poem develops and his internal monologue continues, he speculates about the kind of person who might be the last to visit the place and finally suggests that this last person might be one like himself: 'Bored, uninformed, knowing this ghostly silt/ Dispersed.' Eventually, though, he acknowledges that the church is a 'special shell' that leads to some pleasure: he does not know what the place 'is worth,' a phrase which suggests both monetary and less tangible types of value, and yet 'it pleases me to stand in silence here.' The connection the speaker makes – and what seems to give him the greatest pleasure in the place – is its significance in life cycle events '—marriage, and birth,/ And death, and thoughts of these –' and the speaker continues, in his isolation, to use the church as a place of connection to others, or at least to his thoughts of others. The immaturity of his behavior in the opening stanzas – calling out from the lectern, giving a worthless coin to alms – seems to change by the end of the poem when he wishes for, if only hypothetically, seriousness.

The opening stanza of the poem is the one most often read as dismissive and disrespectful, with Swarbrick, for instance, calling it 'flippant' and 'facetious,' and Larkin himself points to it as evidence of his purposeful lack of knowledge about churches: 'I go to some pains to point out that I don't bother about that kind of thing, that I'm deliberately ignorant of it – 'Up at the holy end,' for instance.'[14] But even in the first stanza, the tone of the poem is far from consistently disrespectful;

> Hatless, I take off
> My cycle-clips in awkward reverence, ...

Indeed, the 'awkward reverence' of removing cycle clips in place of a hat shows the speaker's tense and uncertain relationship with churches and their contents. Roger Day reads the speaker's feelings as 'ambivalent,' noting that he 'experiences 'awkward reverence' yet is studiedly casual in the reference to 'some brass and stuff/ Up at the holy end.'[15] Richard Palmer finds the first two stanzas 'a joyous orgy of adolescent nose-thumbing and arrogantly studied aloof arrogance' and Andrew Motion calls the speaker 'an interloper, slightly goofy, disrespectful, "bored" and "uninformed" ' and says that he 'begins the poem by banishing any signs of holy dread.'[16] For all of these, though, the speaker's actions require explanation since, even in his dismissal of 'holy dread,' his behavior is not entirely disrespectful and suggests inelegance rather than derision.

Larkin claims, in an interview with Ian Hamilton, that 'Church Going' is not a religious poem. Indignantly, he insists that it is 'of course an entirely secular poem... It isn't religious at all.' But he also claims, just two sentences earlier, that 'its popularity is somewhat due to extraneous factors – anything about religion tends to go down well.' So 'Church Going' is a poem about religion – religious symbols, religious meaning, faith – without being religious itself; that is, it does not profess belief in a deity or suggest 'that the affairs of this world are under divine superveillance.'[17] Then, despite having just explained that the poem is not religious but is about religion, he adds a few sentences later that 'of course the poem is about going to church, not religion.' Larkin's emphatic language throughout this section of the interview belies the fact that he seems somewhat unsure himself of whether the poem is about religion, or in what way it is about religion. His hesitancy to categorize the religiosity of the poem is awkward in conversation, and he expresses significant disgust and some anger while telling the story of an American who 'misread' the poem; yet even he appears unclear about how he should categorize or define the poem's relationship to religion. A primary problem in this interview may be the multiple ways in which religion can be defined: in its entirety as belief, practice, ritual, personal and collective history, aesthetic and worldview; or as any subset or single element of that list.

Of course, 'Church Going' is about religion in a very obvious way, and it is more subtly about the loss of religion and the fear of the loss of some elements of religion. It also offers a kind of faith in the desire for faith while remaining resolute about its lack of conventional faith. Thus we can begin to see the poem's connection to believers and the breaking down of the hesitantly mocking tone established at the poem's start. Richard Hoffpauir notes that 'Church Going' highlights not only the church's ability to 'contain and concentrate and so give coherence to our natural needs and most universal of routines' but also that 'the gathering and enclosing that the church encouraged provided a means of preserving human memory.' The faith of the poem, as Hoffpauir reads it, is in ritual 'by means of the absence left in community life by the decline in religious faith'.[18] The faith, then, is not in a god or in any of the formalities of religion but in its bringing together of people and in the realities of people's need for something beyond themselves, although not necessarily something supernatural. In this way it speaks to the concerns of multiple audiences – both believers and non-believers – by presenting a kind of twice-removed faith: the speaker does not have traditional faith, but he has faith in faith; he believes in the power of belief.

Everything in this poem points to its real depth of human feeling, the lack of isolation in a poem that seems on its surface to highlight isolation. Although the speaker is a solitary figure in a solitary environment, the depth of human connection extends to the past, considering the people who were married or christened in the church; to the present ('someone would know' whether the roof was cleaned or restored); to the future ('I wonder who/ Will be the last, the very last...'); from religious to superstitious people to those who are 'bored' and 'uninformed'; and from the living to the dead. The human connection in this poem, despite featuring a speaker who, at least initially, is so isolated and disconnected from others, is quite profound. Perhaps this is why Larkin calls it a 'humanist poem.'[19] The humans to whom the poem connects are both those like the speaker and those fairly unlike the speaker and whose theologies differ from his. And the initial condescension, into which the poem could have fully devolved, is absent by the poem's end, replaced by a belief in people and, by extension, an empathy with their beliefs, if not an agreement with them.

Although the poem, like so many of Larkin's poems, seems constantly to undermine its own statements, it reaffirms again and again the importance of this place, not because of its affiliation with the supernatural – or with superstition – but because of its affiliation with human need (or, as the speaker puts it, compulsion). The speaker of the poem, who resists being fully part of the church's world and dismisses (as Larkin himself does) 'the crew/ That tap and jot and know what rood-lofts were' also recognizes the place as deserving reverence, albeit hesitating, and seriousness. So of course this is far from a purely religious poem; it is far too cynical to be devotional or liturgical. But, as Larkin must certainly know, and as his answer to Hamilton suggests, he realizes that his poem is more complex in its religious attitude – and less perfectly secular – than his answers about the poem superficially indicate.

Steven Cooper suggests that 'the speaker's initial indifference to religion [in 'Church Going'] is ultimately tempered with a rediscovery of the value of faith.'[20] This is an interesting way to define the work, which does not rediscover faith itself but rediscovers 'the value of faith.' The value of faith is not applied personally to the speaker but more generally – it has a social value, and a personal value for others – and the speaker appreciates its worth in those ways even as he continues not to internalize its more dogmatic principles. Recognition of this value of faith permits the speaker to connect to the poem's readers, who are respected not in a simple-minded way but with an open willingness to grapple with real questions, as his readers do, and an understanding of why different people might reach different conclusions. The poem may begin as all-knowing, but it ends conditionally, suggesting that the speaker's answers might be the right ones but that the believers' answers might be right instead, or in addition. Certainly it empathizes with those readers who act upon their instincts differently than the speaker does:

> ... someone will forever be surprising
> A hunger in himself to be more serious,
> And gravitating with it to this ground, ...

In this way the speaker reaches out to readers, validating their compulsions, which he sees as manifested in himself as well – changing his nouns from the particular 'dubious women' and 'ruin-bibber[s]' of the earlier stanzas to the simultaneously more personal and more generic 'someone' and 'himself' of the final stanzas – to include himself and his readers in the last stanza's open-ended possibilities.

Larkin seems rather angry in his interview with Hamilton about the religious readings of the 'Church Going' ('trust the tale and not the teller, and all that stuff'), but in his interview with John Haffenden he seems more sympathetic to religious feeling in general but explains that

"Church Going' isn't that kind of poem: it's a humanist poem, a celebration of the dignity of...' and then cuts himself off with 'well, you know what it says.' Of course, this is a bit of a joke, in that Larkin is perfectly aware that people do not know what it says and that the poem is the subject of significant debate. His statement implies that what the poem says is self-evident, but he has seen (and commented critically on) the various interpretations readers have given of the poem. So he withdraws himself from offering a concrete or definitive poet's interpretation, but the idea that the poem is about dignity is clear even without his finishing the sentence. The dignity is not of religion itself, nor of churches nor of atheism; instead, the poem demonstrates the dignity of the struggle with religious desire – desire for finding meaning and order and a greater significance – and rationality. In the struggle itself is dignity. So while the poem may be secular in the sense that it does not proclaim belief in God or even necessarily desire for belief in God, it very clearly proclaims belief in human longing and in humanity.

James Booth highlights this tension in 'Church Going' by showing two competing views that use the poem as 'a weapon in a kind of class war between the literary avant garde seeking a "new seriousness" in poetry, and a cultural establishment who claimed it on behalf of traditional spirituality.'[21] But, as Booth rightly posits, 'Larkin was not concerned to score points in a debate about religion. His quarrel was not that of a polemicist, with others, but that of a poet, with himself; so the tone remains inextricably mixed.'[22] Indeed, the confusion Larkin seems to present in the interviews, with the poem being about religion but not religious and then not about religion, is reflected in the confusion of the poem itself, which offers an ultimately unresolved view of the attractions and detractions of religion and belief. Nicholas Marsh insightfully argues for the intentionality of the poem's lack of resolution: 'in the literal sense, the poem cannot tell us anything. On the other hand, it presents the speaker as a twentieth-century man wrestling with these questions, and it recreates the sheer complexity and depth of the disturbance they cause him. At the very least, the poem tells us that questions concerning the purpose of existence are central to the experience of a twentieth-century atheist.'[23] Marsh's all-important reading of the line, 'And what remains when disbelief has gone?' notices, as other critics have not, that the real question the speaker seems to be asking ('And what remains when *belief* has gone?') is inverted here and thus 'the problem is how to lose rational cynicism, not the loss of religion at all. ... He struggles to set himself free from his *dis*belief; but he is frightened and has no idea what can take its place.' As Marsh's reading makes clear, the poem cannot accurately be read as merely promotion of religiosity or promotion of atheism. Instead, it is a complex internal argument about the place of religion (both literally and figuratively) in modern life with a palpable tension that is not resolved by either the opening stanza that features an awkward and perhaps irreverent speaker or by the final lines, voiced in a more pious tone. Readers are able to find a place in this debate regardless of their own views on the Church because the poem offers so many possibilities and is not pedantic in its own tentative answers and cautious exploration.

The poem's developmental structure, something we often see in Larkin's poetry, allows the poet to reach out to his audience in several ways. By beginning the poem in one mental and emotional state and ending in another, he carries the reader with him through his growth. The reader, who may think he knows this speaker when the poem opens, is carried on a slightly surprising journey, finding his own understanding developing along with the speaker's. In addition, the poem reaches out to the reader by demonstrating, through its changing attitudes, that confusion is acceptable and even positive. The poem does not lecture its readers, as poems about religion (either pro- or con-) can easily do but instead presents a speaker who thinks he knows how he feels but finds, in the course of seven short stanzas, that he might feel differently, or at least that others feel understandably differently. The wall built up by the speaker in the early stanzas parallels the resistance readers might feel to the premise of the poem, and as the speaker gradually opens himself to a 'rediscovery of the value of faith,' so too the reader is softened to the ideas of the poem, and so the journey through the poem is taken with the reader in mind, breaking down the reader's preconceptions and hesitancies as it presents a breaking down of the speaker's similar feelings. Stojkovic calls this movement the poem's 'subjectivity,' and notes that 'the subjectivity of the speaker in "Church Going" gives the poem coherence and "logical" movement from one sensory impression, or thought, or feeling, to another.'[24] While the poem certainly acts 'logically' in this way, the effect of this movement is not only to illuminate 'the psychological depths, or quirks, of a *persona*,' but also to destabilize the reader's position by disallowing easy judgment, either of the persona or of the church.

The question Larkin avoids is why such a poem exists. If a writer is truly uninterested in churches, why choose to write about them? And if Larkin sees them as useless relics, why memorialize them this way? Through the mere existence of the poem one might argue that Larkin's relationship to religion, or at least to the physical embodiments of spirituality, is far more complicated than he would admit in interviews or prose. In an interview, Larkin claims to have written the poem because he had recently stopped in a church and the poem grew out of that experience. But Larkin seems not to ask this question of himself, at least in his responses to questions about the poem, and he too avoids questioning the root of that 'hunger' that the poems presents as a kind of universal truth.

Interestingly, the speaker claims often to stop in churches despite his awkwardness and, as he later says, his boredom and lack of knowledge.

> Yet stop I did: in fact, I often do,
> And always end much at a loss like this,

After raising the question of his own tendency to stop in churches without consciously knowing why, he drops the point entirely, not following up on his own implicit question of wondering what he's looking for. In his willingness to reach out from his solitude to his readers, he is able to avoid – at least temporarily – the most difficult and probing questions of himself and focus instead on the larger community and make broader sociological pronouncements. Rather than answering his self-posed question, he redirects the questions to others and to wondering what will become of churches in the future, when they 'fall completely out of use'. His self-examination is past and becomes an examination of society and the various types of people who do or will visit churches, including his own unexamined type.

In this way, the poem very much resembles 'Reasons for Attendance,' in which the speaker also begins to question his own motives and then backs off from his introspection: 'Why be out here?' he asks, but rather than answering the question he redirects it at others: 'But then, why be in there?' thus avoiding the most uncomfortable self-interrogation by acting as though the question had not been raised or had been merely rhetorical. The self-questioning hangs in the air of both poems, though, and then returns in the powerfully ambiguous final lines of the poems: 'someone,' the speaker tells us, will always return to this ground,

> Which, he once heard, was proper to grow wise in,
> If only that so many dead lie round.

Just as 'Reasons for Attendance' ends with an 'if,' so does 'Church Going,' and in both cases the final line shows that the self-directed question that seemed for a while to have been forgotten was present all along and has led, however belatedly, to an answer. In each case, the pain and self-recognition of a perfectly straightforward answer is forgone for the discomfiting conditional statement that proves both the speaker's self-awareness and his (grudging or, at least, belated) willingness to admit to uncertainty even when certainty had seemed to be his greatest asset.

The primary suggestion at the poem's end is the one stated: what matters about this spot, what makes it 'serious' and deserving of serious attention, is that it is surrounded by burial places.[25] But that final conditional phrase also leaves open the possibility that the connection here, and the importance, is not only to the place's history and the presence of the dead, but also, perhaps, to something else. Why else might this ground be proper to grow wise in? The final line, which offers the 'tag' about which Ian Hamilton complains, leaves open at least the possibility of a consideration of something bigger and more important than merely the dead lying round.[26] The speaker suggests that there may be something else special about this place, and while he resists thinking of its special importance as religious in any conventional way, he nonetheless ends the poem lacking the atheistic certainty and the anti-religious conviction he seemed to feel earlier in the poem. The 'if' shows his confidence slightly shaken and leaves the poem with an openness to more conventional possibilities for the importance of and potential wisdom in this ground.

The phrase 'if only' contains not only a shaking of confidence but also a kind of wistfulness; it is generally used to suggest wanting something, as in 'If only I had done this' or 'If only we could have that.' In 'Church Going' the phrase suggests a possibility of something bigger than just what follows it. 'Only because so many dead lie round' would change entirely the meaning of the final line, offering a clear confidence in its reasoning; but the addition of 'if' there opens a question and, just as the 'awkward reverence' of the beginning of the poem does, shows the struggle between competing beliefs and desires. The speaker may know what he wants to believe, but he is not able to convincingly demonstrate that he wholeheartedly believes it. And each time he tries to show the conviction of his beliefs, something, like a big 'if,' undermines it.

God is only mentioned directly once in this poem, in the clichéd phrase that is used as an irreverent joke: 'God knows how long.' In this case the phrase has a literal as well as a figurative meaning, having both the sense that no one really knows how long the church has held this 'brewed' silence and, literally, that God – if there is a God – must know since, after all, this is a church. However, a less punning possibility of God is left open in one other place in the poem, when the speaker observes that 'Power of some sort or other will go on/ In games, in riddles, seemingly at random.' This line uses the word 'power' in the sense of 'higher power' but without clarifying what that power might be, and the uncertainty of 'some sort or other' and 'seemingly' suggest that the speaker is far less assured in his views of belief than his earlier immature bravado indicated. The poem leaves us with the desire to *know* and with the resignation to not knowing but to continuing to search, likely fruitlessly. Not a deep and abiding faith, and not quite a pronounced atheism, but a willingness to pursue unanswerable questions and an acknowledgment that those questions exist and are fundamental to humanity; 'our compulsions' are not for finding answers but for admitting that there are questions. In this way the poem again opens itself up to an affiliation with readers by presenting its speaker not as knowing but as asking. He asks, though, in multiple ways and from various perspectives, allowing readers to feel a kinship with him in some part of the poem, if not throughout the whole work. While Booth calls Watson's term 'sacred' 'simply inappropriate to the dispassionate and empty sublimity' of Larkin's poetry, he nonetheless recognizes a distinct brand of religiosity in the poems, 'but the religion is an agnostic one, with no doctrine, no morality, no institutions and no personal god.'[27] And yet the suggestion of 'power' in the poem (which may, indeed, be 'Power' since the word begins a sentence and thus we cannot tell if it might have otherwise been capitalized) hints at a personal god, if not in the way that it is generally imagined. And while there may not be a single, agreed-upon doctrine or morality, the people the speaker imagines visiting the place all have a sense of doctrine and even a sense of morality – if only in their desire to be 'serious' – that recognizes something beyond secularism, if not for the speaker himself than for those others who populate the speaker's imagination.

Simon Petch comments that 'Church Going' is the only poem in *The Less Deceived* that is 'about learning rather than about being "undeceived." The speaker is struggling towards knowledge rather than working his way out of illusion.'[28] But the speaker is indeed working with ideas of illusion rather than just knowledge. Although he does say this ground 'was proper to grow wise in,' he also seems to think of religion not as knowledge but as a kind of necessary and longed-for illusion. Thus, the poem is actually about *unlearning* rather than moving towards knowledge: 'Church Going' 'is the story of a man struggling to divest himself of his twentieth-century secular rationalism.'[29] What the speaker already knows is, in fact, the problem here; his knowledge has replaced the possibility of belief. Again, like 'Reasons for Attendance,' this poem offers a tension between 'believing this' and 'believing that,' or, in this case, 'knowing this' and 'believing that;' the speaker's cerebral nature places him in the 'knowing' camp, but not satisfyingly so. In fact, his ability to 'know' and his confidence in knowing lead both to the sense of intellectual superiority that we see in so many of the poems and to the hesitant but undeniable envy he feels for the relative comfort of a rationality-trumping belief. He claims not to know what draws him to the place but feels some pleasure in being there nonetheless. The poem thus presents what his knowledge convinces him of and what his compulsions, his hunger, his gravitation towards churches tries to say to him but cannot. Knowledge here acts as a barrier that belief cannot permeate, which is reassuring in that it convinces the speaker of his fundamental rightness but disturbing because he longs for belief and sees such longing as both instinctual and, for him, unreachable. In the church, 'all our compulsions meet,' and yet its purpose is constantly becoming 'more obscure.'

Still, we must remember the distance between Larkin and his speakers. Despite the great openness to possibility Larkin presents in 'Church Going' and other poems, readers must remain wary of conflating the emotions and thoughts of the poems' speakers with a full truth about Larkin himself. Larkin seems, frankly, far less ambiguous about his lack of belief than his speakers do. Perhaps he has his moments of wistfulness, but often his presentations of religious sympathy come across as ready-made for his audiences. What is undebatable is Larkin's preoccupation with religion and the meaning it holds for others, if not for him. Nonetheless, he clearly has empathy for and understanding of those who do have faith; and he understands the connection at least to parts of it – perhaps not to the faith itself, but certainly to the idea of the tradition and the need for faith. When he tells Sutton, after a long string of profanity, that 'I think I shall start going to church,' the tone is obviously tongue-in-cheek (particularly since he follows the statement with 'What have I written? Thoughts suitable to a sanitorium'),[30] and yet the issue of religion is one that seems often to be on Larkin's mind, and not only – not even predominantly – in critical ways. Even as early as 1948, he writes wistfully to Sutton, 'in addition to sorrow I can't get used to the fact of death & am trying hard to accept it in a spirit of good faith. But really, what has one any faith in?'[31] He remains preoccupied with religion's attempts to comfort and with its ability to draw people to it in ways that are meaningful to them. 'No one could help hoping Christianity was true, or at least the happy ending – rising from the dead and our sins forgiven. One longs for these miracles, and so in a sense one longs for religion.'[32] His claims of atheism are probably theologically true for him, but his interest in religion lies both in the externalities of religion – the buildings, the relics, the music, the people – and the ways in which belief comforts and reassures others. And while he is almost too desperate to convince Hamilton of his pure secularism, in other places, including the poems, he goes to great lengths to empathize, or to show speakers empathizing, with the religious attachments of his believers.

Larkin's appearance on *Desert Island Discs* certainly shows him trying to make himself as palatable to the public and as 'ordinarily British' as possible, but it is nevertheless striking that he chooses two overtly religious records for overtly religious reasons. He has already expressed, in at least one published interview and one radio program, that anything to do with religion goes down well with the public, and he may have had that in mind when choosing his discs for the popular program with Roy Plomley. He also may have wanted to temper some of the less mainstream jazzy records with more recognizable choices. (This tendency may also explain his choice of Edward Elgar when 'I should just want to lie back and think of England... the Midlands, the South-West Midlands, the meadows, the rivers, the occasional church and cathedral.' This nostalgia sounds more like Betjeman than Larkin, but he presents himself as a much less cynical and more conventionally patriotic and religious character on the desert island.) Even aside from his nostalgic mention of churches as part of England's landscape about which he likes to 'lie back and think,' he tells Plomley that 'I should want something for Sundays, which suggests Church Music.'[33] Is this Philip Larkin speaking? He should want something for Sundays? Is that to suggest that he wouldn't listen to Louis Armstrong or Bessie Smith – two of his other choices – on Sundays because of religious feeling for the day? To learn that Larkin, so firm in his proclamations of atheism, determines musical choices through a kind of aesthetic Sabbath observance is surprising for anyone who knows him at all beyond his poems. Even for a close reader of the poems who fully conflates the speaker with the author, this kind of religious attachment would be odd. But Larkin here uses music as a kind of marker of ordinariness and, furthermore, of likeability. He presents himself throughout the *Discs* program as an utterly loveable poet archetype and uses church music as a marker of that model. With some noticeable differences from the opinions expressed in his letters, he tells Plomley that, being on a desert island, 'I suspect I should miss people and society in general;' that 'over the years I've come to think that I rather like work;' that 'I certainly don't have a great mass of unpublished poems;' that 'I have been very gratified by the offer of [honorary doctorates];' and that he writes so that even somebody 'who has never met you and perhaps isn't even living in the same cultural society as yourself... will read and so get the experience that you had and that forced you to write the poem.' While none of these answers is exactly untrue (except perhaps for the great mass of unpublished poems, depending on how one defines a 'great mass'), the jocularity of tone and smoothing of rough edges around the answers shows a conscious attempt at making himself pleasant and living up to a kind of popular image. He does unashamedly admit to his lack of attachment to formal religion on the program as well, but he also claims that 'Church music is a kind of music I like very much in the same way as jazz,' which, if true, is not something he talked about much. For all the hundreds of pages of writing about jazz – in the reviews, the letters, the personal essays – the subject of its similarities to Church music just is not there.

He also suggests to Plomley that perhaps 'agnostics are naturally romantic about religion,' another assertion that seems contrary to other statements about his religious feeling. It is interesting to note, as well, that he refers to himself here as an 'agnostic,' a milder and more palatable term than the more inflammatory 'atheist' he usually uses. He had written in 'The Savage Seventh' in 1959 that 'it was that verse about becoming again as a little child that caused the first sharp waning of my Christian sympathies. If the Kingdom of Heaven could be entered only by those fulfilling such a condition I knew I should be unhappy there.'[34] In a review of the poets Vernon Scannell and Peter Redgrove for *Guardian* in1960, consciously channeling Shaw, he writes, 'What is religion? Lies. What is patriotism? Lies. What is our hope for the future, our faith in ourselves, our love of our neighbor? Lies, lies, lies...'. Perhaps a poem like 'Church Going' hints at this romance, but for other audiences, outside of the very large audience of *Desert Island Discs*, he chooses not to articulate the 'natural romance' he may feel for religion.

As if his choice of Thomas Tallis' Forty-part Motet to be used as 'Sunday music' isn't enough, just two records later, Larkin explains, 'Well, I would like a record for Christmas. That argues that I would only play it once a year but I would probably play it more often than that. ... This suggests to me... the Christmas of the illuminated manuscripts and the books of hours with the red and blue robes and the gold crowns and the gold haloes and the snow, and so forth.'[35] This statement is interesting not merely because it is so out of character but also because it demonstrates sentimental feelings for the accoutrements of Christmas. Throughout his *Desert Island Discs* appearance, Larkin remains perfectly accepting of religious tradition, not hostile at all, which demonstrates both the tension we see in the poems' attitudes towards religion and also the canny way in which he presents himself as a man of the people. His apparent affinity for religiosity, if not religion itself, highlights a divide in his poems as well: religion is separable into several parts, and the theological segment is not necessary to having religious feeling and attachments to other aspects of religion, including its artistry and its ability to fulfill some instinctual human need.

This desire to recognize something fundamentally natural about religious belief is presented as well in a poem that offers more distance between the speaker and religion. In 'Faith Healing,' another poem that deals with religion but in a way that involves the speaker less personally in the poem's action, Larkin presents a scene as ambiguous as that of 'Church Going.' The poem begins, typically, with a description of a scene as presented from afar: a group of women file into a room dominated by a single male figure, a religious leader, dressed respectably and formally. Stewards push the nondescript women towards this silver-haired man,

> Within whose warm spring rain of loving care
> Each dwells some twenty seconds.

Here the sarcasm increases as the speaker points out the preacher's hypocrisy in promising these women something he obviously cannot deliver.

While the poem could easily be read as condescending toward gullible believers, whose gullibility is here compounded by their all being women, and toward their leaders, who prey on their inanity, it also offers moments of empathy and understanding that confuse what might otherwise be a clear message about the corruption of religion. The fact that the preacher's 'loving care' is lavished on each woman for only 'some twenty seconds' shows that the preacher's proclaimed love is superficial at best and, at worst, a complete deception. The women, too, are criticized and condescended to by the speaker, who speculates that some of the women 'sheepishly stray' from the central figure while others remain paralyzed there

> ... twitching and loud
> With deep hoarse tears, as if a kind of dumb
> And idiot child within them still survives
> To re-awake at kindness.

The insult of these lines is inescapable and leads readers like Germaine Greer to call the ideas in Larkin's poems 'anti-intellectual, racist, sexist, and rotten with class consciousness.'[36] But such analyses work only if one reads sections of the poem – like the one above – in isolation from the rest of the text. A reading of the whole work complicates this uncontextualized interpretation and allows John Banville to write that 'Faith Healing' is 'a poem that no true misogynist could have written.'[37]

In the third stanza, for instance, the speaker changes his pronouns to show his sympathy for the women and his willingness to affiliate himself with them, noting that

> In everyone there sleeps
> A sense of life lived according to love.

What seems to have been a harsh judgment against the women who fall so easily for the preacher's obvious performance becomes a larger statement about human nature and the human need for love. Larkin's telling use of pronouns again underscores the universalizing tendencies in what seems initially to be a poem of unremitting critique. The move from a discussion of 'the women' in the poem's opening lines to the use of 'everyone' – a general and obviously inclusive pronoun – in the last stanza not only tempers the earlier appraisal of these 'twitching,' 'dumb,' 'sheepish' women but includes the speaker of the poem with them, implicitly noting that his fundamental tendencies are the same as theirs and, by extension, the same as the readers'. In addition, the 'some' and 'others' dichotomy the speaker had just established in the second stanza, presenting the women as animals or hysterics, is rethought in the third stanza with a self-inclusive effacement: 'some' think of love as the difference they could effect on others, but others feel love as something that would have fuelled and motivated them. By including the speaker in the 'everyone' of this later dichotomy, Larkin presents a speaker open to questions and willing to acknowledge his part in a common humanity, even one that has the potential to be unappealing and irrational.

Just as the speaker of 'Church Going' comes to realize at the end of the poem that seriousness is a valuable goal, which he may hold for himself and which the church (but not the Church) may provide, the speaker of 'Faith Healing' ultimately reveals his recognition that love is a human necessity and that it may be provided by religion, even religion that seems to be a sham. The sympathy in this poem is not for religion itself, but religion permits the speaker to see more clearly the hunger for love (like the hunger for seriousness in 'Church Going') and understand how intertwined are the secular desire for love and the religious desire for belief, how easily they meld. And for those many who cannot find love elsewhere, like the women in the poem but not exclusively like those women, they look to the imaginary love of 'the voice above/ Saying *Dear child.*' The poem's criticism of what is presented as an elaborate lie is consistently condemning, but its assessment of those who are taken in by the lie is surprisingly sympathetic. The change in tone near the end of this poem – from an outsider's criticism to an inclusive sympathy – is unexpected and, as in so many of Larkin's poems, presents multiple sides of an issue. Readers are left to wonder whether the first tonality is the one we trust – in this case, the one that criticizes the American preacher and derides the almost ridiculous women – or if the final, developed, empathetic voice – the one that universalizes the women's experiences and internalizes their deep needs – has the figurative, as well as the literal, final word.

Andrew Swarbrick recognizes that the women of the poem, at least initially, 'are victims not only of delusion, but of a narrator who seems determined to mock them.' But, he adds, 'even at their most foolish and ugly, there is compassion for them, not explicitly stated but suggested in the poem's narrative technique which situates us in the women's collective consciousness.'[38] But the compassion is not merely suggested and is, at least in those couple universalizing lines, explicitly stated. By opening the possibility that the speaker himself contains 'a sense of life lived according to love,' and that we readers also contain that sense, the poem explicitly sympathizes with the women and show compassion for their neediness in an unforgiving and too loveless world. As Swarbrick wisely notes, 'Indeed, *The Whitsun Weddings* repeatedly thinks of 'being them:' Mr Bleaney, the widow, the women in 'Faith Healing,' all of them in some way damaged, or failures, or casualities.'[39] A great strength of the religious-themed poems is the extent to which the speaker imagines himself as someone else, as a believer, and so the insularity and self-absorption of which Larkin is often accused is almost always present in the poems but almost never consistent throughout each work. The poems often begin with harsh judgment and a sense of the speaker's superiority and then open up to a more sympathetic ambivalence and a genuine attempt to imagine the experience of being other and to embody, at least for a few moments, the other. In fact, 'Church Going' and 'Faith Healing' speak directly to the issue of insularity by presenting a speaker who revels in his solitary, secular superiority until he begins to question that stance and, eventually, moves toward a posture of understanding others, if not being in full agreement with them.[40]

The speaker's rationality prevents him from fully exiting himself, which leads to the sense that he remains detached and superior, but that posture, too, is ultimately framed as a failure on the metacognitive speaker's part rather than as arrogant self-satisfaction. The last stanza of 'Faith Healing' begins by quoting the preacher's earlier question to the naïve and searching women:

> What's wrong! Moustached in flowered frocks they shake:
> By now, all's wrong.

The preacher asks 'What's wrong' without really meaning it, 'scarcely pausing' for the women to answer him. When the speaker rephrases that question as an aghast exclamation, he similarly insults the women, not through neglect but through ridicule, noting their moustaches, their unfashionable dresses, and their ludicrous behavior. Unlike the preacher, though, who moves past his question of 'what's wrong' to clasp the women's heads 'abruptly,' the speaker of the poem discontinues his mocking lines and suddenly seems to reconsider himself: 'By now, all's wrong.' That 'all' is all-encompassing. It is not merely in regard, anymore, to what is wrong with the women but what is wrong with him too; and in case we have missed this inclusiveness, the second half of that line moves from a distanced discussion of the moustached and frocked women to a general statement about people, their needs and unifying qualities. The preacher remains separate and condescending throughout the poem; the speaker began that way too but reconsiders that stance and presents it, ultimately, as both unfair and self-deluding.

What seems to interest Larkin about religion in both 'Church Going' and 'Faith Healing,' then, is not the way that organized religion works but the way that it appeals to something fundamental in people. His use of the pronoun 'one' in the final stanzas of both poems moves the speaker away from the distanced judgment-making of the early stanzas and towards a more nuanced understanding of human tendency and human need. And, of course, the use of 'one' also opens the possibility that the speaker is himself included in his depictions of people's spiritual needs. Modulating from the distanced 'they' and 'them' of the poems' early stanzas, and the condescending name-calling of 'dubious women,' 'some ruin-bibber,' or 'Christmas addict,' and the insulting descriptions of the women's 'thick tongues' and moustaches, the speaker presents universal descriptions that encompass both the seemingly ignorant religion-seekers and himself.

The reader seems to be included as well, and so also cannot stand entirely outside this scene, and, because of the universalizing statements, cannot continue to judge either the women (as the speaker initially does) or the speaker himself, since in both poems he is included, albeit passively, in the speaker's humanitarian awakening. As in 'Church Going,' Larkin almost sneakily persuades the reader to judge with his speakers at the beginning of the poem and feel, as the speaker does, condescension towards and superiority to the poem's subjects by stating his criticisms of the subjects as though they are foregone conclusions and simple binaries. By aligning readers with the speaker this way, the speaker's self-probing prompts similar behavior on the part of the reader, who cannot remain complacently judgmental throughout the whole poem. This rhetorical move both destabilizes readers and manipulates their expectations for poetic conventions; readers likely anticipate a speaker who knows his feelings and expresses them rather than one who uses the poem as a means of developing, and radically altering, his feelings. Larkin's poetry is thus discomfiting, and Larkin considers the reactions his readers will have without enabling them to inhabit the easiest or most comfortable readerly position. His ability to move readers not only physically through the scene but temporally through his speaker's discoveries and developments prevents them from occupying a distanced reader's role or from passing dispassionate judgment.

Janice Rossen argues that 'Faith Healing' 'clearly suggests an attitude of contempt for women on the part of the poet, and also a deeply rooted fear of them' and adds that 'part of the problem inherent in religion, as Larkin portrays it, is that it does not have any power to unite anyone to something greater than him or herself.'[41] But these statements overlook the potential inclusion of the speaker himself and intentional manipulation of pronouns from the first to the third stanzas of the poem. They also ignore the obviously uniting elements of the final stanza, in which universal emotions and needs are present, oblivious to issues of gender or nationality that were presented as central earlier in the poem. In other words, Rossen's interpretation does not allow for the development of the speaker's character throughout the course of the poem, despite the fact that unstable and inconsistent characters are hallmarks of Larkin's style. The surety of early stanzas, again and again, is replaced by a questioning introspection, but Rossen approaches the poems as though the speaker's opinions are fully formed from the start rather than works in progress.

Simon Petch notes the development of the speaker in 'Church Going,' writing that 'the most interesting aspect of 'Church Going' is the development of the speaker's attitude; and so unobtrusive is the poet's technique in this respect that by the time we have become involved in the gravity and seriousness of the end of the poem we may have forgotten the casually informal tone of the poem's opening stanzas.'[42] We may indeed have forgotten that attitude, but it seems more likely that we would have been confused by it. We think we had understood the speaker initially, and then we find ourselves startled by the change in his manner and come to realize that the whole poem was a process of exploration rather than a confirmation of the speaker's initial posture. The question of whether we are more willing to trust the outlook of the first stanzas or the more pensive attitude of the final stanzas is thus less applicable than whether we are able to move through the stages of the speaker's thought process with him and see the continuing discomfort that is masked first by immaturity and later by more staid speculation. Neither the beginning nor the ending of the poem offers answers, but by considering equally the beginning and ending, we are able to see that 'Church Going' and 'Faith Healing' are not poems about answers but about ongoing questions of self-definition and of the individual's relationship to his fellow humans.

In both these poems, but most obviously in 'Faith Healing,' the speaker's condescension toward the masses, borne of his cerebrality, is almost a desire rather than a truth for the speaker, who wants to remain separate from the masses and superior in his separation, but who finds himself drawn to these masses: to observing them but also to understanding their ways of thinking and ways of feeling and to finding parallels between them and the self-inclusive 'one' or 'everyone' the speaker invokes with such apparent authority. He wishes to keep himself apart from others, as is demonstrated so clearly in the physical and emotional separateness of the speaker in these religion poems as well as 'Reasons for Attendance' and poems on non-religious topics, but the lives of the masses consistently engage him and so his desire for intellectual remove is tempered as the poems progress by attempts to lessen the distinctions between himself and others and to find places of emotional intersection. 'Faith Healing' illustrates this pull toward the believers who begin as the subjects of scorn, and thus the criticism of the poem ends up applying not to the praying women but only to the preying preacher. He, like the speaker, had initially posited himself as superior to the women but, unlike the speaker, he is never redeemed through an eventual leveling with the masses. Larkin's speaker, by developing beyond his initial self-righteous impressions of the scene, fails in his attempts to maintain full intellectual separation from the masses of women, but he far surpasses the morality of the preacher by ultimately identifying with the needs, if not the beliefs, of the believers.

The third most evidently religious of Larkin's poems is 'Water,' written in 1954, the same year as 'Church Going,' but not published until ten years later in *The Whitsun Weddings*. This poem is often read as an explicitly secular approach to religiosity, as by Rossen, who says that the poem 'offers a deliberately detached, unemotional view of religion, and perhaps constitutes something close to Larkin's ideal in the matter'[43] and also by Swarbrick, who argues that 'the poem makes use of the traditionally religious associations of water (as in baptism) and secularises them.'[44] Certainly the tensions between religious and secular are less pronounced here than in 'Church Going' and 'Faith Healing,' particularly since the speaker himself is unconflicted in 'Water' and does not change his attitude during the course of this short poem. He simply presents a brief hypothetical situation (with the 'If' of the poem appearing here in the first line rather than the last) and says that the symbolism for his religion would be essentially identical to already existing religious symbolism but without any mention of a deity.

> If I were called in
> To construct a religion
> I should make use of water.

Most readers note the similarity between the imagery of water in the poem and in Christianity, as Swarbrick comments on the use of water in baptism. Others also find the symbolism Larkin chooses to be explicitly Christian, like Roger Day, who calls Larkin's 'devout drench' 'a colloquial description of the basis of Christian life – the Sacrament of Baptism' and notes that 'the water in a glass would be turned to the East (which saw the birth of Christianity).'[45] Richard Palmer notes that, in 'Water,' 'every image or idea resonates with long established religious practice, Christian or otherwise,'[46] but nonetheless finds Larkin's water imagery to be almost exclusively Christian, noting, for instance, that the 'all-capable flood' from the poem 'Going' suggests 'both baptism and the Holy Spirit, carrying us safe to the shores of heaven.'[47] Janice Rossen writes similarly that 'in the religion which he would construct, a prominent role would be given to the images of baptism and rebirth.'[48]

Interestingly, to readers outside the Christian tradition, perhaps the most notable thing about Larkin's choice of water as opposed to a more obviously and exclusively Christian symbol (say, a Cross or Crucifix) is that water is almost universally religious and far from exclusively Christian. While the 'furious devout drench' may most closely resemble baptism for Christian readers, for Muslim readers it probably sounds most like *ghusl*, the daily ablutions in preparation for prayer, following sex, in order to touch the Koran, before feasts, and as part of the burial rituals. For Jews, it sounds like the *mikveh*, in which the devout dunk themselves entirely before marriage and in preparation the annual Day of Repentance and in which women immerse themselves monthly. For Hindus the phrase almost certainly conjures images of the daily morning washing ritual and the mandatory bath before entering a Temple. Adherents of Shinto may think of the 'devout drench' as the ever-present preparatory water purification before worship or the holiness ascribed to waterfalls. The liturgy of all of these non-Christian religions, too, relies on water imagery. Judaism and Islam use the story of the Great Flood, as Christianity does, but with different nuances of interpretation; Judaism emphasizes the crossing of the Red Sea and miracles that occurred with a kind of 'devout drench' there; both Hinduism and Zoroastrianism have Great Flood stories central to their liturgies.[49] While Larkin may not have been intimately familiar with all of these variations on religious water usage, he nonetheless chose the symbol most widely used across all varieties of religions and least exclusive to a particular religious denomination, despite the many readers who see the poem as posited directly against, or alongside, Christianity.

Larkin's argument in 'Water' is not for or against religion, exactly, but in favor of a recognition of human connection to a single symbol. The universality of water as a religious symbol is underscored in this poem, which forgoes an emphasis on differences among religions, or on privileging one religion above another, and instead shows that the basic tendencies towards 'constructing a religion' are universal and inherently human. The final image of the poem – a raised glass of water, 'in the east. ... Where any-angled light/ Would congregate endlessly' – suggests a unity among believers of any denomination and those outside of established faith who might, for unstated reasons, have been 'called in/ To construct a religion.' Of course the speaker 'should make use of water' (with the dual meaning of 'should:' both 'would do' and 'ought to do') because everyone else who has constructed a religion has made use of water, and the speaker, in his apparent secularism, feels and submits to the same fundamental tendencies as all other religious founders. The poem, like 'Church Going' and 'Faith Healing,' highlights a fundamental need that religion can fulfill and speaks to something that the speaker of the poems believes to be instinctive; the instinct draws some people to supernatural belief, some to superstition, and others to rationality, but all three of these poems underscore the fact of a similar tendency that prompts such behaviors in everyone.

Swarbrick reads 'Water' as a poem of personal identity, 'even to make oneself different from oneself,' much in the vein of 'This Whitsun Weddings' or 'Lines on a Young Lady's Photograph Album;' but he also notes that 'the light in the final image represents coherence, difference becoming unity.'[50] While one might read the poem personally, the unity Swarbrick observes need not be merely personal, and nothing in the poem suggests that the speaker thinks autobiographically about his theological choice. If one sees the choice of water as a universalizing symbol, then the unity Swarbrick reads in the final lines of the poem is more communal than individual unity. The poem thus recognizes something about 'everyone,' just as 'Faith Healing' does; as Rossen writes, the poem 'remains unencumbered by fonts, rood-lofts, buttresses, carved choirs and other significant though largely uninterpretable religious symbols which connect the church with England, tradition, and a sense of nationalism.'[51] It creates this separation not just by dismissing the import of these specific symbols but by choosing a universal symbol that connects to audiences in a variety of ways and moves well outside the insular British, secular-Christian world with which Larkin is most frequently associated.[52]

All of these poems deal with a topic in which, according to popular lore, Larkin had no interest and of which he had very little knowledge. Certainly he presents himself as uninterested and ignorant much of the time. And yet these poems demonstrate not only knowledge of the trappings and details of religion but also thoughtfulness about the impetus for religion. Repeatedly, the poems promote the notion that the impulse that manifests itself in the particularities and details of religious belief – with all its superficialities and potential for corruption – is universal and can lead to love, to seriousness, and to 'congregation' in its best possible sense. And, as is implicit in all three poems, it can lead to basic understanding and to empathy as well. The speakers of these poems model for readers how a position that focuses on the problematic specifics of religion can be opened up into a position simultaneously more inclusive and more deeply understanding of human nature. These poems also present an understanding of difference and argue that certain human tendencies remain consistent regardless of how they manifest themselves, thus presenting religion as one of several options for negotiating the self in the world. While this option is not one that the poet himself has chosen, it is one that his poems acknowledge and work to understand at the same time that they push readers towards similar multivalent approaches to their own strongly-held beliefs, whatever those might be.

The empathy these poems present, not only for their created characters but also for their implied readers, demonstrates one of the most profound ways that Larkin reaches out to audience. And so, in addition to speaking explicitly about and to his readers; using multiple voices to create dialogue as well as confound reader expectations; writing candidly about the interaction between individuals and memory; and presenting himself and his speakers as members of a viewing, listening audience, Larkin also chooses a topic about which his own skeptical views are widely known and offers nuanced connections to people whose views are utterly different from him own. The presumed incomprehensibility of others' minds is made comprehensible in these religiously-themed poems, wherein a poet so often accused of insularity, provinciality, narrow-mindedness and self-absorption creates characters who reach outside themselves, look elsewhere for answers, expand their perspectives, and embrace the needs of others. And, in doing so within the confines of the poem, with fictional speakers and fictional characters, Larkin reaches out to his real readers as well, illustrating for them the process of moving from self-confidence to self-questioning and from judgmentalism to empathy.

Conclusion: Two Philips

And finally, an anecdote. An acquaintance recently said this to me: 'My problem with Larkin is that he's a dirty old man. Exemplar of Englishness and all that, but just a dirty old man in the end. And I think he's an example of the worst sort of Freudianism.' Not sure what he meant, I asked him to explain himself. 'Well, you know, 'They fuck you up, your mum and dad,'' he offered by way of explanation. I suggested that 'This Be the Verse' isn't really typical of Larkin and listed 'Dockery and Son' or 'Church Going' as offering more nuanced views of procreation and a more thoughtful solemnity about life. 'Oh, I only really know "They fuck you up," he told me, 'so maybe you're right about his other poems. I don't know.' At the conclusion of this conversation, this man who admittedly knew almost nothing of Larkin offered a final observation of which I had often thought myself: 'He's just like Philip Roth in that way. People love him, but he's a dirty old man too.' And so, now, after having offered my own interpretations of Larkin's poems, I would like to present a brief comparison of these two very different (but often similarly received) writers and to suggest that Larkin precedes – subtly, quietly, and with much self-conscious masquerading – the postmodern tradition of the great American novelist who so candidly confuses author and narrator; who so boldly upends audience expectations; and who so assuredly forces his audience to confront its assumptions and readerly conventions.

Certainly Philip Roth's critical reception has, in important ways, mirrored Larkin's, with the important exception that Roth's reputation suffered early and has been, largely, redeemed while Larkin's reputation, taking its greatest hit posthumously, continues to require concerted efforts at redemption. The characteristics that have often been emphasized in their writings, however, are remarkably similar. Roth, for instance, is often seen as a quintessentially American artist. He is said to capture a particular kind of 'Americanness' through his evocation of American history and of suburban landscapes as well as certain fundamentally 'American success stories.'[1] Catherine Morley argues that Roth's *American Trilogy* 'self-consciously addresses the role of the writer in the construction of a mythical national identity' and calls the focus of the three novels 'the dream of a self-reliant American identity.'[2] And although Roth's early work in particular was often affixed with the 'Jewish-American' label, his more recent pieces have become, in the words of Max Falkowitz, 'vital American reading,' leaving aside the ethnic qualifier.[3] Like Larkin, Roth writes discomfitingly about sex and gender and uses unexpectedly foul language.[4] In addition to widespread discomfort with the novelist's use of obscenity and vulgarity, many critics have accused Roth of, at best, insensitivity toward women and, at worst, encouraging active hatred of women.[5]

Philip Larkin, too, has long been labeled a representative of national identity. Seamus Heaney points to him as the embodiment of a particular British voice, saying that Larkin is 'urban modern man, the insular Englishman, responding to the tones of his own clan, ill at ease when out of his environment. He is a poet, indeed, of composed and tempered English nationalism.'[6] John Bayley argues that Larkin's late poems are 'the most refined and accurate expression possible of a rational as well as a universal area of awareness' and that 'they are very English in fact.'[7] Simon Petch calls Larkin 'representatively English,'[8] and Donald Davie claims that Larkin represents 'British poetry at the point where it has least in common with American.'[9] John Osborne cites no fewer than seven additional scholars who emphasize 'Larkin's position as a belated national poet' and his 'enduring Englishness.'[10] Larkin's depiction of rural scenes, his frequent play with ideas of 'here and elsewhere,' and his self-presentation as wary of travel have prompted many readers to see him as possessing a representative Britishness.[11]

Accusations of vulgarity, not merely in the sense of obscenity but also in the broader sense of 'commonness' with which Irving Howe uses it in relation to Roth, have followed Larkin too, particularly since the publication of his letters. Lisa Jardine asks how students can be advised seriously to study Larkin's poetry when the student who consults a copy of the *Selected Letters* 'confronts a steady stream of casual obscenity, throwaway derogatory remarks about women, and arrogant disdain for those of different skin colour or nationality,' all of which are, according to Jardine, evident in the poems as well. Joseph Bristow writes, of the "chummy democratic appeal" of Larkin's obscenity, that it 'is informed by prejudices that are not by any means as ordinary, commonplace, or acceptable as the poetic language in which they are so plainly spelled out.'[12] According to Bristow, Larkin was transformed from 'the bard of the nation who spoke both of and to an Englishness we could cherish into the man from whom we could only recoil.'[13] In particular, Bristow highlights Larkin's use of ' "fuck," "crap" and "piss" ' as 'four-letter words issued from a conservatism that the nation had increasingly come to despise'[14] while Peter Ackroyd calls Larkin 'a foul-mouthed bigot.'[15] In all these cases, the use of taboo words in the poems is interpreted as reflecting something insidious about Larkin's beliefs, just as Roth's use of vulgarity in the novels is seen as a moral failing on the author's part.

Perhaps most noticeably, both writers' works are read in almost exclusively biographical ways despite offering complex and contradictory insights into how biographical – or not – their writings really are. Their populism, provincialism, sexism, gender bias, self-absorption, and depressive attitudes are found almost indiscriminately in their works and their lives. About Larkin, John Osborne points out that 'the stark truth is that the overwhelming majority of the poems tell one nothing about the gender, race, class or nationality of either their narrators or their addressees, but that both the poet's champions and detractors fill in the missing information by jumping to the conclusion that the protagonist is always and only a white, male, middle-class Englishman named Philip Larkin.'[16] In other words, as well-intentioned as readers may be, they seldom avoid assuming that Larkin's characters resemble – or, even more problematically, are – Larkin himself. Roth's novels suffer a similar fate, and Carlin Romano goes so far as to defend the imposition of biography onto Roth's novels' characters: 'Criticism 101 warns tyro students not to confuse protagonist and author. But here's a tip from Criticism 501: When you're still getting indistinguishable jerk characters like Kepesh after more than 20 novels, that's the author talking.'[17] As Kevin R. West more moderately writes, 'Critics have not been altogether kind to Kepesh, especially in his egotism and attitude toward women, and this unkindness toward his character often mirrors as unkindness toward Roth himself.'[18] Osborne and West make explicit the way in which both writers' characters are read not as creative and fictional but as derivative and autobiographical. The conflation of the lives and works of these two writers has resulted in Larkin's poetry being criticized for what he did in his life and Roth's life criticized for what he writes in his novels and stories.[19]

The critical barrier between life and work is almost entirely erased for both of these writers, but that erasure is an error. For both of them, though, this erasure is at least in part an honest error, committed because the writers invite it. Both of them play with their audiences by intentionally complicating the relationship between author and speaker and by asking readers to question the authenticity of their writings' voices.[20] Larkin hints, on more than one occasion, that his poetry is 'true,' telling *Paris Review*, for example, that 'you've seen this sight, felt this feeling, had this vision, and have got to find a combination of words that will preserve it by setting it off in other people. The duty is to the original experience,' thus implying that his poems are somehow empirical, even reportage.[21] As we can see from criticism and analysis of 'The Whitsun Weddings,' though, that reporter's sensibility is a conscious falsehood on Larkin's part. His claims that the poem 'only needed writing down' and that 'anybody could have done it' are easily dismissed by James Booth and, more importantly, by the poem itself, which is entirely unlike reportage regardless of Larkin's (most likely tongue-in-cheek) claims.

Roth's play with audience expectations is, by now, fairly well recognized and thoughtfully analyzed by a number of his best current readers. Larkin's work, however, is less frequently subjected to similar critical analysis and continues largely to be read as straightforward and uncomplicated, as though the Larkin of the interviews can be fully trusted, a trap into which Roth's writing is less likely to fall due to his more obvious game-playing. For instance, many readers have noted Larkin's dismissive treatment of the American who misreads 'Church Going' as 'a great religious poem,' about which Larkin remarks, 'he knows better than me – trust the tale and not the teller, and all that stuff.' Readers take Larkin's apparent frustration with D.H. Lawrence's sentiment to mean that readers should trust the teller above the tale, seemingly in keeping with the most straightforward possible interpretations of Larkin's work, those that agree with his statement that one can't say much about his work and that, once one has read the poem, it is all perfectly clear and requires no further explication.[22] Larkin implies, in an answer to Ian Hamilton about 'Church Going,' that the speaker is the equivalent of the writer, suggesting that because he (Larkin) emphasizes his ignorance of church architecture and detail in the poem, he (the poem's speaker) is identically ignorant of such things. Such hints at the identity of the poem's speaker jibes well with his answers in others interviews about the same poem: '['Church Going'] came from the first time I saw a ruined church in Northern Ireland, and I'd never seen a ruined church before – discarded. It shocked me.'[23] These answers that suggest Larkin's inseparability from his speaker fit in well with readers' perceptions of Larkin as an utterly personal poet. Of course, the church in 'Church Going' is not ruined and discarded: it contains brownish flowers that had been cut for Sunday, and the speaker has to pause before entering to be sure that 'there's nothing going on,' so, presumably, the building cannot look as ruined or discarded as did the church that apparently inspired the poem.

Those superficial concerns aside, though, what most readers overlook is Larkin's own playing with his placement as the poem's speaker in the interview: just a few moments after he subtly suggests that he is present in the poem, he distances himself from the speaker of 'Church Going,' saying 'I think one has to dramatize oneself a little. I don't arse about in churches when I'm alone. Not much, anyway.' That final tag – 'not much, anyway' – manipulates readers precisely as Roth does, since Larkin had first implied that readers should trust the teller and not the tale – himself rather than the poem – and had at other times suggested that the poem was based on a personal and very real experience; but he then lets readers know that, in fact, the speaker of the poem is a 'dramatization' of the poet since the poet himself would not be found 'arsing about' in churches. And, finally, Larkin throws in, as an apparently unimportant aside, that he *does* sometimes 'arse about' in churches. The tone is obviously joking, but the implications for readers are profound and highlight the unknowability of Larkin's speakers as well as the conscious game-playing concerning his relationship to his speakers. Is Larkin the speaker of 'Church Going' or not? I believe he is not, because the creator of the poem is both more savvy and more self-aware than the speaker, but Larkin encourages us to believe that he is the speaker at the same time that he purposely distances himself from that speaker and then, subtly, lessens that distance.

In other words, as Roth names his protagonists 'Philip Roth,' presents characters who grew up in his exact circumstances, in his hometown, with a family identical to his, and then demands that readers recognize the fiction of his creations, so Larkin presents Larkinesque speakers with potentially autobiographical stories who are, subtly but unmistakably, pushing readers to see beyond those parallels and consider more complicated, multivalent possibilities for what his poems are doing.[24] While Roth is notably outspoken for his efforts at undermining readerly assumptions – and criticized for appealing too much to a scholarly audience – Larkin's similar attempts are largely ignored, and he is criticized for appealing too *little* to a scholarly audience. In large part, though, this ignoring of Larkin's subtle but unmistakable postmodern tendencies – the shifting speakers in 'Places, Loved Ones;' the rhetoric of false binary in 'Poetry of Departures;' the speaker as viewed subject in 'The Whitsun Weddings;' the reader implicated in the poem's action in 'Reasons for

Attendance,' 'The Old Fools,' and 'Faith Healing;' and the complicating of earlier works, building on and unsettling literary tradition, as in 'Sad Steps' and 'Sympathy in White Major' – develops from Larkin's successful creation of a persona and convincing arguments for his own simplicity. In addition, much like Roth, Larkin enacts his experimentalism in a genre that very much resembles a pre-Modern tradition from which it grows. Roth's novels in most ways resemble traditional novels just as Larkin's poems contain the major hallmarks of earlier poetic forms, and while Roth very explicitly manipulates ideas of characterization, history, truth, and fiction, Larkin raises similar questions but with more camouflage.[25] His ability to create nontraditional poetry within the confines of traditional form and using conventional language shows him occupying a unique place in twentieth-century verse, not as a loud and obvious practitioner of experimentalism but as someone who has thoughtfully taken stock of developments in his genre, who is completely familiar with and very much part of the trajectory of poetic development, and who is able to meet a public desire for accessibility and realism while offering profound innovations in character, persona, audience, and voice, among many other things.

The comparison between these two very different Philips – one British and one American, one born Christian and one Jewish, one a poet and one a novelist, one considered insufficiently intellectual and the other overly so – shows not only how similarly they have both been understood (and misunderstood) but can also illuminate directions in which Larkin criticism might move. The kind of criticism to which Roth's fiction has been subjected – a criticism that, at least in recent years, takes as its starting points Roth's intentional and ongoing manipulation of the reader and his undermining of the reader's expectations and received wisdom about novels – is a direction in which Larkin criticism could move as well. Larkin's poetry has such evident value beyond its ability to reflect details of Larkin's life that critics would do well to learn from the books of Debra Shostak, Derek Parker Royal, Ben Siegel and others who approach Roth's works with the presumptions of his sophistication, his thoughtfulness about the nature of writing and literary form, and his ability and desire to upset audience expectations. Larkin's work, while subtler, is no less sophisticated than Roth's and no less attuned to the concerns of genre, assumptions about authorial intention, and the significant ways in which including the reader in the text forces upon him necessary questions of his responsibility to the reading experience. Just as Shostak asserts that Roth's novels challenge readers 'to transcend the anxiety of the interpretive act, to embrace and be liberated by the duplicity of reality itself and not merely the duplicity of language,' so Larkin's poetry prompts readers to recognize the duplicity of language alongside the inevitable duplicity of the reader's role in the poem and the necessity of entangling himself in the unreal world created by the reality of the poem. Roth scholarship, for all its early similarities to Larkin scholarship, has moved well beyond finding parallels between the life and work and proving the work's literary worth by defending it against charges of populism and anti-intellectualism. Larkin deserves no less.

One final point of comparison may be useful here as well: Larkin's earliest literary works, those that I have barely mentioned in the preceding pages, were novels. He commented in many interviews that he really wanted to be a novelist but that novels didn't 'find' him the same way poetry did. He tells the *Observer* that 'You must realize I didn't want to write poems at all, I wanted to write novels. I still think novels are much more interesting than poems... I think they were just too hard for me.'[26] Three years later he reiterated to *Paris Review* that 'I wanted to 'be a novelist' in a way I never wanted to 'be a poet,' yes. Novels seem to me to be richer, broader, deeper, more enjoyable than poems' and that 'I didn't choose poetry: poetry chose me.'[27] Novels, he remarked several times, 'are about other people and poems are about yourself.'[28]

In one of his last interviews, in March of 1984, Larkin reiterates and clarifies his earlier statements about novels and poems:

> I say somewhere that poems are about yourself, whereas novels are about other people. I suppose I didn't really know enough about other people, or perhaps I wasn't interested enough in other people to be a novelist. At the same time, I do think that the novel, at its best, is a better picture of the human situation than the poem, because it has a broader impact; and the poem, or the lyric poem at any rate, is simply one emotion from one person; and OK, you do that and it's very piercing. But the novel is a kind of diffused impact of a great many emotions of a number of people, interacting and referring back to those circumstances and so on, which I think is much more difficult to do, but in the end much more impressive.[29]

These self-assessments seem to have very little to do with Larkin's actual poetry, however. In fact, his poems demonstrate an almost uncontrollable fascination with other people and endless attempts to inhabit and embody them. Larkin's poems are often misread as 'one emotion from one person,' but as my readings here have shown, they are far more complex than that assessment allows. In fact, almost none of the poems contains just 'one emotion,' and the wildly divergent criticisms of Larkin's poems demonstrate how impossible it is to pin a single emotion to any of his poems. The idea that Larkin's poems feature only 'one person' is belied by the poems as well, which often feature, or at least open themselves to the possibility of, multiple speakers, as Osborne has demonstrated of 'Sympathy in White Major' and I have shown in 'Places, Loved Ones' and 'Poetry of Departures,' among others. As I hope I have proven, Larkin's seemingly straightforward statement that poems are about oneself is brought into question by the actual poems, which do not support that assertion, or at least do not support it in the strictly autobiographical way that it might be interpreted. We might argue that Larkin's poems *are* about himself to the extent that they illustrate his humor, his multiplicity of voices, and the degree to which he plays games with his audience and undermines the received wisdom of the audience's passive role in the reading experience; but those kinds of 'personal' details do not seem restricted by genre, nor do they seem to be the sort of thing to which Larkin refers when he says that poems are 'about oneself.'

Larkin's novels, however interesting they are as precursors to his poems, never move beyond relatively standard storytelling to play with identity or to destabilize the role of audience in relation to speaker as so many of his poems successfully do. Roth's novels, however, constantly destabilize their readers and undermine expectations. We can see the ways in which Roth confounds audiences through his novels in both the texts themselves and in the critical responses to the texts. Throughout the decades of his work, we see Roth challenge readers to think more consciously about their own reading experience, to confront their expectations for the novel as a genre, and to challenge their assumptions about the relationship between writer and speaker. Larkin's poems, unlike his novels, embody similar concerns and push the genre's boundaries in similar ways, inviting interpretations that highlight the poem's internal contradictions and easy movement between truth and 'truth.'

Based on Larkin's poems, we might say that Philip Roth is the sort of novelist that Larkin would have liked to have been had his novelistic ambitions succeeded. While it is likely that Larkin would have publicly denied and made less explicit the concerns Roth enacts, Roth's fiction can nonetheless serve as a model of the audience concerns Larkin demonstrates and the ways in which literature can intentionally destabilize its audience and ask readers to question their complicity and their assumptions. Certainly the two writers' willingness to undermine literary decorum is parallel, but so is their conscious dividing of the pleasure-seeking audience from the scholarly audience. Larkin, as I have shown, thinks just as much about the scholarly audience as any other twentieth-century poet but pretends not to, while Roth certainly writes for the pleasure-seeker but uses language and conventions that seem ideal for literary critique. Perhaps because of this difference in their approaches and because of Roth's overt manipulations and Larkin's very subtle ones, Larkin's work has not been subjected to the same kind of metatextual criticism that Roth's has, but Larkin criticism has much room to develop in this direction.

My explorations in this project, drawing attention to Larkin's active engagement of audience in various ways – by directly addressing them, by imagining what it is like to *be* them, by leaving spaces for them in which they can place themselves – offer a reconsideration of Larkin and his verse. His interest in audience, his use of multiple voices, and his complicated approaches to past and present all suggest a forward-looking poet who understands the broad canon of literature (not merely British) and who plays games with his readers through intentionally misleading critical approaches to his work and the creation of a persona. His poems about temporality, jazz and religion specifically illustrate the complexity of his poetic creations and the unique ways he reaches out to his audiences. By recognizing what Larkin's poetry does – well beyond and quite apart from what he claims it does – we can both do justice to his marvelous work and begin to envision more fully the extent to which this supposedly self-absorbed poet writes for his readers, challenging us, confronting us, and ultimately asking us to take our role in the 'fundamental nexus between poet and audience' as seriously as he does.

Notes

Preface

1. Saussure has argued for this figurative back-and-forth in linguistic terms, while Bakhtin has presented it in terms of both conversation and literary texts; Stanley Fish's discussion of 'interpretative communities,' like Iser and Jauss' theories of production and reception, demonstrates the ways that interpretation is shaped not only by a fixed text but by the reader's interaction with the text, which is necessarily mutable.

2. I have chosen, throughout this project, to use masculine pronouns for the singular 'reader.' While in my case, the pronoun is inaccurate, I wish to be clear throughout the text that I refer to readers generally and not to myself in particular. I fear that the use of 'her' and 'she' may be unnecessarily distracting, and the use of plural pronouns is not always possible. My choice of masculine pronouns, therefore, is not one of politics or ideology but of practicality and clarity.

3. Easthope, Anthony. *Englishness and National Culture*. London: Routledge, 1999. p. 185.

4. Bakhtin, M.M. 'The Problem with Speech Genres.' *Speech Genres and Other Late Essays*. Eds Michael Holquist and Caryl Emerson. Austin, Texas: University of Texas Press, 1986. p. 94.

5. Bradford. Richard. *First Boredom, Then Fear*. London: Peter Owen Publishers, 2005. p. 76.

6. Motion, Andrew. *Philip Larkin: A Writer's Life*. New York: Farrar, Straus, Giroux, 1993.

7. Cooper, Stephen. *Philip Larkin: Subversive Writer*. Brighton: Sussex Academic Press, 2004.

8. Due to some ambiguity in Larkin's will, Anthony Thwaite was able to publish the letters, but one suspects that the publication would not have been Larkin's choice, despite his assertion, which Motion quotes in his defense of the publication, that 'Unpublished work, unfinished work, even notes towards unwritten work, all contribute to our knowledge of a writer's intentions' and his address to the Manuscripts Group of the Standing Conference of National and University Libraries on the 'Neglected Responsibility' of preserving writers' manuscripts as well as 'diaries, notebooks, letters to and from, even photographs and recorded tapes: anything, in fact, that makes up the archive of a creative writer's life and constitutes the background of his works' (*RW* 99). Larkin seems to believe that his private words will be destroyed rather than published, as when he tells Motion, 'When I see the Grim Reaper coming up the path to my front door I'm going to the bottom of the garden, like Thomas Hardy, and I'll have a bonfire of all the things I don't want anyone to see' (qtd. in Banville). Perhaps fear of his own impending death or the nature of his final illness prevented the implementation of such a plan.

9. B.J. Leggett wisely points out that this interview, with *The Paris Review*, was conducted in writing, so if Larkin hadn't known of Borges, which is unlikely, he had ample time to find out more before answering the question. His answer, when read, sounds like an honest immediate reaction to the question, but when the reader recognizes the interview situation and the amount of time potentially involved in producing each answer, he realizes that this innocence on Larkin's part was probably less genuine than it initially seems. In addition, Larkin seems to have been much better read than he lets on in interviews, as has been noted by James Booth, Andrew Swarbrick and others.

10. Shakespeare, John. 'Larkin's First Interview.' *The Times Literary Supplement.* 1 April 2009.

11. Stojkovic, Tijana. *Unnoticed in the Casual Light of Day: Philip Larkin and the Plain Style.* New York: Routledge, 2006. p. 150.

12. Garcia, Damaso Lopez. 'Post-Metropolitan Larkin.' *Hugarian Journal of English and American Studies.* Fall 2003. 81–9. p. 88.

13. Marsh, Nicholas. *Philip Larkin: The Poems.* Basingstoke: Palgrave Macmillan, 2007. p. 154.

14. Osborne, John. *Larkin, Ideology and Critical Violence: A Case of Wrongful Conviction.* Basingstoke: Palgrave Macmillan, 2008. p. 54.

15. Day, Gary. ' "Never Such Language Again": The Poetry of Philip Larkin.' *British Poetry from the 1950s to the 1990s: Politics and Art.* Eds Gary Day and Brian Docherty. New York: Macmillan, 1997. 33–47. pp. 46 and 34.

16. Motion, Andrew. *Philip Larkin.* London: Methuen, 1983. p. 11.

17. Larkin, Philip. *Required Writing: Miscellaneous Pieces.* New York: Farrar, Straus and Giroux, 1983. p. 82.

18. Banville, John. 'Homage to Philip Larkin.' *New York Review of Books.* 23 Feb. 2006. pp. 8–9.

19. Banville, 'Homage to Philip Larkin.'

20. J.R. Watson makes an excellent case for the parallels between Larkin and Browning, noting that 'for Browning (as, I think, for Larkin) there was a brave deception in the strong and engaging surface, which hid a complex and sensitive disturbance within' (Watson, J.R. 'The Other Larkin.' *Critical Quarterly* 1975. 347–60. p. 348).

21. Phelan, James. *Reading People, Reading Plots: Character, Progression, and the Interpretation of Narrative.* Chicago: The University of Chicago Press, 1989. pp. 5–7.

1 Larkin and Audience

1. *RW* p. 80. In this he anticipates Roland Barthes, among others, who argues in *S/Z* that the act of reading is equivalent to textual creation: 'to read is to struggle to name, to subject the sentences of the text to a semantic transformation' (Barthes, Roland. *S/Z.* New York: Hill and Wang, 1975. p. 92). By locating the text's very existence in the reader rather than in the physical body of the text, Larkin, like Barthes, both privileges the reader's experience and relinquishes some degree of authorial control over a fixed text.

2. *RW* pp. 293–4.

3. Rabinowitz, Peter. *Before Reading: Narrative Conventions and the Politics of Interpretation*. Ithaca, New York: Cornell University Press, 1987. p. 95. Rabinowitz also calls the narrative audience an 'imitation audience,' one that is privy to knowledge of certain cultural and social conventions and can thus understand the 'imitation of some nonfictional form (usually history, including biography and autobiography)' in which the novelist engages. Rabinowitz further argues that 'the narrator of the novel (implicit or explicit) is generally an imitation of an author' (p. 95).

4. While Rabinowitz writes of the novel as the point at which the actual audience and the narrative audience meet, Larkin – a self-proclaimed aspiring, and failed, novelist – creates poetic scenes that employ audience in ways very similar to novels and that feature miniaturized narrative structures but surprisingly detailed and complex characterizations.

5. To a great extent, readers have been taught similarly about poetry, and examples ranging from Donne to Browning to Eliot demonstrate that readers know better than to assume the poet is identical to the narrator of 'The Flea' or 'My Last Duchess' or 'The Love Song of J. Alfred Prufrock.' And yet, at least subtly, the perception of poetry as a more 'personal' genre has persisted, from the works of the so-called Confessional poets (about whose confessionalism much debate has arisen) to the popular perception that laymen, people in pain or love, and angsty teenagers might best express themselves through the writing of poetry. Again, this may lie simply in the genre's potential for brevity, but it may also be a function of what my students believe to be poetry's ability to 'mean anything to anyone' with no fixed rules of interpretation and to be a genre that is uniquely personal and, consequently, non-fictional. This layman's definition of poetry – 'Do you write poems? Me too!' – leads to more frequent conflation of speaker with artist in poetry than in novels.

6. Rabinowitz's concept of narrative and authorial audiences is related to Bakhtin's idea that all readers 'imagine to ourselves what the speaker *wishes* to say. And we also use this speech plan, this speech will (as we understand it), to measure the finalization of the utterance' ('The Problem of Speech Genres' p. 77). Thus, as we will see, Larkin's tendency to move from surety to questioning, rather than the more conventional pattern of a speaker who 'raises questions, answers them himself, raises objections to his own ideas, responds to his own objections, and so on' (p. 72) calls into question as well the finalization of his utterances, which ask for participation from readers in a way different from more conventional speech patterns. The poems' uncertain endings – their pattern of answering questions and then raising them, responding to objections and then raising them – leaves readers uncertain when and where they fit into the poems. In the way, Larkin manipulates traditional audience expectations through a re-visioning of discursive language.

7. Larkin, Philip. *Selected Letters*. Ed. Anthony Thwait. London: Faber and Faber, 1992. p. 6.

8. *SL* pp. 5–6.

9. Larkin, Philip. *All What Jazz*. New York: Farrar, Straus and Giroux, 1985. p. 18.

10. *RW* p. 80.

11. *RW* p. 92.

12. *RW* p. 82.
13. Osborne, *Larkin, Ideology, and Critical Violence*, pp. 51 and 56. By his statement about Modernist music, Osborne seems to mean that Larkin loved jazz, a modernist musical genre, rather than that he loved Schoenberg or Antheil or other classical Modernist composers. He writes 'by pretending that jazz only became Modernist in the 1940s he is able, at a cosmetic level, to square his love of the former with his supposed loathing of the latter' and further that 'whatever his claims to the contrary, then, Larkin's real critique of the Parker generation is not that it renders jazz threateningly Modernistic, but that it renders the jazz which had always been Modernistic less accessible, converting it into a minority cult and relinquishing the mass audience to the genuine but rhythmically less sophisticated pleasures of rock 'n' roll' (p. 31).
14. Larkin, Philip. *Further Requirements*. Ed. Anthony Thwaite. London: Faber and Faber, 2001. p. 49.
15. *RW* p. 74.
16. This all sounds pleasant enough but is hardly reinforced in his private correspondences: 'Life here varies from dreary to scarcely bearable... I've no friends and no gramophone and find this address far from satisfactory' (*SL* p. 248) and, in the same year as that pleasant interview with the *Observer*, he writes (among many other complaints), 'Have my 'Spring Cough,' along with my spring headache, spring aching bones, spring depression... I spend long hours slumped in front of the TV, holding a large glass of weak whisky & water, and watching sports and old films' (*SL* pp. 600–1).
17. *FR* p. 25.
18. *FR* p. 52.
19. *FR* p.48.
20. *FR* p. 52.
21. *RW* p. 60.
22. *RW* p. 65.
23. *RW* p. 79.
24. Swarbrick, Andrew. *Out of Reach: The Poetry of Philip Larkin*. Basingstoke: Palgrave Macmillan, 1997. pp. 55–7.
25. Petch, Simon. *The Art of Philip Larkin*. Sydney: International Scholarly Book Services, 1981. p. 55.
26. Rossen, Janice. *Philip Larkin: His Life's Work*. University of Iowa Press, 1989. p. 52.
27. Swarbrick, *Out of Reach*. p. 56.
28. Crosman, Robert. 'Do Readers Make Meaning?' *The Reader in the Text*. Eds Susan Rubin Suleiman and Inge Crosman Wimmers. Princeton University Press, 1980. p. 162.
29. Wolfgang Iser's discussion of blanks is also useful here. Iser argues that a speaker is comprehensible to the extent that his words benefit from 'observed connectibility,' which is disrupted by blanks. Iser posits that such blanks can 'point up the difference between literary and everyday use of language,' but 'they might also, as in the case of Larkin's verse, point up the difference between an authorial assertion and a reader's creation of meaning through his own placement in the blanks. The connectibility thus comes not simply from a reader's 'acts of ideation' but from an author's manipulation of blanks to create a place and a voice for the reader. Iser highlights everyday language as

distinct from the language of fiction, and exposition as employing language differently from fiction: 'the multiplicity of possible meanings must be constantly narrowed down by observing the connectability of textual segments, whereas in fictional texts the very connectability broken up by the blanks tends to become multifarious' (Iser, Wolfgang. *The Act of Reading: A Theory of Aesthetic Response*. Johns Hopkins University Press, 1978. p. 184). Larkin's verse, among other things, complicates this binary in that it is neither expository nor – at least in most readers' views – fictional. Its self-conscious hints at its own nonfictionality help to fill in most blanks for readers predisposed to biographical readings of the poems; once, however, poems are read as more closely aligned with fiction than with exposition, the blanks open themselves more obviously to places for the reader to insert himself, necessarily, into the text to create meaning.

30. Qtd. in Cooper, *Philip Larkin, Subversive Writer* p. 124.
31. Cooper, *Philip Larkin: Subversive Writer* p. 124
32. *FR* p. 106.
33. Cooper, *Philip Larkin: Subversive Writer* p. 125.
34. Ibid. pp. 126–7.
35. Swarbrick, *Out of Reach* p. 129.
36. Bakhtin, *Speech Genres and Other Late Essays* p. 68.
37. Ibid. p. 69.
38. Osborne, *Larkin, Ideology, and Critical Violence* p. 118.
39. Rossen argues that Titch Thomas, the poem's defacer, indulges a 'sexual fantasy expressed in the form of sadistic violence,' seeking to 'punish and humiliate her image in pointedly sexual terms.' This suggests, to Rossen, that the poet himself 'seems to justify violence against women by suggesting that access to the woman is something men have been unfairly deprived of; therefore, she is fair game.' By saying she is 'too good for this life,' 'the poet somehow puts the burden back on her, implying that she tempts men out of her own vanity and that she also comprises the source of their deprivation. As a siren, she drives men to commit bizarre and brutal acts in response; as a prostitute, according to this logic, she deserved the punishment anyway' (pp. 74–5).
40. Swarbrick goes on to say that 'The poem's satirisation of the female fantasy figure gives way to the gleeful destruction of an erotic icon; behind that destruction there lies an attitude of sexual self-disgust' (p. 118). Swarbrick does not say explicitly that it is Larkin's own self-disgust, but he certain implies that.
41. Booth, James. *Philip Larkin: The Poet's Plight*. Basingstoke: Palgrave Macmillan, 2005. p. 186.
42. Gray, Jeffrey. 'Larkin's 'Sunny Prestatyn.'' *The Explicator*. Spring 2003. pp. 175–7. p. 177.
43. Rossen, *Philip Larkin: His Life's Work* p. 75.
44. Bradford, *First Boredom, Then Fear* p. 192.
45. It has been suggested to me that the stages of the poster's defacement may also serve as an allegory for the debate about the poem itself, or even about Larkin's poetry generally. It is extremely unlikely that Larkin anticipated that potential analogy but interesting nonetheless. Gary Day, rather similarly, speculates that the poem 'dramatises at some level Larkin's poetic

development. Put simply, the poster offers an unrealistic view of life which corresponds to the sort of ideas found in Larkin's early verse. His later work correct that view and this is reflected in the spifflication of the poster. ... There is, in other words, no reality behind the text except another text and this calls into question the accepted view of Larkin as a poet of the real' (p. 39). Again, I find it unlikely that Larkin would have considered this analogy, but the fact that the objects observed in this poem are paper does, perhaps, hint at the possibility of their parallels to poems.

46. Swarbrick, *Out of Reach* p. 128.
47. Petch, *The Art of Philip Larkin* p. 95.
48. Ibid.
49. Booth, *Philip Larkin: The Poet's Plight* p. 191.
50. Ibid. p. 192.
51. As Larkin tells Ian Hamilton, 'One of the things I do feel a slight restiveness about is being typed as someone who has carved out for himself a uniquely dreary life, growing older, having to work, and not getting things he wants and so on.' My expectation, after reading this line, is that Larkin would defend his life as not particularly dreary; what he objects to, it turns out, is not the 'dreary' bit but the 'uniquely' bit. He goes on, 'Is this so different from everyone else? I'd like to know how all these romantic reviewers spend their time – do they kill a lot of dragons, for instance? If other people have wonderful lives, then I'm glad for them, but I can't help feeling that my miseries are over-done a bit by the critics' (*FR* p. 21). His defense, in other words, is not that his life isn't dreary but that it's no drearier than everyone else's life. His miseries are over-done not because he's not miserable but because everyone else is probably equally so.

2 Larkin's Voices

1. Swarbrick, *Out of Reach* p. 70.
2. Ibid. p. 173.
3. Ibid. p. 61.
4. Marsh, *Philip Larkin: The Poems* p. 12.
5. James, Clive. 'Don Juan in Hull.' *Reliable Essays: The Best of Clive James*. London: Picador, 2001. p. 182.
6. Carey, John. 'The Two Philip Larkins.' *New Larkins for Old*. Ed. James Booth. Basingstoke: Palgrave Macmillan, 2000. pp. 51–65. pp. 52–3.
7. Ibid. p. 65.
8. Petch, *The Art of Philip Larkin* p. 82.
9. Motion, *Philip Larkin: A Writer's Life* p. 288.
10. Easthope, *Englishness and National Culture* pp. 185–6.
11. Rossen, *Philip Larkin: His Life's Work* p. 57.
12. Robert Frost's 'The Figure in the Doorway' raises similar issues and offers a speaker similarly positioned on a passing train who also recognizes that the observations he makes through the train window are reciprocated by those on the other side: 'Nor did he lack for common entertainment./ That I assume was what our passing train meant./ He could look at us in our diner eating,/ And if so moved uncurl a hand in greeting.' The apparent protection and

isolation offered by the glass is upended in both these poems, and the speaker in both cases acknowledges his dual positions as watcher and watched.

13. Easthope, *Englishness and National Culture* p. 186.
14. *FR* p. 57.
15. Booth, Review of *Englishness and National Culture*. *British Journal of Aesthetics*, April 2000. pp. 274–7. p. 274.
16. *FR* p. 57.
17. Shakespeare, John. 'Larkin's First Interview.' *The Times Literary Supplement*. 1 April 2009.
18. Bradford, *First Boredom, Then Fear* p. 210.
19. Swarbrick, *Out of Reach* p. 168.
20. Ibid. p.174.
21. Kacandes, Irene. *Talk Fiction: Literature and the Talk Explosion*. Lincoln, NE: University of Nebraska Press, 2001. p. 145.
22. Andrew Motion writes that, in 'Poetry of Departures,' Larkin (not a speaker) 'accused himself of meanness without apologizing for it' (p. 428) and that 'Larkin had – finally – deliberately turned away from Ruth, just as he had more recently let Winifred and Patsy go. In 'Toads,' as in 'Poetry of Departures' and 'Reasons for Attendance,' he addresses the elements in his personality that have allowed this to happen – the passivity and the need for solitude – and has tried to persuade himself that they are inevitable and desirable' (p. 237).). Janice Rossen asserts that the poem 'satirises the appeal of this wanderlust by showing its attraction to the poet, longing for immediacy and action' (p. 53). Richard Bradford writes that in 'Poetry of Departures,' 'the predominant mood is that of stoic resignation, an acceptance that some aspects of [Larkin's] world cannot be altered but are by their intransigence recognizable to him as appropriate, albeit distorting mirrors of his termperament' (p. 119). James Booth writes that the technical precision of the poem 'reveal the poet to be, as he concedes, perfectly house-trained, with a pusillanimous regard for the decorums of room and stanza,' arguing that the poet is speaking about himself in this work (*Philip Larkin: The Poet's Plight* p. 158).
23. Marsh, *Philip Larkin: The Poems* p. 24.
24. As Bakhtin comments of Dickens' *Little Dorrit*, 'his entire text is, in fact everywhere dotted with quotation marks that serve to separate out little islands of scattered direct speech and purely authorial speech, washed by heteroglot waves from all sides' (Bakhtin, M.M. *The Dialogic Imagination*. Ed. Michael Holquist. Trans. Caryl Emerson and Michael Holquist. Austin, Texas: University of Texas Press, 1988. p. 307). This 'hybrid construction' is precisely what Larkin enacts, but in a far briefer and, perhaps, less likely form. Bakhtin calls this style 'parodic,' particularly in its pre-Dickensian use (in Smollett, Fielding, and, especially, Laurence Sterne), and the element of parody is certainly present in Larkin's text as well. The short lyric form, though, along with the lack of developed, novelistic characters and the reader's uncertain expectations – one is three-quarters of the way through the poem before even its basic premise is fully clear – lend a gravity to what otherwise might be more obvious parody. As it is, though, Larkin's hybrid construction heightens the poem's mystery at least as much as it lends to the poem's humor.
25. Rossen, *Philip Larkin: His Life's Work* p. xv.

26. Booth, *Philip Larkin: The Poet's Plight* p. 16.
27. James, 'Don Juan in Hull' p. 183.
28. James writes that 'When Larkin's narrator in 'A Study of Reading Habits' said 'Books are a load of crap,' there were critics – some of them, incredibly, among his more appreciative – who allowed themselves to believe that Larkin was expressing his own opinion. ... It should be obvious at long last, however, that the diction describes the speaker. When the speaker is close to representing Larkin himself, the diction defines which Larkin it is – what mood he is in' (p. 182).
29. Ibid. p. 178.
30. Cooper, *Philip Larkin: Subversive Writer* p. 123.
31. Republished in Amis, Martin. *The War Against Cliché*. New York: Vintage Books, 2001.
32. Ibid.
33. Bradford, *First Boredom, Then Fear* p. 15.
34. *SL* p. 596.
35. Bradford, *First Boredom, Then Fear* p. 96.
36. It is worth noting, as well, that Amis' letters to Larkin strike a remarkably similar tone and are sometimes even harsher, as though the two men are trying to outdo each other. For instance, before appearing on a television show to talk about the welfare state, Amis writes to Larkin, 'My message will be simple: *Do* some *work* and *pay* for it *yourselves*, you LAZY GREEDY F U C K E R S' (Amis, Kingsley. *The Letters of Kingsley Amis*. Ed. Zachary Leader. New York: Hyperion, 2001. pp. 824–5). More disturbingly, and demonstrating the same self-awareness and identical diction as a number of Larkin's letters, Amis writes within days of the birth of his daughter, 'The baby is quite hefty and looks no worse than might be expected. Rather better, really. I hope she has a lovely childhood and has a lovely time at school and makes a lot of lovely chums and brings them home. A girl ought to feel she can bring her friends in an introduce them to her parents the trouble with you is you're just a' (p. 361). Indeed, Amis is expressing a sexual interest in the future school girl friends of his days-old daughter. Perhaps because the situation is so extreme, the untruthfulness – the posing – of Amis' statement is more evident than in some of Larkin's letters, but the same game-playing and use of multiple voices are particularly evident when the correspondences are read as paired rather than in isolation.
37. *RW* pp. 260–1.
38. *SL* p. 493.
39. Roberts, Neil. *Narrative and Voice in Postwar Poetry*. London: Longman, 1999. pp. 7–8.
40. Bradford, *First Boredom, Then Fear* p. 34.
41. *SL* p. 277.
42. Bradford, *First Boredom, Then Fear* p. 176.
43. Ibid. p. 59.
44. Cooper, *Philip Larkin: Subversive Writer* pp. 6–7.
45. Ibid. p. 126.
46. Mulvey, Laura. 'Visual Pleasure and Narrative Cinema.' *Film Theory and Criticism*. Eds. Leo Braudy and Marshall Cohen. Oxford University Press: 1999. pp. 746–57. p. 751.

47. Conquest, for example, once sent a fake notice to Larkin accusing him of trafficking in pornography and threatening immediate arrest. Larkin was beside himself and spent a day meeting with his solicitor about how to protect himself. Bradford argues that Larkin responded with some bitterness to Conquest's later admission of responsibility and was never fully able to look at the incident as a harmless joke.
48. *SL* p. 304.
49. Booth, *Philip Larkin: The Poet's Plight* p. 137.
50. Rossen, *Philip Larkin: His Life's Work* p. 52.
51. Easthope, *Englishness and National Culture* p. 185.
52. Swarbrick, *Out of Reach* p. 11, and Roberts, *Narrative and Voice in Postwar Poetry* p. 8.
53. Bradford, *First Boredom, Then Fear* p. 17.
54. Palmer, Richard. *Such Deliberate Disguises: The Art of Philip Larkin*. London: Continuum, 2008. p. 66.
55. Bradford, *First Boredom, Then Fear* p. 210.

3 Memory and Change

1. Motion, *Philip Larkin: A Writer's Life* p. 111.
2. *AWJ* p. 226.
3. *AWJ* p. 18.
4. *RW* p. 50.
5. *RW* p. 25.
6. *RW* p. 39.
7. Falck, Colin. 'Philip Larkin.' *British Poetry Since 1970: A Critical Survey*. Eds Peter Jones and Michael Schmidt. Manchester: Carcanet, 1980. pp. 403–11. p. 410.
8. Bayley, John. 'Larkin and the Romantic Tradition. *Critical Quarterly* Spring/Summer 1984. pp. 61–6. p. 61.
9. Martin, Bruce. *Dictionary of Literary Biography*. Detroit, Michigan: Thomas Gale Publishers, 2005.
10. King, Peter. *Nine Contemporary Poets: A Critical Introduction*. London: Methuen, 1979.
11. Rossen, *Philip Larkin: His Life's Work* pp. 50–1.
12. In *First Boredom, Then Fear*, Bradford writes that 'Jane Exall, a friend of Ruth's, would later be presented as the "bosomy English Rose" of his 1962 poem "Wild Oats".' He goes on to say that 'There is no evidence that Larkin kept copies of all of his letters, but it is almost certain that he did with this one [written to Amis in 1947], given that it reads as a prose version of the poem he would write thirteen years later, "Wild Oats".' His single example of the similarities between the poem and the letter is this: 'In the poem Ruth is referred to as 'her friend in specs I could talk to,' the one he 'took out,' despite the attraction of Jane, the bosomy rose. In the letter Ruth and he 'got on... because we are really quite alike,' she being less attractive, less a reminder of his own inadequacies and in whose company he could 'start thinking about something else' – something other than sex' (p. 71). While these similarities are fine, as far as they go, the letter hardly seems a prose version of the poem,

and the sentiment expressed in the poem differs significantly from that of the letter. In fact, the part of the letter in which Larkin says, according to Bradford, that Ruth is 'less attractive, less a reminder of his own inadequacies' does not actually appear in the letter except in Bradford's reading into it. Larkin writes that he and Ruth are 'quite alike,' which Bradford takes to mean that she is the 'friend in specs I could talk to'. Being able to talk to someone and being 'quite like' someone are obviously not the same thing, and the language of the poem is utterly different – in tone, vocabulary, self-consciousness, voice, and meaning – from the language of the letter Bradford cites.

13. Bradford, *First Boredom, Then Fear* pp. 71–2.
14. Ibid. p. 97.
15. Rossen, *Philip Larkin: His Life's Work* p. 92.
16. Swarbrick, *Out of Reach* p. 61.
17. Osborne, *Larkin, Ideology, and Critical Violence* p. 140.
18. Marsh, *Philip Larkin: The Poems* p. 166.
19. Qtd. in Motion, *Philip Larkin: A Writer's Life* pp. 500–1.
20. Lehman, David. 'Foreword.' *Required Writing*. Ann Arbor: The University of Michigan Press, 1999. p. xv.
21. *FR* pp. 31–2.
22. Bradford, *First Boredom, Then Fear* p. 102.
23. *SL* p. 551.
24. *FR* p. 55.
25. Ibid.
26. Swarbrick, *Out of Reach* p. 52.
27. Pritchard, William. 'Larkin's Presence' *Philip Larkin: The Man and His Work*. Ed. Dale Salwak. Iowa City: University of Iowa Press, 1989. pp. 71–89. p. 78.
28. Marsh, *Philip Larkin: The Poems* p. 151.
29. *AWJ* p. 27.
30. Osborne, *Larkin, Ideology and Critical Violence* p. 53.
31. Ibid. p. 259.
32. Regan, Stephen. 'Philip Larkin: A Late Modern Poet.' *The Cambridge Companion to Twentieth-Century English Poetry*. Ed. Neil Corcoran. Cambridge University Press, 2007. pp. 147–58.
33. *FR* p. 19.
34. Ibid.
35. Whalen, Terry. 'Philip Larkin's Imagist Bias.' *Critical Quarterly*. June 1981, pp. 29–46. p. 30.
36. *RW* p. 79.
37. *FR* pp. 19–20.
38. *RW* pp. 69–70.
39. *SL* p. 138.
40. Swarbrick, *Out of Reach* p. 84.
41. *RW* p. 72.
42. *RW* p. 125.
43. Booth, *Philip Larkin: The Poet's Plight* p. 43.
44. *FR* p. 66.
45. *AWJ* p. 23.
46. *SL* p. 138.

47. Osborne, *Larkin, Ideology and Critical Violence* p. 64.
48. Bristow, Joseph. 'The Obscenity of Philip Larkin.' *Critical Inquiry*. Autumn 1994, pp. 156-181. p. 174.

4 Jazz and Audienceship

1. Rasula, Jed. 'Jazz and American modernism.' *The Cambridge Companion to American Modernism*. Ed. Walter Kalaidjian. Cambridge University Press, 2005. p. 157. Quite a number of writers have explored the issue of jazz's Modernism, as Alfred Appel, Jr. does. In *Jazz Modernism*, he argues that 'As singers, Armstrong, Waller, Teagarden, and Holiday typically had to modify or tear apart and rebuild poor or mediocre Tin Pan Alley material in a pro-creative manner analogous to the ways in which modernists such as Picasso begot paper collage, wood assemblage, and metal sculpture' (Appel, Alfred. *Jazz Modernism: From Ellington and Armstrong to Matisse and Joyce*. New Haven: Yale University Press, 2004. p. 1). Although jazz's inherent Modernism is not the emphasis of my argument, understanding the error of a presumption that bebop is Modernist while other jazz forms are not can illuminate Larkin's arguments in *All What Jazz* as well as demonstrate the kinds of attachments Larkin has to Modernism beyond his explicit objections to the sounds of bebop.
2. Leggett makes much, for instance, of Larkin's use of the opening lines of 'Aubade,' finding parallels in the language of Blues singers. He writes that Larkin's line 'I work all day, and get half drunk at night' 'read in another context, could as easily be attributed to Sleepy John Estes or Blind Lemon Jef-ferson,' and calls the line 'a jazz/blues intertext inhabiting the Larkin canon that may be glimpsed now and then' (p. 43). He also writes that 'only in one line of the poem do the blues make a direct appearance, yet the poem as a whole is shaped by an attitude that is closer to the music of the American South than to the poetry of a long English tradition' (pp. 14–15).
3. Leggett, BJ. *Larkin's Blues: Jazz, Popular Music and Poetry*. Louisiana State University Press, 1999. p. 43.
4. Qtd in Leggett, *Larkin's Blues* p. 12.
5. Leggett, *Larkin's Blues* p. 18.
6. Rasula, 'Jazz and American Modernism' p. 162.
7. Leggett, *Larkin's Blues* pp. 91–2.
8. Ibid. p. 18.
9. *The Letters of Kingsley Amis* p. 1036.
10. Watts, Cedric. 'Larkin and Jazz.' *Critical Essays on Philip Larkin: The Poems.* Eds Linda Cookson and Bryan Loughrey. Harlow, Essex: Longman: 1989. pp. 20–7. p.25.
11. Swarbrick, *Out of Reach.*
12. *AWJ* p. 116.
13. Terry Teachout's comparison of Beiderbecke and Armstrong, for instance, explains that Beiderbecke 'played with precise, at times almost fussy articu-lation and a rounded, chime-like tone whose sound Eddie Condon famously likened to 'a girl saying yes,' sticking mostly to the middle register and avoid-ing the interpolated high notes that became an Armstrong trademark. His

improvised solos had an architectural balance similar to Armstrong's, but they were more subdued in their emotional impact' (Teachout, Terry. 'Homage to Bix.' *Commentary* Sept. 2005. pp. 65–8.), but despite these significant differences, both remained attached to traditional compositional structures and varied their sound only to the extent that it remained melodic. Gary Giddins calls Armstrong 'an indefatiguable propagandist for playing straight melody and seductive rhythms' (Giddins, Gary. *Satchmo*. New York: Doubleday, 1988. p. 14) and notes that he 'advocated and perfected purity of tone and obeisance to melody' (p. 7). On the other hand, Ben Ratliff writes that Coltrane 'was looking for a music that stepped outside of history' (Ratliff, Ben. *Coltrane: The Story of a Sound*. New York: Farrar, Straus and Giroux, 2007. p. xvii) and writes, of bebop in the 1940s – music most widely considered 'modern' and that Larkin regards as Modernist – that 'it came to be associated with fast tempos, asymmetrical melodic lines, and chord harmonies inspired by Stravinsky, Debussy, and Bartok' (p. 9).

14. *AWJ* p. 19.
15. Ibid. p. 248.
16. Ibid. p. 175.
17. Ibid. p. 246.
18. Ibid. pp. 260–1.
19. Ibid. p. 21.
20. Bradford, *First Boredom, Then Fear* p. 291.
21. *AWJ* p. 15.
22. Ibid. p. 15.
23. Ibid. p. 226.
24. Rasula, 'Jazz and American modernism' p. 162.
25. *RW* p. 56.
26. Rasula, 'Jazz and American modernism' p. 159.
27. Motion cites several of Larkin's most offensive racial comments, including that Larkin called the Labour government 'nigger-mad' in a letter to Amis; that he wrote to his mother that she must 'be pleased to see the black folk go from the house over the way'; and the now-famous song lyric he sent to Robert Conquest: 'Prison for strikers, Bring back the cat, Kick out the niggers, What about that?' Motion includes the song lyric's title – 'How to Win the Next Election' – but neglects to point out that the title disowns the lyric from necessarily being a 'true' statement of Larkin's own feelings about race.
28. *AWJ* p. 24.
29. Ibid. p. 87.
30. Ibid. p. 68.
31. Ibid. p. 87.
32. Ibid.
33. Ibid. pp. 31 and 87.
34. Osborne, *Larkin, Ideology, and Critical Violence* pp. 244–5.
35. *RW* p. 56.
36. Watts, 'Larkin and Jazz' p. 27.
37. Ibid. pp. 22–3.
38. *AWJ* p. 23.
39. *RW* p. 56.
40. *AWJ* p. 16.

41. As he writes of Clifford Brown and other Bop musicians in 'From Clifford to Connie' in 1966, their music was 'nervous and hostile' as though the musicians were saying of their audience that this is 'something they can't steal because they can't play it.' Two years later, composing the Introduction to the volume of reviews, he uses the same line and directs it more obviously toward issues of race: 'This new mode seemed to have originated partly out of boredom with playing ordinary jazz six nights a week... and partly from a desire to wrest back the initiative in jazz from the white musician.' And while in other places he expresses empathy for the African-American impulse to be self-protective, he nonetheless presents it as an affront to his own audienceship.
42. Watson, 'The Other Larkin' p. 347.
43. Alvarez, Al. *The New Poetry.* Harmondsworth: Penguin, 1966. p. 20.
44. *AWJ* p. 28.
45. Ibid.
46. Ibid. p. 29.
47. Ibid. pp. 75–6.
48. *FR* p. 78.
49. This stanza features a typical interaction between the speaker and subject of the poem, as Larkin's poems never do: 'How many are you, then,' said I,/ 'If they two are in heaven?'/ Quick was the little Maid's reply,/ 'O Master! we are seven.'
50. Timms, David. *Philip Larkin.* Edinburgh: Oliver and Boyd, 1973. p. 21.
51. *RW* p. 80.
52. *FR* p. 3.
53. Ibid. p. 23.
54. *AWJ* p. 137.
55. *RW* pp. 81–2.
56. Ibid. p. 72.
57. As Istvan Racz writes, Larkin was familiar with Cezanne's 'Card Players' series and called one of the paintings 'wonderful' in a letter to James Sutton. Racz suggests that 'this picture, and Cezanne's mature pictures in general, could serve as emblems for the kind of Movement poetry that Larkin and his contemporaries are associated with. ... What Larkin discovered in the picture and recreated in his poem is the act of constructing an allegory of timelessness in a heavy and monumental vision' (Racz, Istvan. 'Space in Larkin and Cezanne.' *Hugarian Journal of English and American Studies.* Fall, 2003. pp. 119–25. pp. 123–4).
58. *RW* p. 54.
59. *AWJ* p. 85.
60. Ibid. p. 167.
61. Ibid. p. 198. As opposed to hearing about 'anything in Latin or Cuban or 5/4 rhythm, any freedom music 'in which the beat is often suspended, distended or ignored at certain points', anything with electric or electronic sounds, anything ethnic or with sitars...'.
62. *RW* p. 72.
63. Giddins, Gary. 'Something Else.' *The New Yorker.* 14 April 2008.
64. *AWJ* p. 16.
65. *RW* p. 72.

66. Jost, Ekkhard. 'Free Jazz.' *The Story of Jazz: from New Orleans to Rock Jazz.* Ed. Joachim E. Berendt. Englewood Cliffs, NJ: Prentice-Hall, 1978. p. 133.
67. Although 'Ornithology' is a Charlie Parker tune, unlike some of Parker's pieces, it uses the backdrop of an earlier piece, 'How High the Moon,' for its chord progression.
68. Jost, Ekkhard. *Free Jazz: The Roots of Jazz.* New York: Da Capo Press, 1981. pp. 17–18.
69. Jost, 'Free Jazz' p. 133.
70. *AWJ* p. 26.
71. Ibid.
72. *RW* p. 125.
73. *FR* p. 319.
74. Pp. 342–4.
75. *AWJ* p. 20.
76. *FR* p. 112.
77. *AWJ* p. 19.

5   Religion and Empathy

1. 'I hated everybody when I was a child, or I thought I did. When I grew up, I realized that what I hated was children' (*FR* p. 47). 'As far as I can see, all women are stupid beings' (*SL* p. 63). 'England may be full of dishonesty and unpleasantness and sordidity etc. but I (naturally, I suppose) have a prejudice in favor of it. Fuck America. God Fuck America' (*SL* p. 67). 'Not many niggers round here I'm happy to say. Except the Paki doctor next door' (*SL* pp. 699–700). 'What dreary no-good cunts these foreigners are' (*SL* p. 291).
2. Kissick, Gary. 'They Turn on Larkin.' *The Antioch Review.* Winter 1994. pp. 64–70. p. 64.
3. Easthope, *Englishness and National Culture.*
4. Stojkovic, *Unnoticed in the Casual Light of Day* p. 94.
5. *FR* p. 106.
6. Motion, *Philip Larkin* p. 60.
7. Hoffpauir, Richard. *The Art of Restraint: English Poetry from Hardy to Larkin.* Newark, Delaware: The University of Delaware Press, 1991. p. 263.
8. Hughes, Noel. 'The Young Mr. Larkin.' *Larkin at Sixty.* Ed. Anthony Thwaite. London: Faber and Faber, 1982. p. 22.
9. Phillips, D.Z. *From Fantasy to Faith.* New York: St. Martin's Press, 1991. pp. 51–2.
10. Almond, Ian. 'Larkin and the Mundane: Mystic Without a Mystery' *New Larkins for Old.* Ed. James Booth. Houndmills, Basingstoke: Palgrave Macmillan, 2000. pp. 182–9. p. 189.
11. Day, Roger. ' "That Vast Moth-Eaten Musical Brocade:" Larkin and Religion.' *Critical Essays on Philip Larkin: The Poems.* Eds. Linda Cookson and Bryan Loughrey. Harlow, Essex: Longman: 1989. pp. 81–92.
12. Booth, James. *Philip Larkin: Writer.* New York: St. Martin's Press, 1992. p. 136.
13. Motion, *Philip Larkin* p. 60.
14. *FR* p. 22.
15. Palmer, *Such Deliberate Disguises* p. 85.

16. Motion, *Philip Larkin: A Writer's Life* pp. 104 and 241.
17. *FR* p. 22.
18. Hoffpauir, *The Art of Restraint* pp. 277–8.
19. *FR* p. 57.
20. Cooper, *Philip Larkin: Subversive Writer* p. 140.
21. Booth, *Philip Larkin: The Poet's Plight* p. 126.
22. Ibid. p. 129.
23. Marsh, *Philip Larkin: The Poems* p. 119.
24. Stojkovic, *Unnoticed in the Casual Light of Day* p. 135.
25. The final reference to 'the dead' also hearkens back to an earlier, more casually mentioned reference: 'the holy end.' When first used, 'the holy end' has the studied throwaway tone of dismissal for the church's physical features, but in conjunction with the imagery of death and churchyard burial in the poem's final lines, it suggests another sort of holy end altogether.
26. Hamilton notes that 'a number of poems in *The Less Deceived* seem to me to carry a final kick in the head for the attitudes they have seemed to be taking up. ... Somehow the whole poem doubles back on itself.' He calls this change in attitude 'a kind of elaborate self-imprisonment.' When Larkin does not respond to this question directly, Hamilton presses the issue by saying that 'what I do rather feel is that many of [the poems] carry this kind of built-in or tagged-on comment on themselves' (*FR* p. 23). Larkin, kindly, tries to make Hamilton feel better for what he calls his own 'stupid question' by answering, disingenuously, 'It's a very interesting question and I hadn't realized I did that sort of thing.'
27. Booth, *Philip Larkin: Writer* pp. 165–6.
28. Petch, *The Art of Philip Larkin* p. 57.
29. Marsh, *Philip Larkin: The Poems* p. 118.
30. *SL* p. 4.
31. *SL* p. 145.
32. *FR* pp. 56–7.
33. *FR* p. 105.
34. *RW* p. 111.
35. *FR* p. 109.
36. Greer, Germaine. 'A Very British Misery.' *The Guardian* 14 Oct. 1988.
37. Banville, 'Homage to Philip Larkin.'
38. Swarbrick, *Out of Reach* pp. 98–9.
39. Ibid. p. 124.
40. It may be worth noting here, as well, that both 'Church Going' and 'Faith Healing' – poems with developmental speakers that ask for development from their readers – employ *active* titles, with the participle verb form, which opens each title to a double reading with contrasting meanings. As a number of readers have pointed out, 'Church Going' includes a pun on going to church versus the church itself 'going.' But, as has not been pointed out as far as I know, 'Faith Healing' can be read similarly: the phrase is popularly used to describe the activity in which this unappealing preacher engages, but it also suggests the possibility that faith does, indeed, heal.
41. Rossen, *Philip Larkin: His Life's Work* pp. 44–5.
42. Petch, *The Art of Philip Larkin* p. 55.
43. Rossen, *Philip Larkin: His Life's Work* p. 45.

44. Swarbrick, *Out of Reach* p. 99.
45. Day, ' "That Vast Moth-Eaten Musical Brocade:" Larkin and Religion' p. 86.
46. Palmer, *Such Deliberate Disguises* p. 100.
47. Ibid. p. 92.
48. These many instances of, presumably, Christian writers finding resonant Christian imagery in Larkin's poem – whether they think that Larkin embraces or dismisses those images – reinforces my argument that Larkin indeed speaks to every reader. These critical readers conveniently find in Larkin's imagery their own faith traditions reflected, despite the fact that the poem offers no hint of Christianity beyond the use of the words 'religion' and 'water,' both used utterly generically.
49. Abrams, Paula. 'Water in Religion.' *The Water Page*. Water Policy International Ltd. 2000. http://www.africanwater.org/religion.htm. Date accessed 26 Apr. 2009.
50. Swarbrick, *Out of Reach* p. 99.
51. Rossen, *Philip Larkin: His Life's Work* pp. 45–6.
52. Although nothing in Larkin's writings suggests that he was intimately familiar with Wallace Stevens' work, 'Water' can be likened to two of Stevens' poems: Danielle Pinkstein goes so far as to say that 'Water' 'could not have been written without' Stevens' 'Anecdote of the Jar.' Water is Stevens' anecdote in a [sic] jar, its pellucid distorting shadow, a symbolic lighthouse holding dominion' (Pinkstein, Danielle. 'The Summer of 'Essential Beauty." *Hugarian Journal of English and American Studies*. Fall, 2003. pp. 63–79. p. 76). Perhaps a more likely parallel, though, is Stevens' 'The Glass of Water,' which includes these lines: 'Here in the centre stands the glass. Light/ Is the lion that comes down to drink.' This is a decidedly secular poem that focuses instead on metaphysics and poetry while using imagery very similar to Larkin's, which suggests both a depth of allusion seldom attributed to Larkin and a reinforcing of the universality I have argued for above.

Conclusion: Two Philips

1. For example, Swede Levov in *American Pastoral*: 'grandson of Jewish immigrants, star high-school athlete and prosperous owner of the family glove factory in Newark, civic-minded in his public life, kind and tolerant in private.' (http://www.cnn.com/SPECIALS/2001/americasbest/pro.proth.html).
2. 'Bardic Asperations: Philip Roth's *Epic of America*.' *English*. Oxford Journals. Vol. 57, no. 218. pp. 171–98.
3. Review of *Indignation* at bookreporter.com.
4. Ellen Gerstle writes of Roth that his work 'calls up questions about obscenity and art, subjects that have drawn him into conflict with his readers. Not surprisingly, a number of critics found [*The Dying Animal*] as slender intellectually as it is physically. ... Some complaints had a disturbingly familiar ring, echoing earlier rebukes of misogyny and sexual perversion. Other objections claimed Roth was overworking past themes' ('*The Dying Animal*: The Art of Obsessing or Obsessing about Art?' *Turning Up the Flame: Philip Roth's Later Novels*. Eds. Jay Halio and Ben Siegel. University of Delaware Press, 2005. pp. 194–206. p. 194). Chaim Bermant writes, scathingly, of Roth that he works in

a tradition of 'the foul-mouth, whose influence [Irving] Howe has described in the context of show-business, now invading the sacred realms of literature' (Bernant, Chaim. *The Jews*. London: Weidenfeld and Nicolson, 1977. p. 158). According to Howe, Roth developed from the prodigy author of *Goodbye, Columbus*, whose stories were 'lovely chronicles of his generation's limited aspirations' (*The Boston Globe* 1981) to a purveyor of vulgarity with 'the wish to pull down the reader in common with the characters of the work, so that he will not be tempted to suppose that any inclination he toward the good, the beautiful, or the ideal merit anything more than a Bronx cheer' (Howe, Irving. 'Philip Roth Reconsidered.' *Commentary*. Jan. 1972. pp. 69–77).

5. For example, Linda Grant writes of Roth, in the *Guardian*, 'it has now become apparent to many admirers, male and female, that there is a dark distaste for women, a repugnance that can only be described by the word misogyny. One must resist the urge to psychoanalyse or to conflate Roth with his male creations, but the palpable sense of disgust towards the women characters has certainly intensified. It's deeply rooted, almost medieval' (17 April 2007). Grant obviously recognizes the desirability of separating author from speaker, but her use of the 'existential there' ('there is a dark distaste for women') allows her simultaneously to accuse Roth while apparently remembering the principles of critical distance. Isabel Coixet, the director of the film version of *The Dying Animal*, calls Roth 'one of the most misogynistic writers of his generation' (*Moviemaker*, 8 August 2008), and Vivian Gornick asks why Roth, along with Bellow and Mailer, 'hate[s] women.' Bellow and Roth, according to Gornick, offer readers 'barely filtered 'declarations of insult and injury" which are driven 'by an anger at the women in their lives. (Both writers, she suggests, left little imaginative space between author and narrator)' (Qtd. in *Harvard Gazette*. 14 Feb. 2008). As with Larkin, these Roth readers emphasize Roth's conflation with his characters and the apparent inseparability of his, perhaps, misogynistic characters from the author himself. They also overlook the possibility that, just as Larkin and Roth's works complicate notions of speaker, audience, religion, personal identity, and realities, they might also complicate and play with conventional notions of gender and characterization.

6. Heaney, Seamus. *Preoccupations: Selected Prose 1968-1978*. New York: Farrar, Straus and Giroux, 1980. p. 167.

7. *Times Literary Supplement* June, 1974.

8. Petch, *The Art of Philip Larkin* p. 2.

9. Davie, Donald. *Thomas Hardy and British Poetry*. New York: Oxford University Press, 1972. p. 188.

10. Qtd. in Osborne, *Larkin, Ideology, and Critical Violence*, pp. 132–3.

11. Larkin's Britishness has frequently been used against him as well. For example, Lisa Jardine famously argued against teaching Larkin, offering the interpretation that his 'Little Englandism... sits uneasily within our revised curriculum, which seeks to give all of our students, regardless of background, race or creed, a voice within British culture.' She explains that Larkin's poetry occupies a place 'at the heart of the traditional canon of English Literature. Its place, that is, within that body of works cherished by defenders of British culture as the repository of the Best of British – those sentiments and ideas which allow our culture to reflect the standards and values which the educated world

considers universally valid' despite the fact that, for her, the letters prove that Larkin is 'not the benevolent, modest, librarian with an extraordinary ear for a quintessentially British kind of detail of A-level anthologies, but rather a casual, habitual racist, and an easy misogynist' (Jardine, Lisa. 'Saxon Violence.' *The Guardian.* 8 Dec.1992, p. 24).

Joseph Bristow, as well, in his influential *Critical Inquiry* piece, uses Jardine's assault on Larkin to support his argument that Larkin's 'work and his life proved almost inseparable from one another as his career developed over time... Rarely have the personality of the poet and his poetic persona been conflated into one and the same image. Larkin, in this respect, appeared to live up to the ordinariness upon which his reputation as a writer had been built' ('The Obscenity of Philip Larkin' 161).

12. Bristow, 'The Obscenity of Philip Larkin' pp. 157 and 160.
13. Ibid. p. 161.
14. Ibid. p. 160.
15. Qtd. in Osborne, *Larkin, Ideology and Critical Violence* p. 14.
16. Osborne, *Larkin, Ideology and Critical Violence* p. 21.
17. Qtd. in West, Kevin R. 'Professing Desire.' *Philip Roth: New Perspectives on an American Author.* Ed. Derek Parker Royal. Westport, CT: Praeger, 2005. pp. 226–39. p. 232.
18. West, 'Professing Desire' p. 232.
19. To offer just one of many possible examples, as part of the attack on Larkin's depiction of women, Janice Rossen garners details, almost indiscriminately, from Larkin's biography as well as from his creative works. For instance, she begins the chapter entitled 'Difficulties with Girls' in *Philip Larkin: His Life's Work* with this remarkable intersection of Larkin's life and work: 'Larkin's fury against women is not so much a declared state of siege against them personally as it is an internal battle raging within himself. In a world characterized largely by deprivation, women come to stand for the fact that:

> Life is an immobile, locked,
> Three-handed struggle between
> Your wants, the world's for you, and (worse)
> The unbeatable slow machine
> That brings what you'll get.

Rossen continues, 'People – and life in general – seem to have disappointed Larkin enormously. Still, deprivation often takes a uniquely feminine cast for him. Larkin is constantly encountering difficulties in his relations with girls – experiencing the pain of 'Love again: wanking at ten past three', the inability to work out why things should be so impossible (being unable to 'say why it never worked for me'), and the frustration of trying to accommodate his own needs.' Rossen quotes the poetry as support for her assertions about Larkin's life and offers, in these opening lines, no support outside of the verse for her assertions of Larkin's 'fury against women' (p. 66). For her, the unnamed – and often ungendered – speaker of the poems is inevitably Larkin, and Larkin is indistinguishable from the 'I' of every first-person poem. Thus, for Rossen, an objectionable sentiment about women in the letters can meaningfully be read onto the poems, and a poetic line about relationships is the emotional equivalent of a diary entry. Larkin's literary misogyny is 'proven' for Rossen by uncontextualized lines taken from disparate poems in conjunction with knowledge about Larkin's romantic relationships, and, not surprisingly, Roth's characters and personal life have been used in similarly uncritical ways to uncover his perceived disgust for women and to support accusations of self-hating Judaism, among other criticisms.

20. Margaret Smith argues that 'Roth contrives to blur the boundaries of fiction and autobiography as narrative strategy; indeed, this can be understood as his own personal stance regarding his work' (Smith, Margaret. 'Autobiography: False Confession?' *Turning Up the Flame. : Philip Roth's Later Novels*. Eds. Jay Halio and Ben Siegel. University of Delaware Press, 2005. pp. 99–114. pp. 99–100.). And Ben Siegel points out that 'From the start, Roth has shrewdly manipulated his readership into wondering how much of his fiction is fact and how much fiction... But, then, where would Philip Roth be today as a writer if readers had not responded willingly to his teasing, suggestiveness, and trickiness?' (Siegel, Ben. 'Reading Philip Roth.' *Turning Up the Flame: Philip Roth's Later Novels*. Eds Jay Halio and Ben Siegel. University of Delaware Press, 2005. pp. 17–30. p. 24).

21. *RW* p. 58.

22. Ibid. p. 54.

23. *FR* p. 56.

24. As Roth famously wrote in *Deception*, 'I write fiction and I'm told it's autobiography, I write autobiography and I'm told it's fiction, so since I'm so dim and they're so smart, let them decide what it is or it isn't.' To further complicate matters, this isn't Roth's own voice speaking but the voice of 'Philip,' the protagonist in a novel that seems to mine Roth's own life for its biographical details. (Roth, Philip. *Deception*. New York: Vintage. 1997.)

25. Roth, for instance, writes to Zuckerman, in the beginning of *The Facts*, 'I'm using the word 'facts' here, in this letter, in its idealized form and in a much more simpleminded way than it's meant in the title. Obviously the facts are never just coming at you but are incorporated by an imagination that is formed by your previous experience. Memories of the past are not memories of facts but memories of your imagining of the facts' (8). And later, Zuckerman 'writes' back to Roth, "As for characterization, you, Roth, are the least completely rendered of all your protagonists... Your acquaintance with the facts, your sense of the facts, is much less developed than your understanding, your intuitive weighing and balancing of fiction. You make a fictional world that is far more exciting than the world it comes out of... By now what you are is a walking text' (Roth, Philip. *The Facts: A Novelist's Autobiography*. New York: Farrar, Straus and Giroux, 1988. p. 162). This conversation between two fictional characters, or perhaps between one fictional and one 'real' character, echoes the language of Larkin's 'Maiden Name,' but Larkin's poem omits much of Roth's overt self-consciousness – the obvious inclusion of the reader in the joke – when making similar statements about truth and fiction.

26. *RW* p. 49.

27. Ibid. pp. 62–3.

28. Ibid. p. 49.

29. *FR* p. 115.

Bibliography

Abrams, Paula. 'Water in Religion.' *The Water Page*. Water Policy International Ltd. 2000. http://www.africanwater.org/religion.htm. Date accessed 26 Apr. 2009.

Almond, Ian. 'Larkin and the Mundane: Mystic Without a Mystery.' *New Larkins for Old*. Ed. James Booth. Basingstoke: Palgrave, 2000. 182–9.

Alvarez, Al. *The New Poetry*. Harmondsworth: Penguin, 1966.

Amis, Kingsley. *The Letters of Kingsley Amis*. Ed. Zachary Leader. New York: Hyperion, 2001.

Amis, Martin. *The War Against Cliché*. New York: Vintage Books, 2001.

Appel, Alfred. *Jazz Modernism: From Ellington and Armstrong to Matisse and Joyce*. New Haven: Yale University Press, 2004.

Bakhtin, M.M. *The Dialogic Imagination*. Ed. Michael Holquist. Trans. Caryl Emerson and Michael Holquist. Austin, Texas: University of Texas Press, 1988.

Bakhtin, M.M. 'The Problem with Speech Genres.' *Speech Genres and Other Late Essays*. Eds. Michael Holquist and Caryl Emerson. Austin, Texas: University of Texas Press, 1986.

Banville, John. 'Homage to Philip Larkin.' *New York Review of Books*. 23 Feb. 2006.

Barthes, Roland. *S/Z*. New York: Hill and Wang, 1975.

Bayley, John. 'Larkin and the Romantic Tradition. *Critical Quarterly*. Spring/ Summer 1984. 61–6.

Bernant, Chaim. *The Jews*. London: Weidenfeld and Nicolson, 1977.

Booth, James. *Philip Larkin: The Poet's Plight*. Basingstoke: Palgrave Macmillan, 2005.

Booth, James. Review of *Englishness and National Culture*. *British Journal of Aesthetics*, Apr. 2000. 274–7.

Booth, James. *Philip Larkin: Writer*. New York: St. Martin's Press, 1992.

Bradford. Richard. *First Boredom, Then Fear*. London: Peter Owen Publishers, 2005.

Bristow, Joseph. 'The Obscenity of Philip Larkin.' *Critical Inquiry*. Autumn 1994, 156–81.

Brennan, Maeve. *The Philip Larkin I Knew*. Manchester University Press, 2002.

Carey, John. 'The Two Philip Larkins.' *New Larkins for Old*. Ed. James Booth. Houndmills, Basingstoke: Palgrave, 2000. 51–65.

Cooper, Stephen. *Philip Larkin: Subversive Writer*. Brighton: Sussex Academic Press, 2004.

Crosman, Robert. 'Do Readers Make Meaning?' *The Reader in the Text*. Eds Susan Rubin Suleiman and Inge Crosman Wimmers. Princeton University Press, 1980.

Crouch, Stanley. 'John Coltrane's Finest Hour.' *Slate*. 10 Mar. 2006.

Davie, Donald. *Thomas Hardy and British Poetry*. New York: Oxford University Press, 1972.

Day, Gary. ' "Never Such Language Again": The Poetry of Philip Larkin.' *British Poetry from the 1950s to the 1990s: Politics and Art*. Eds Gary Day and Brian Docherty. New York: Macmillan, 1997. 33–47.

Day, Roger. ' "That Vast Moth-Eaten Musical Brocade:" Larkin and Religion.' *Critical Essays on Philip Larkin: The Poems*. Eds Linda Cookson and Bryan Loughrey. Harlow, Essex: Longman: 1989.

Easthope, Anthony. *Englishness and National Culture*. London: Routledge 1999.

Ellman, Richard and Robert O'Clair. Notes. *Modern Poems: A Norton Introduction*. New York: Norton, 1989.

Falck, Colin. 'Philip Larkin.' *British Poetry Since 1970: A Critical Survey*. Eds Peter Jones and Michael Schmidt. Manchester: Carcanet, 1980. 403–11.

Finney, Brian. 'Roth's Counterlife: Destabilizing the Facts.' *Biography*. Fall 1993. 370–87.

Garcia, Damaso Lopez. 'Post-Metropolitan Larkin.' *Hugarian Journal of English and American Studies*. Fall 2003. 81–9.

Giddins, Gary. *Satchmo*. New York: Doubleday, 1988.

Giddins, Gary. 'Something Else.' *The New Yorker*. 14 Apr. 2008.

Gerstle, Ellen. 'The Dying Animal: The Art of Obsessing or Obsessing about Art?' *Turning Up the Flame: Philip Roth's Later Novels*. Eds Jay Halio and Ben Siegel. University of Delaware Press, 2005. 194–206.

Gray, Jeffrey. 'Larkin's "Sunny Prestatyn." ' *The Explicator*. Spring 2003. 175–7.

Greer, Germaine. 'A Very British Misery.' *Guardian*. 14 Oct 1988.

Heaney, Seamus. *Preoccupations: Selected Prose 1968–1978*. New York: Farrar, Straus and Giroux, 1980.

Hoffpauir, Richard. *The Art of Restraint: English Poetry from Hardy to Larkin*. Newark, Delaware: The University of Delaware Press, 1991.

Howe, Irving. 'Philip Roth Reconsidered.' *Commentary*. Jan. 1972. 69–77.

Hughes, Noel. 'The Young Mr. Larkin.' *Larkin at Sixty*. Ed. Anthony Thwaite. London: Faber and Faber, 1982.

Iser, Wolfgang. *The Act of Reading: A Theory of Aesthetic Response*. Johns Hopkins University Press, 1978.

James, Clive. 'Don Juan in Hull.' *Reliable Essays: The Best of Clive James*. London: Picador, 2001.

Jardine, Lisa. 'Saxon Violence.' *Guardian*. 8 Dec. 1992, 24.

Jost, Ekkhard. *Free Jazz: The Roots of Jazz*. New York: Da Capo Press, 1981.

Jost, Ekkhard. 'Free Jazz.' *The Story of Jazz: from New Orleans to Rock Jazz*. Ed. Joachim E. Berendt. Englewood Cliffs, NJ: Prentice-Hall, 1978. 133.

Kacandes, Irene. *Talk Fiction: Literature and the Talk Explosion*. Lincoln, NE: University of Nebraska Press, 2001.

King, Peter. *Nine Contemporary Poets: A Critical Introduction*. London: Methuen, 1979.

Kissick, Gary. 'They Turn on Larkin.' *The Antioch Review*. Winter 1994. 64–70.

Larkin, Philip. *All What Jazz*. New York: Farrar, Straus and Giroux, 1985.

Larkin, Philip. *Collected Poems*. Ed. Anthony Thwaite. New York: Farrar, Straus and Giroux, 1993.

Larkin, Philip. *Further Requirements*. Ed. Anthony Thwaite. London: Faber and Faber, 2001.

Larkin, Philip. 'Introduction.' *Collected Poems of John Betjeman*. Boston: Houghton Mifflin, 1971.

Larkin, Philip. *Philip Larkin: Collected Poems*. Ed. Anthony Thwaite. New York: Farrar, Straus and Giroux, 2004.

Larkin, Philip. *Required Writing: Miscellaneous Pieces*. New York: Farrar, Straus and Giroux, 1983.

Larkin, Philip. *Selected Letters*. Ed. Anthony Thwait. London: Faber and Faber, 1992.

Lehman, David. 'Foreword.' *Required Writing*. Ann Arbor: The University of Michigan Press, 1999.

Leggett, BJ. *Larkin's Blues: Jazz, Popular Music and Poetry*. Louisiana State University Press, 1999.

Lowell, Robert. *Life Studies*. New York: Farrar, Straus and Giroux, 1969.

Mailloux, Steven. *Interpretive Conventions: The Reader in the Study of American Fiction*. Ithaca, New York: Cornell University Press, 1982.

Marsh, Nicholas. *Philip Larkin: The Poems*. Basingstoke: Palgrave Macmillan, 2007.

Martin, Bruce. *Dictionary of Literary Biography*. Detroit, Michigan: Thomas Gale Publishers, 2005.

Motion, Andrew. *Philip Larkin*. London: Methuen, 1983.

Motion, Andrew. *Philip Larkin: A Writer's Life*. New York: Farrar, Straus, Giroux, 1993.

Mulvey, Laura. "Visual Pleasure and Narrative Cinema.' *Film Theory and Criticism*. Eds Leo Braudy and Marshall Cohen. Oxford University Press: 1999. 833–44.

O'Connor, William Van. *The New University Wits and the End of Modernism*. Carbondale: Southern Illinois University Press, 1963.

Osborne, John. *Larkin, Ideology and Critical Violence: A Case of Wrongful Conviction*. Basingstoke: Palgrave Macmillan, 2008.

Osborne, Thomas. 'Polarities of Englishness: Larkin, Hughes and National Culture.' *The Critical Quarterly*. Spring 2006. 43–67.

Palmer, Richard. *Such Deliberate Disguises: The Art of Philip Larkin*. London: Continuum, 2008.

Petch, Simon. *The Art of Philip Larkin*. Sydney: International Scholarly Book Services, 1981.

Phelan, James. *Reading People, Reading Plots: Character, Progression, and the Interpretation of Narrative*. Chicago: The University of Chicago Press, 1989.

Phillips, D.Z. *From Fantasy to Faith*. New York: St. Martin's Press, 1991.

Pinkstein, Danielle. 'The Summer of "Essential Beauty."' *Hugarian Journal of English and American Studies*. Fall 2003. 63–79.

Pritchard, William. 'Larkin's Presence.' *Philip Larkin: The Man and His Work*. Ed. Dale Salwak. Iowa City: University of Iowa Press, 1989. 71–89.

Rabinowitz, Peter. *Before Reading: Narrative Conventions and the Politics of Interpretation*. Ithaca, New York: Cornell University Press, 1987.

Racz, Istvan. 'Space in Larkin and Cezanne.' *Hugarian Journal of English and American Studies*. Fall 2003. 119–25.

Rasula, Jed. 'Jazz and American Modernism.' *The Cambridge Companion to American Modernism*. Ed. Walter Kalaidjian. Cambridge University Press, 2005.

Ratliff, Ben. *Coltrane: The Story of a Sound*. New York: Farrar, Straus and Giroux, 2007.

Regan, Stephen. 'Philip Larkin: A Late Modern Poet.' *The Cambridge Companion to Twentieth-Century English Poetry*. Ed. Neil Corcoran. Cambridge University Press, 2007. 147–58.

Ricks, Christopher. 'Introduction.' *Collection of Poems*. Alfred Lord Tennyson. New York: Doubleday, 1972.

Roberts, Neil. *Narrative and Voice in Postwar Poetry.* London: Longman, 1999.

Rossen, Janice. *Philip Larkin: His Life's Work.* University of Iowa Press, 1989.

Roth, Philip. *American Pastoral.* Boston: Houghton Mifflin, 1997.

Roth, Philip. *Deception.* New York: Vintage. 1997.

Roth, Philip. *The Facts: A Novelist's Autobiography.* New York: Farrar, Straus and Giroux, 1988.

Rowe, M.W. 'Unreal Girls: Lesbian Fantasy in Early Larkin' *New Larkins for Old.* Ed. James Booth. Basingstoke, Hampshire: Palgrave, 2000. 79–96.

Shakespeare, John. 'Larkin's First Interview.' *The Times Literary Supplement.* 1 Apr. 2009.

Sidney, Philip. *Defense of Poesie, Astrophil and Stella, and Other Writings.* Ed. Elizabeth Porges Watson. London: Tuttle, 1997.

Siegel, Ben. 'Reading Philip Roth.' *Turning Up the Flame: Philip Roth's Later Novels.* Eds Jay Halio and Ben Siegel. University of Delaware Press, 2005. 17–30.

Smith, Margaret. 'Autobiography: False Confession?' *Turning Up the Flame. : Philip Roth's Later Novels.* Eds. Jay Halio and Ben Siegel. University of Delaware Press, 2005. 99–114.

Stevens, Wallace. *Collected Poems.* New York: Knopf, 1954.

Stojkovic, Tijana. *Unnoticed in the Casual Light of Day: Philip Larkin and the Plain Style.* New York: Routledge, 2006.

Swarbrick, Andrew. *Out of Reach: The Poetry of Philip Larkin.* Hampshire: Palgrave Macmillan, 1997.

Teachout, Terry. 'Homage to Bix.' *Commentar.y* Sept. 2005. 65–8.

Thwaite, Anthony. Introduction to *Further Requirements.* London: Faber and Faber, 2001.

Timms, David. *Philip Larkin.* Edinburgh: Oliver and Boyd, 1973.

Watson, J.R. 'The Other Larkin.' *Critical Quarterly* 1975. 347–60.

Watson, J.R. 'Philip Larkin: Voices and Values.' *Philip Larkin: The Man and His Work.* Ed. Dale Salwak. Iowa City: University of Iowa Press, 1989. 90–111.

Watts, Cedric. 'Larkin and Jazz.' *Critical Essays on Philip Larkin: The Poems.* Eds Linda Cookson and Bryan Loughrey. Harlow, Essex: Longman: 1989. 20–7.

West, Kevin R. 'Professing Desire.' *Philip Roth: New Perspectives on an American Author.* Ed. Derek Parker Royal. Westport, CT: Praeger, 2005. 226–39.

Whalen, Terry. 'Philip Larkin's Imagist Bias.' *Critical Quarterly.* June 1981, 29–46.

Wordsworth, William. *Lyrical Ballads and Other Poems.* Eds James Butler and Karen Green. Ithaca, New York: Cornell University Press, 1992.

Index